24.40

Economics of
International Trade

Economics of International Trade

Richard I. Leighton

Associate Professor of Economics
State University of New York
at Binghamton

McGraw-Hill Book Company

New York St. Louis San Francisco
London Sydney Toronto Mexico Panama

Economics of International Trade

For Marguerite

Preface

This text is intended for a one-semester course in international trade. The object is to provide an articulated view of international trade in length which can be covered in this limited time period. Since the coverage is necessarily not broad, the instructor will probably want to add particular theoretical, historical, or institutional material of especial interest to him; it is hoped that the book will lead him into such discussions without leaving him pressed for time. Furthermore, illustrations based on historical material and material current at the time of writing have been kept to a bare minimum; the world meetings on tariffs and the monetary crises are supplying illustrations considerably more meaningful to the student than those based on facts many years old. It is use of these current events that makes a course on international trade dynamic and meaningful to the student.

The development of the text is rather orderly and straightforward. First the relation of price to trade is discussed; the usual arguments of comparative advantage are discussed along with other factors which influence price. Second, the relation of national income to trade is taken up; the mutual determination of the levels of trade and national income is set forth and the international trade multiplier is derived. Third, the consequences of capital flow on trade are introduced; this is basically the transfer problem. Fourth, the total trade induced by these variables is accounted for in the discussion on the balance of payments. The remainder of the text deals with maintaining equilibrium in the balance of payments.

To reach the largest possible audience, I have explained the theoretical tools introduced; it is hoped that students without knowledge beyond the principles level will find the text understandable. For those who have had intermediate theory, this repetition should prove a useful review and opportunity to see the theory extended to the larger economy. Also the multipliers have been derived in detail with simple algebra in the appendix of Chapter 5; it is my intent to make the proof intelligible also to those not mathematically equipped.

I am indebted to the *South African Journal of Economics* for permission to use excerpts from my article in the December issue of 1966. I am also indebted to my colleague, Dr. Kenneth Kurihara, distinguished professor of economic theory, for reading and commenting on a large proportion of the manuscript. Prof. John Matthews of the College of William and Mary read the entire manuscript and offered a number of very useful suggestions. Dr. Ana Eapen also read the entire manuscript and suggested areas of clarification and correction. Dr. Kenji Takeuchi of the World Bank kindly read portions of the manuscript. To all I am greatly indebted. Marguerite Leighton edited the entire manuscript and made a large number of revisions which greatly improved the clarity and style. She also typed the entire manuscript. Without her assistance, this book would never have been written. Even though the collective shoulders of all these kind persons are broader than mine, I must alone take responsibility for all errors and shortcomings.

Richard I. Leighton

Contents

Economics of
International Trade

1.

The Rationale of International Trade

Under a system of perfectly free commerce, each country naturally devotes its capital and labour to such employments as are most beneficial to each. This pursuit of individual advantage is admirably connected with the universal good of the whole. By stimulating industry, by rewarding ingenuity, and by using most efficaciously the peculiar powers bestowed by nature, it distributes labour most effectively and most economically: while, by increasing the general mass of productions, it diffuses general benefit, and binds together by one common tie of interest and intercourse, the universal society of nations throughout the civilised world.

David Ricardo
Principles of Political Economy

Classical economists were oriented primarily toward growth economics, and their main concern was explaining how the "wealth of nations" was increased. In explaining increased output, specialization and division of labor were given special attention. Adam Smith's description of how a larger number of pins could be produced when labor was specialized by detail functions as opposed to handcraft methods was widely quoted and generalized. The extent of specialization and division of labor was dependent upon the size of the market; a larger market would encourage a greater degree of specialization and division of labor.

Questions as to the contribution of foreign trade to the "wealth of nations" arose. It appeared clear that foreign trade enlarged the market and allowed further gains from specialization and division of labor. However, it was still necessary to set down the argument clearly: to show what goods would be imported and exported and to show the gains from trade. The theory developed is called the *law of comparative advantage.*

The Law of Comparative Advantage

The law of comparative advantage states that each nation produces and trades that good which it can manufacture cheaply and imports the commodity which it can produce only at great sacrifice. For classical economists, the value of a good is determined by the cost of production, with the relative cost of production of various goods revealed by the labor content. Thus the more labor required to produce a good, the more expensive it is. A nation, according to classical economists, exports a commodity which it can produce with relatively little labor and imports the commodity which, if produced at home, would require relatively large amounts of labor. A given commodity cannot be produced with the same amount of labor in all countries. Favorable resources allow a nation to produce a good with less labor than a nation not as favorably situated. For example, a nation with coal resources near the surface will need to devote smaller amounts of labor per ton than a nation with coal resources at great depths.

The law of *absolute advantage* is illustrated in Table 1-1 under the assumptions of perfect competition—two countries and two commodities. The two nations, England and France, are both able to produce wine and textiles. England can produce 20 yards

Table 1-1 *Output per man-year of labor*

	Textiles, Yards	Wine, Bottles
England	20	10
France	10	20

of textiles with one man-year of labor, whereas France can produce only 10 yards. However, France can produce 20 bottles of wine per man-year of labor to England's 10 bottles. In England 20 yards of textiles must exchange for 10 bottles of wine, since the amount of labor required is the same for these quantities of the two commodities. Ten yards of textiles must exchange for 20 bottles of wine in France. Clearly, textiles are cheap in England; one has to give only 10 bottles of wine for 20 yards of textiles, whereas in France one has to give 20 bottles of wine for only 10 yards of textiles. Simultaneously, wine is cheap in France, since 10 yards of textiles will buy 20 bottles of wine, whereas in England 20 yards of textiles are required to buy only 10 bottles of wine. An exchange which would reduce the price of wine in England and the price of textiles in France would be mutually desirable to the two countries.

An exchange rate which lies between the rates at which textiles exchange for wine in the two countries, i.e., 20 to 10 for England and 10 to 20 for France, will improve the well-being of both countries. An exchange rate of, say, 10 to 10 might emerge on the international market. England would find trade advantageous; to produce 10 bottles of wine, it had to give up 20 yards of textiles, but with free trade it can specialize in textiles and exchange 10 yards of its output for 10 bottles of wine. Wine now costs less in terms of textiles exchanged. France likewise gains; to produce both commodities, it must give up 20 bottles of wine for every 10 yards of textiles desired. But with free trade it can produce only wine and exchange on the world market 10 bottles of wine for every 10 yards of textiles desired. Specialization improves the well-being of both nations. With trade, England would produce textiles and France wine. Each nation has a clear absolute advantage; England can produce textiles more cheaply than wine, and France can produce wine more cheaply than textiles.

Even if one of the two nations should have an absolute advantage in the production of both commodities, there are still gains to be reaped from international trade. In Table 1-2 England is more efficient in the production of both textiles and wine than is France. A man-year of English labor is more efficient in the production of wine and textiles than is a man-year in France. If England can get more than 30 bottles of wine for 50 yards of textiles, it can gain from trade. Suppose France will give 40 bottles of wine for 50 yards of textiles; if England diverts one man-year of labor from textiles to wine, it will lose 50 yards of textiles and gain 30 bottles of wine. Instead it might produce 50 yards of textiles to trade with France for 40 bottles of wine. England gains 10 bottles of wine through trade, rather than trying to produce the wine itself. This arrangement would be quite satisfactory to France. Two man-years of French labor will produce either 20 yards of textiles or 40 bottles of wine. Trading 40 bottles of wine for 50 yards of textiles yields France a net gain of 30 yards of cloth over what it could produce at home. France has a comparative advantage in wine and England in textiles.

Specialization and trade increase the economic well-being of both nations regardless of whether one of the nations has a comparative or absolute advantage. An additional illustration might help to clarify the case of comparative advantage. Imagine a physician whose time is valued at $50 an hour; he is also a champion typist and can type twice as many words per minute as his secretary. The secretary is paid $2 per hour. Clearly, this physician has an absolute advantage over his secretary in both medicine and typing. However, it is more profitable for him to practice medicine, earn $50 an hour, and pay his secretary $2 for the typing. If he did the typing himself, he would save $4 for every hour spent at his typewriter, since he types twice as fast as his secretary. But by devoting his time entirely to medicine he earns $50 per hour rather than the $4 per hour for any typing.

Table 1-2 *Output per man-year*

	Textiles, Yards	Wine, Bottles
England	50	30
France	10	20

Opportunity Cost

The above discussion is presented in terms of what labor will produce. But labor is not the only factor of production; capital and land are also required. Since land, labor, and capital are not used in the same proportions in the production of all commodities, the amount of labor required to produce two alternative goods does not necessarily reveal their relative costs of production. Quantities of two commodities requiring the same amount of labor but different amounts of capital must have different prices. Thus the law of comparative advantage must be illustrated without using the value of labor as representative of the cost of production.

Instead of comparing the alternative outputs which a given quantity of labor can produce, the theory may be reformulated to show the total output of various commodities obtained when a nation's total resources are utilized. In Table 1-3 it can be seen that if England puts all its resources—land, labor, and capital— into textiles, it can produce 300 million yards, and if it puts all its resources into wine production, it can produce 100 million bottles. Thus the opportunity cost of producing 300 million yards of textiles is said to be 100 million bottles of wine; the *opportunity cost* is the amount of one good which must be given up in order to provide resources for the expansion of a second commodity. France can produce 100 million yards of textiles or 200 million bottles of wine—the opportunity cost of producing one yard of textiles in France is two bottles of wine, assuming constant costs. Trade will benefit both nations as long as the international rate of exchange for the two commodities lies between the opportunity costs of the two nations, i.e., 300 to 100 and 100 to 200. For England to produce 300 million yards of textiles, the opportunity cost is only 100 million bottles of wine, whereas the opportunity cost in France is 600 million bottles of wine. Likewise, France

Table 1-3 *Alternative outputs for given resources*

	Textiles, Million Yards	Wine, Million Bottles
England	300	100
France	100	200

can produce 200 million bottles of wine at an opportunity cost of 100 million yards of textiles, whereas England's opportunity cost is 600 million. Comparative advantage expressed in terms of opportunity cost indicates that England should specialize in textiles and France in wine, and that the two nations should trade.

Suppose, for illustration purposes, that an international rate of exchange of 2 yards of textiles for 1 bottle of wine should emerge. By diverting the resources required to weave 3 yards of textiles into wine production, England could produce 1 bottle of wine, and the cost of a bottle of wine, therefore, is 3 yards of textiles. If, however, on the international market it need give only 2 yards of textiles for a bottle of wine, the wine is less expensive by 1 yard of textiles. Surely England would maximize its well-being by specializing in textiles and trading for the desired amount of wine. France can likewise gain from specialization and trade. For France to produce a unit of textiles requires giving 2 bottles of wine. Two yards of textiles can be had for 1 bottle on the world market. France will maximize its economic well-being by specializing in wine production and trading for the desired amount of textiles.

Production Possibilities Curve

A *production possibilities curve* is a simple device for depicting all possible combinations of two goods which a nation might produce with given resources. The shape of the curve depends on the assumptions made about the opportunity costs. It may be assumed that the opportunity cost is constant. In this case the amount of commodity N given up to allow additional production of T is the same, regardless of the amount of N and T being produced. In contrast, it may be assumed that the opportunity cost is one of increasing cost; this means that every time an additional unit of T is produced, ever-increasing amounts of N must be given up in order to provide the resources for expanding T's output.

CONSTANT COSTS Suppose that a team of technical experts establishes empirically that if nation W employed all its resources, it could produce the amounts of N and T set forth in Table 1-4. The marginal rate of transformation (mrt) is the amount of one good N which must be given up in order to release resources

Table 1-4 *Alternative outputs of N and T when all W's resources are utilized*

Combination	N	T	mrt
a	40	0	
b	32	1	8/1
c	24	2	8/1
d	16	3	8/1
e	8	4	8/1
f	0	5	8/1

necessary to produce an additional unit of a second good T. In the table, each additional unit of T has the same cost in terms of N; resources capable of producing eight units of N must be diverted to increase output of T by one unit, regardless of the level of production of N and T. Constant cost means that the marginal rate of transformation is constant. It is the result of each factor of production being equally effective in producing both goods; i.e., a factor is not more suited to the production of one good than to another.

The above data are illustrated graphically in Figure 1-1. Units of commodity N are measured on the vertical axis and units of T on the horizontal axis. Combination a of 40 units of N and zero units of T lies on the vertical axis of country W and is labelled a. Likewise all combinations a through e of Table 1-4

Figure 1-1

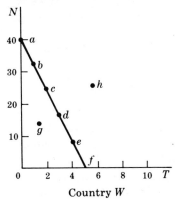

Country *W*

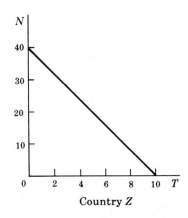

Country *Z*

are plotted in Figure 1-1. The points are connected, and the resulting line is a production possibilities curve. A production possibilities curve then shows all possible combinations of two commodities which a nation might produce. The particular combination to be chosen lies on the curve. Points inside the curve, such as *g*, represent outputs at less than full employment and are therefore not considered. Points beyond the curve, such as *h*, require more resources than the country possesses and are therefore also beyond consideration. The full-employment outputs under consideration must lie on the production possibilities curve.

The slope of the production possibilities curve is the marginal rate of transformation (mrt). The slope shows the reductions required in one commodity in order to increase the output of the second commodity. Since the marginal rate of transformation is constant, the slope must be constant, and thus the production possibilities curve must be a straight line.

Establishing and plotting all possible combinations of goods *N* and *T* which country *Z* can produce with all its resources fully employed yields the second part of Figure 1-1. It can be seen that the marginal rate of transformation of *N* for *T* is 4 to 1; reducing the output of *T* by one unit will provide resources sufficient to expand output of *N* by four units. Country *Z* has a comparative advantage in the production of *T*; less *N* has to be given up for each additional unit of *T*. On the other hand, country *W* has the comparative advantage in the production of *N*; less *T* has to be given up to produce an additional unit of *N*.

The two graphs can be combined into one in Figure 1-2 to

Figure 1-2

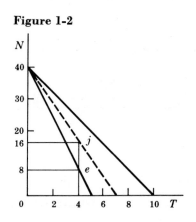

show country *W*'s gain from trade, but it will not show the consequences of trade for country *Z*. Now, suppose that country *W* specializes in the production of *N* and exchanges *N* for *T* with country *Z*. *W*'s gain depends on the bargain struck between the two countries. Let us assume that an exchange rate of 6 to 1 becomes established. (How the exchange rate becomes established will be discussed later.) The dotted line represents the exchange rate and has a slope of 6 to 1. The very fact that it is further out from the origin than *W*'s production possibilities curve shows that there are gains to *W*.

Now if country *W* decides that it must have 4*T*, then with economic independence it has remaining resources sufficient to produce 8*N*, represented by point *e* in Figure 1-2. However, if *W* participates in international trade and specializes in the production of 40 units of *N*, then, with an exchange rate of 6 to 1, it need give only 24*N* for the desired 4*T*, leaving 16*N*. Thus with trade nation *W* still has its 4*T* plus 16*N*, represented by point *j* in Figure 1-2, whereas it could only have 8*N* with 4*T* under a policy of autarchy, represented by point *e* in Figure 1-2. Thus the gain from trade to country *W* is 8*N*.

Table 1-5 shows *W*'s gains for different levels of exports. *W* specializes in the production of *N* and its output is listed in column 1. In column 2, alternative amounts of *N* are assumed to be consumed at home. Subtracting the amount consumed at home from the country's output yields the amount available for export in column 3. The alternative amounts available for export are traded at the exchange rate of 6*N* for 1*T*, with the results in column 4. A comparison of the amounts of *N* and *T* in columns 2 and 4 with the amounts available under autarchy in Table 1-4

Table 1-5

1 Production of N	2 Consumed at Home	3 Exports (1 − 2)	4 T Received	5 Gains in Terms of N
40	40	0	0	0
40	34	6	1	2
40	28	12	2	4
40	22	18	3	6
40	16	24	4	8
40	10	30	5	10

yields the gains from trade in column 5 of Table 1-5. In this table the gains are expressed in terms of commodity N. However, the gains from trade may be taken in either or both commodities as taste patterns dictate.

As long as the international exchange rate lies between the values of the mrt in the two countries, both nations gain from trade. For example, the above-mentioned exchange rate of 6 to 1 lies between W's mrt of 8 to 1 and Z's mrt of 4 to 1; consequently trade is profitable to both nations. To produce T, W had to use resources capable of producing $8N$. With trade, W need give only $6N$ for the $1T$. For country Z to produce $4N$, it had to transfer resources capable of producing $1T$. With trade, it can get $6N$ for the $1T$, a gain of $2N$. Clearly, both nations have gained from trade.

If the international exchange rate should coincide with the mrt of one of the countries, then only the other nation can gain from trade. For example, an exchange rate of 8 to 1 results in W being unable to gain from trade. To produce T, W must direct resources capable of producing $8N$ into T production. To obtain T by trade, W must give $8N$. The cost of acquiring T is the same through production as through trade. But for Z it is a different story. Reduction of T output by one unit will allow the expansion of N by four units. In trade, one unit of T will bring eight units of N. Obviously Z gains greatly from trade; as a matter of fact, it alone reaps the entire gain from trading.

Finally, the international exchange rate cannot lie outside of the two nations' mrt. It would be impossible for an exchange rate of 2 to 1 to exist. Each nation would be willing to exchange two of N for one of T, but neither nation would be willing to give $1T$ for $2N$; each could obtain more N by directing resources from the production of T to the production of N. Likewise, an exchange rate of $10N$ for $1T$ will not induce any trade. Both nations will want to give up T for N and neither will be willing to give up N for T. Consequently, trade cannot take place.

With constant returns to scale, trade can take place only when each nation has a different mrt. The gains from trade for a particular nation depend on how much the international exchange rates differ from that nation's mrt. The greater the difference, the greater the gains from trade. The gains from trade rest, further, upon the amount of trade taking place. Obviously, a larger amount of trade allows larger gains from trade and a greater increase in the standard of living.

INCREASING COSTS   It would seem unlikely that most nations would be confronted with constant costs over a substantial range of production. Constant costs imply that all resources are of equal quality and that they are all equally suited to the production of both commodities. For example, if the United States were to increase the agricultural output and reduce the output of manufactured goods, it would not necessarily be the case that factory workers would be as productive in agriculture as the farmers. Nor would farmers be as productive in industry as factory workers, if the decision were to increase manufactured goods and reduce agricultural output. The resources are not equally suited to the production of both commodities. If the output of one good is to be increased, it can be done only by employing resources less suited to this good. Consequently the cost of production rises with output.

Increasing opportunity costs mean that for each additional unit of N produced, ever-increasing amounts of T must be given up. At first as N is increased, resources suited to N but not to T are used to increase greatly the output of N and reduce the output of T by little. But eventually the resources being transferred are not well suited to N but highly suited to T, and consequently N's production increases by little and T's falls by a great deal. Increasing opportunity costs can best be explained by the use of Table 1-6. Suppose we take a given amount of land, labor, and capital, and experimentally find out how much N and T we can produce. If all our resources are devoted to the production of N, we find we can produce 40 units of N. If we want 36 units of N, we find that we can have 1 unit of T with all our resources fully employed. If we want 2 units of T, we can have only 30 units of N.

Table 1-6   *Alternative combinations of N and T with all resources fully employed*

N	T	*mrt*
40	0	
36	1	4/1
30	2	6/1
20	3	10/1
0	4	20/1

With 3 units of T, we can have only 20 units of N. The first unit of T costs 4 units of N, the second 6, and the third 10. The marginal rate of transformation of N for T is rising; larger amounts of N must be given up for additional units of T. This is what is meant by increasing opportunity costs. It must be clear that this is not a market or accounting cost or price. It is purely a technical statement derived from experimentation on the possible combinations of N and T which can be produced with a specified amount of land, labor, and capital. Thus increasing opportunity costs is a technical statement about the increasing mrt as more of a good is produced. The economist takes this as a given physical attribute. It tells us nothing about the economic variables of price and income. It does not even tell us the combination which will be produced, only the possible combinations. Price must be introduced before the particular combination can be set forth.

The data in Table 1-6 may be presented graphically as a transformation curve. First, a combination of $40N$ and $0T$ is plotted in Figure 1-3, then 36 of N and 1 of T, etc. The connected

Figure 1-3

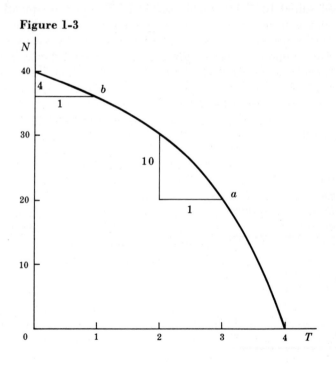

points yield a production possibilities curve, the slope of which is the marginal rate of transformation. The production possibilities curve is concave toward the origin, showing that the substitution rate is not constant but increasing. At a combination of $20N$ and $3T$, represented by point a in Figure 1-3, 1 unit of T may be substituted in production for 10 of N. But at the combination of $36N$ and $1T$, represented by point b in Figure 1-3, the resources required to produce $1T$ can be used alternatively to produce 4 additional units of N.

Now the production possibilities curve shows all possible combinations of N and T which can be produced at full employment. To be inside the curve is to be at less than full employment; there are not sufficient resources to go beyond the curve.

With the production possibilities curve given, the economy must decide which particular combination out of the entire range to produce. The price of the two goods is all-important in determining the quantities of the two commodities to be produced. For example, assume a closed economy in which the domestic price of N is 25 cents and the price of T is 50 cents. In this case, 40 units of N and no units of T would be produced. To produce one unit of T, the resources which will produce $4N$ must be devoted to T; therefore, $4 \times \$0.25$ or \$1 in revenue will be lost from the reduction in the output of N and only 50 cents will be gained from the production of T. Shifting the resources from N to T will result in the net loss of 50 cents. To attempt to expand production of T even further will result in even greater losses, because of the assumption of increasing cost. To attempt to produce a second unit of T means that six units of N must be given up in order to provide the resources needed for the additional unit of T; the loss of revenue on $6N$ is \$1.50 and the gain from T is 50 cents, yielding an additional net loss of \$1.

However, if the price of N were 25 cents but the price of T were \$8, then only T would be produced. Four T would be produced with a total revenue of \$32. If the resources needed to manufacture 1 unit of T were transferred to the production of N, then 20 units of N would be produced. Producing 20 units of N would yield \$5, and the reduction of 1 unit of T would reduce revenue by \$8. The net result of transferring resources from T to N would be a loss of \$3.

A price ratio must be introduced into our graph of the production possibilities curve in order to determine the output of the two commodities. The price ratio is a barter price ratio;

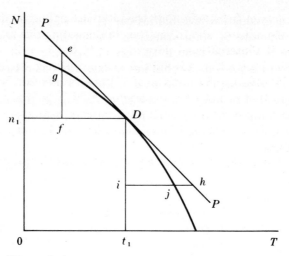

Figure 1-4

i.e., it tells us that so many units of N exchange for one unit of T, and it is called the *barter terms of trade*. For example, two units of N exchange for one unit of T. (The money price of N must be half the money price of T for two units of N to be equal in value to one unit of T.)

With the assumption that nation W has a closed economy, the domestic price ratio is drawn tangent to the production possibilities curve in Figure 1-4. The equilibrium output is at point D, where n_1 of N and t_1 of T are produced. One way to determine whether the equilibrium point represents the best combination is to examine other points. Would it be desirable to move to some point to the left of D, say g? To move from D to g would require giving up Df and using the released resources to produce fg. But the price ratio tells us that quantity fe is of equal value to quantity Df. Since the transferred resources can earn only fg, losses equal to ge would be incurred by moving to point g. Therefore it would not be profitable to move to the left of point D. Now a point to the right of D needs to be examined, such as j. To move from D to j would require giving up Di of N and using the resources to expand production of T by ij. However, the price ratio indicates that Di is of equal value to ih. Losses of jh would be incurred by moving to point j. Clearly then, any movement from D incurs losses, and D is the equilibrium position.

If country W should abandon its policy of autarchy and

open its markets to free trade, then the international price ratio will be the determinant rather than the old domestic price ratio. In Figure 1-5 the international price ratio $P_I P_I$ has been drawn tangent to the production possibilities curve, yielding equilibrium point D_2 with n_2 of N and t_2 of T being produced. Now suppose nation W does not want to consume n_2 of N but only n_1. It can trade on the international price market $n_1 n_2$ ($=SD_2$) for $t_2 t_3$ ($=SD_3$) of T. Nation W now has t_3 of T and n_1 of N, a clear gain of $t_1 t_3$.

Also in Figure 1-5, the domestic price ratio and the produc-

Figure 1-5

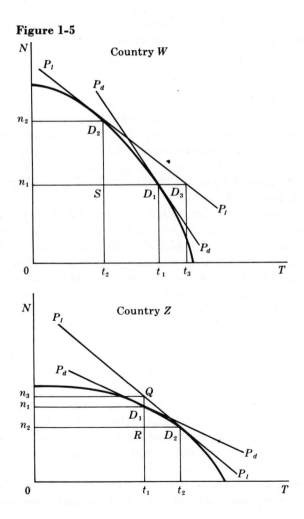

tion possibilities curve of country Z are drawn to yield the equilibrium point D_1 with n_1 of N and t_1 of T produced. The freeing of trade introduces the international price ratio $P_I P_I$. The output of T is induced to expand to t_2, and the output of N is reduced to n_2. Now suppose that country Z does not want to consume t_2 of T but wants to continue to consume t_1; then it can trade $t_1 t_2$ $(= D_2 R)$ for $n_2 n_3$ $(= RQ)$. Nation Z now has t_1 of T and n_3 of N, a clear gain of $n_1 n_3$ over the closed economy.

Now the consequences of free trade are that country Z exports T and imports N and reaches a higher standard of well-being. Simultaneously, country W exports N and imports T, resulting in a higher standard of living for its citizens. Clearly trade has improved the well-being of both nations.

Factor Proportions

As discussed above, the classical economists explained comparative advantage in terms of labor productivity. More modern theory, originated by A. Heckscher and B. Ohlin, explains the difference in opportunity costs from country to country in terms of factor endowments. All nations, for example, do not have the same ratio of labor to capital. Thus the price of labor compared to capital will differ.

Imagine country W as one with large amounts of labor and relatively little capital. A given expenditure will purchase large quantities of labor but little capital. For purposes of illustration, we shall suppose that $100 will purchase 20 man-weeks of labor or 5 machine-weeks of capital. Twenty man-weeks of labor must be equal in value to 5 weeks of capital. In Figure 1-6, the 20 man-weeks and 5 machine-weeks have been marked off and the two points connected by a straight line. The slope of this line is 20 to 5 or 4 to 1 and represents the price ratio; i.e., on the market 4 man-weeks of labor exchange for 1 machine-week. Where the line meets the axis is determined by the expenditure in question. In this case it is $100. The line is called an *isocost curve* and shows all combinations of labor and capital which can be purchased for a specified amount of money.

Larger expenditures of labor and capital produce an isocost curve farther out from the origin. A $200 expenditure would buy 40 man-weeks of labor or 10 machine-weeks of capital. The isocost curve representing $200 is drawn in Figure 1-6 and is parallel to the one representing $100 expenditure because the price

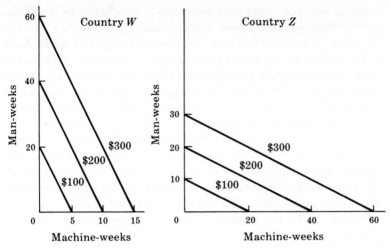

Figure 1-6

ratio of 4 to 1 still holds. Isocost curves of any expenditure level can be drawn, and as long as the same price ratio is assumed, all isocost curves will be parallel.

Also in Figure 1-6 the isocost curves for country Z are drawn. Here it is assumed that country Z has much capital and little labor. Consequently, in this country, a $100 expenditure will buy 10 man-weeks of labor, or 20 machine-weeks of capital, or any combination of labor and capital represented by the $100 isocost curve. Clearly, 1 man-week of labor is equal to 2 weeks of machinery; the price ratio is 1 to 2. All the isocost curves for country Z have the slope of 1 to 2 and show all possible combinations of machinery and labor which can be purchased for the specified amount of total expenditures of $100, $200, and $300.

Obviously country W would find that it could produce more cheaply goods requiring much labor and little capital, and country Z would find that it could produce most cheaply goods requiring much capital and little labor. But that is not the whole story. Rarely can a good be produced by one particular combination of capital and labor. Instead, there are usually varying proportions in which labor and capital can be combined to produce a good. For example, a dam built by natives carrying baskets of gravel to the damsite would represent a high labor-to-capital ratio. The use of wheelbarrows would somewhat reduce the labor-to-capital ratio, and the use of trucks would reduce it still further. The question then is not only what good a nation will produce but also how it will produce it.

The above question can be answered with an isoproduct curve together with an isocost curve. An *isoproduct curve* represents a technical statement about all possible combinations of inputs which will produce a specified quantity of output. In Figure 1-7 the isoproduct curve shows all combinations of labor and capital which will produce 20 units of *N*. An isoproduct curve showing all combinations of labor and capital which will produce 50 units of *T* is also shown in Figure 1-7. Comparing the two isoproduct curves, one notes that the curve for *N* lies further in the vertical distance, and the curve for *T* lies further out in the horizontal plane. The position reveals that *N* requires primarily labor, but capital can be substituted for labor within limits. Likewise *T* is produced with capital, but labor may be substituted within limits. That is, although a good can be produced with varying proportions of capital and labor, the range of such combinations is finite. One further point: note the slope of the isoproduct curve which is the marginal rate of factor substitution. As one substitutes capital for labor, the first unit of capital will substitute for a large number of work-weeks, but as one continues, a great deal of capital will substitute for little labor. The curve indicates that there are increasing costs in substituting one factor for another.

Figure 1-7

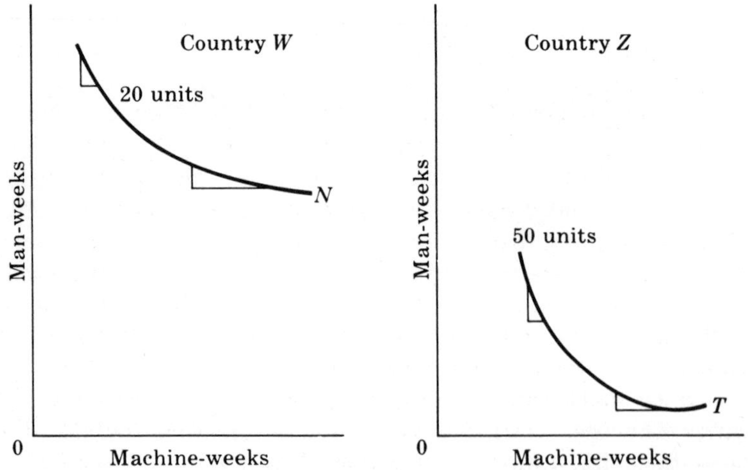

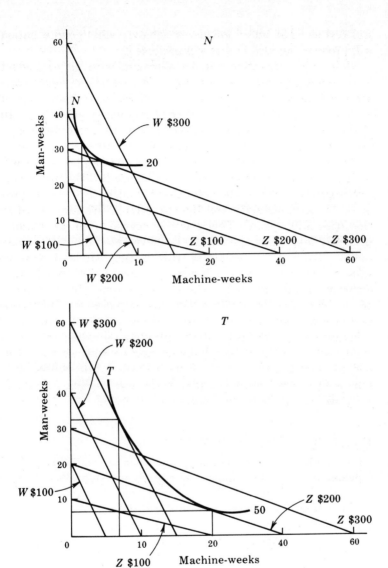

Figure 1-8

The isoproduct curves and isocost curves are drawn together
in Figure 1-8. A line tangent to an isoproduct curve represents
the lowest cost at which the output represented by the isoproduct
curve can be produced. As can be seen at point *a*, country *W*
can produce 20 units of *N* at a cost of $200 by using 32 man-

weeks of labor and 2 machine-weeks of capital. Country Z can produce 20 units of N at a cost of $300 by using 25 man-weeks of labor and 5 machine-weeks of capital (point b). Country Z is the high-cost producer of N because of its scarcity of labor and the limited extent to which capital can be substituted for labor. Country W can produce 50 units of T at a cost of $300 by using 32 man-weeks of labor and 8 machine-weeks of capital. But country Z can produce the 50 units of T at a cost of $200 by combining 8 man-weeks of labor with 20 machine-weeks of capital.

Once again it can be seen that there are gains to be had from free trade—each nation should produce that commodity which it can manufacture most cheaply and trade. Furthermore, it can be seen that in autarchy each country will try to use its abundant factor to produce all commodities; country W uses larger quantities of labor in the production of N and T, and country Z uses larger quantities of capital. But commodities may be somewhat specialized to a particular factor of production, and thus there may be severe limits of a nation's substitution of its abundant factor for the factor required intensely. Or it might be said that whenever a nation produces a commodity, it will attempt to substitute its abundant factor for any other factor in short supply. If it can substitute readily, it will be able to produce the good just as cheaply. If the substitution is limited, it will have to use scarce resources and produce at a high cost.

Factor-Price Equalization

As country W expands the production of commodity N and demands more labor, wages will rise. Similarly, as W reduces the output of commodity T which requires W's scarce factor of production, the returns to capital will fall with the reduced output of T. In Figure 1-9, the supply and demand schedules D_1 and S give a wage rate in country W of S_1 and a return to capital of R_1 in the absence of free trade. Opening the country to free trade brings increased output of N, requiring relatively more labor, and reduced output of T, which requires for its production relatively more capital. The consequences of substituting the production of N for T are increased demand for labor and reduced demand for capital. The demand for labor shifts to D_2; the wage rises to S_2 and employment to L_2. Furthermore, the demand for capital falls to D_2 with a reduced rate of return of R_2 and with quantity of capital used reduced to C_2.

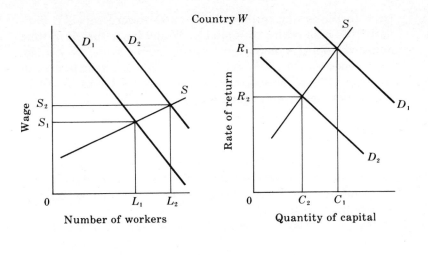

Country W

Number of workers

Quantity of capital

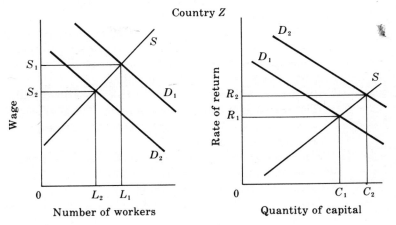

Country Z

Number of workers

Quantity of capital

Figure 1-9

Country Z, with a greater relative abundance of capital, substitutes the production of T for N with the freeing of trade. Since N requires relatively more labor, the demand for labor will fall from D_1 to D_2 with wages falling from S_1 to S_2 and employment falling from L_1 to L_2. The increased output of T will bring a rise in the rate of return of capital to R_2 and the quantity of capital used to C_2.

The pretrade position was one of high wages in Z and low wages in W. Free trade reduced the wages in Z and increased them in W, serving to make them move toward equality. Similarly, the high return to capital in W and low return in Z were adjusted toward equality by the move to free trade. Free trade, then, tends to equate the return to a factor of production in all countries; this is the substance of the so-called Heckscher-Ohlin theorem of factor-price equalization.

Summary

Law of comparative advantage states that each nation produces and trades that good which it can manufacture cheaply and imports the commodity which it can produce only at great sacrifice.

1. For classical economists, the difference in cost of production was revealed by difference in labor costs.
2. An opportunity cost is the amount of one good which must be given up to produce a unit of a second good.
3. Difference in supply of factors of production makes for difference in cost of production in the various countries.
   a. Constant cost—costs do not change with level of output; leads to complete specialization.
   b. Increasing cost—eventually costs rise with output. The nation is not likely to specialize. Trade changes only the quantities produced, not the commodities which will be produced.
4. Factor proportions—quantities of the factors of production determine the relative prices in the various countries. Each country will produce goods by using the abundant factor and those goods suited to the use of the abundant factor.
5. Heckscher-Ohlin theorem of factor-price equalization —free trade tends to equate the returns to a factor of production in all countries.

Selected Readings   (*See list at end of Chapter 2.*)

Price Difference
and International
Trade

So far we have seen how the difference in factor endowment from one country to another causes different prices for these factors in the various countries. The commodity requiring for its production primarily the nation's abundant factor will have a relatively low price compared to the good which requires mainly the country's scarce factor. Thus the difference in endowment causes the price of producing a commodity to vary from one country to another. As long as there are price differences, international trade can occur profitably. Goods flow to the market in which the greatest price is earned.

Thus the necessary condition for international trade is price difference for the various commodities. Any characteristic which may cause prices to differ from country to country is a sufficient condition for international trade, but the price difference alone is the necessary condition. Different factor endowments may cause prices to differ and, therefore, are a sufficient condition for international trade. But price difference alone may be brought about by causes other than factor endowments. Consequently, different factor endowments are only a sufficient but not a necessary condition, since price difference may exist without difference in factor endowment.

The object of this chapter is to introduce *indifference maps* to further illustrate the improvement in economic welfare which comes from participation in international trade. The factors conducive to international trade in this illustration will be (1) different production possibilities, a repetition of Chapter 1, and (2) difference in taste.

Analysis

Before employing indifference maps to illustrate the gains from trade, a word of warning is needed. It is not at all certain that this is a legitimate tool on the national level, as opposed to the individual level. Since there exists no recognized method of quantifying utility on the individual level, it becomes necessary to talk about preference in an ordinal sense, i.e., choice by ranking. But how do you sum ordinal choices for individuals to obtain a national indifference curve? In the following discussion all these theoretical problems are swept under the rug, and it is assumed that we do have a national indifference map.

An *indifference curve* is a graphical depiction of all possible combinations of two commodities yielding a constant level of satisfaction. Indifference curve I in Figure 2-1 shows all combinations of N and T which yield the same level of satisfaction for citizens of country Z. They would be indifferent between particular points on the curve and, consequently, could not choose between points such as k and l. Indifference curves farther out from the origin represent higher levels of satisfaction. An indifference curve can be drawn in for any level of satisfaction. I_2 is a higher level of satisfaction than I_1; how much greater cannot be said. Indifference curves can be ranked only in ascending order of satisfaction. A nation desires to reach the highest level of satisfaction or indifference curve.

The slope of the indifference curve is the marginal rate of psychological substitution (mrps). The marginal rate of psychological substitution indicates the amount of one commodity

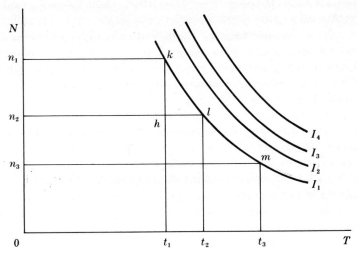

Figure 2-1

the nation must be given in exchange for one unit of a second commodity, so that the level of satisfaction remains unchanged. For example, in indifference curve I_1 in Figure 2-1, nation Z must be given hl of commodity T in exchange for kh of N, so that the country is on the same indifference curve but at a point l rather than k. Now the mrps is not a constant, but changes along an indifference curve. As can be seen in Figure 2-1, a smaller amount of N has to be given up for the same quantity of T in the move from l to m, as opposed to the move from k to l. The marginal rate of psychological substitution diminishes. As N is given up and T increased, T becomes less and N more significant. Thus the nation must be compensated with larger amounts of T (item of less significance) for the loss of N (item of increased significance).

The diminishing rate of psychological substitution requires that the indifference curve be convex to the origin. If the indifference curve were linear, it would indicate that the mrps were constant; one's preference for a commodity would not be affected by the quantity of the commodity possessed. Similarly, a concave indifference curve would indicate that the more of a commodity one had, the more he desired an additional unit; the sixth raspberry soda is more desirable than the first, a taste pattern limited to alcoholics and narcotics. Thus the normal or usual type of indifference curve is one convex to the origin.

It is assumed that two indifference curves cannot have a point in common. The reasoning underlying this assumption can best be illustrated by showing the logical inconsistency which arises when two indifference curves are drawn with a point in common, as in Figure 2-2. Since d and e are on the same indifference curve, they must represent points of equal satisfaction. Likewise, d and f are on the same indifference curve and must be of equal satisfaction. Since $f = d$ and $d = e$, then $f = e$. But as can be seen, e is on a higher indifference curve than f and is thus a higher level of satisfaction. Thus, indifference curves drawn with a point in common lead us to an inconsistency which can be avoided by postulating that two indifference curves can never have a point in common.

Finally, our indifference curves must slope downward from left to right. The alternative would be to slope upward from left to right as in Figure 2-3. But indifference curve I_1 tells us that all points are ones of equal satisfaction. But as can be seen, point h contains more of both goods and must be preferable to g. Therefore, an upward-sloping indifference curve is not consistent with our previous definition.

Thus an indifference map is purely a depiction of taste or psychological preference, without regard to price or availability of goods. From an indifference curve alone it is not possible to determine how much of the good will be purchased and consumed. It is possible to say that steak is preferred to hot dogs, but not

Figure 2-2

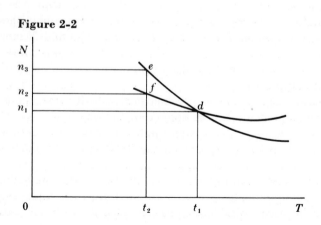

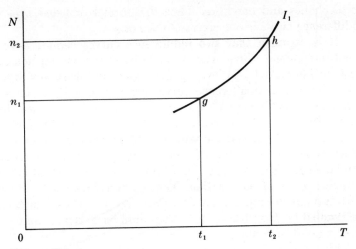

Figure 2-3

whether money will be spent on steak or hot dogs. If steak and hot dogs were the same price per pound, one would expect steak to be purchased. On the other hand, if steak cost 20 times the price of hot dogs, one might reasonably expect some hot dogs to be bought. The next step, then, is to add a price ratio to the indifference curves.

In Figure 2-4, the price ratio is combined with the indifference curves in order to determine how much of the two commodities will be purchased. Once again the price ratio is a barter price ratio; it tells us how much of N will be exchanged on the market for one unit of T. The price ratio passes through points E_1, E_2, and E_3; the equilibrium position must be one of these (or points on any other indifference curve which might be drawn in on the price ratio). At point E_2, ef would exchange for fg to stay on the same level of satisfaction, but the market will give fh for ef, an amount gh more than required to maintain the level of satisfaction. Thus fh gives a greater satisfaction than ef; consequently a move to E_3 must be made under the assumption of welfare maximization. Point E_2 cannot represent a stable equilibrium position. At point E_3, an exchange of ij for hi would leave the nation on the same level of satisfaction; thus the nation would be indifferent between the two points on the curve. However, the market is willing to give ik for hi, an amount jk in excess of what it takes to be equally well off. The assumption of maximization requires

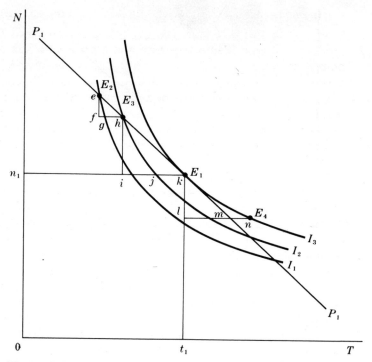

Figure 2-4

that hi be given up for ik, so that the higher level of satisfaction is attained. Accordingly, E_3 does not represent a stable equilibrium position. We may now generalize to say that any point to the left of E_1 will not represent a stable equilibrium for reasons already argued.

Next consider a point to the right of E_1, such as E_4. E_4 is on the same indifference curve as E_1. Hence E_4 and E_1 must represent points of equal satisfaction, and indifference must be expressed between these points. For quantity kl, ln must be given to remain on the same indifference curve. But the market will give only lm for lk, not an amount sufficient to remain on the same indifference curve. The acceptance of lm for kl would lower the level of satisfaction, and since welfare maximization is assumed, the exchange must be rejected. Thus E_1 is the equilibrium position, representing a combination of n_1 of N and t_1 of T when the price ratio is p_1p_1 and the nation's taste pattern is that depicted by the indifference maps of Figure 2-4.

We have seen so far that a production possibilities curve and a price ratio will determine the quantities of two goods to be produced. Also an indifference map and a price ratio will determine how much of two commodities will be consumed. In a closed economy, the quantities of the two commodities produced must be equal to those consumed. The market mechanism will ensure that quantities produced equal quantities demanded at the equilibrium price. If the quantity produced is not equal to the quantity demanded, price must change and bring about the equality.

In Figure 2-5, the production possibilities curve, price ratio, and indifference curve are drawn for countries W and Z. Country W's resources will produce relatively larger quantities of N than T ($ON_1^W > OT_1^W$). With its resources, country Z can produce relatively larger quantities of T than N ($OT_1^Z > ON_1^Z$). Assuming identical taste patterns in the two countries, the price ratios are different in the absence of trade—N is cheap and T expensive in W, and N expensive and T cheap in Z. The price ratios, as a result, have different slopes, $p^W p^W$ in W and $p^Z p^Z$ in Z. Country W's equilibrium is at point E_1^W and produces n_1^W of N and t_1^W of T; country Z's equilibrium is at E_1^Z, with the production and consumption equal at n_1^Z and t_1^Z.

Resorting to international trade does not affect the production possibilities curve or the indifference map, only the price ratio. It is no longer necessary for a nation's production and consumption of a particular good to be equal; it is possible to import or export a good. As a result of moving to international trade, the new price line for both nations is $P^I P^I$ in Figure 2-5. The new price ratio induces nation W to produce more N and less T for a new combination of n_2^W of N and t_2^W of T. Nation W now produces more of N and less of T than it wishes to consume. The desired consumption combination is given by the tangency of $P^I P^I$ to an indifference curve; in this case, the equilibrium point is E_2^W, representing a combination of n_3^W of N and t_3^W of T. Consumption of T exceeds production by $t_2^W t_3^W$, an amount which must be imported. Likewise, production of N exceeds consumption by $n_3^W n_2^W$, an amount which must be exported.

Nation Z's output of T exceeds consumption by $t_3^Z t_2^Z$, and consumption of N exceeds production by $n_2^Z n_3^Z$. Nation Z must export $t_3^Z t_2^Z$ and import $n_2^Z n_3^Z$. In a two-country model, the amount of a good imported by a country must be equal to the amount of that good exported by the other nation. Therefore,

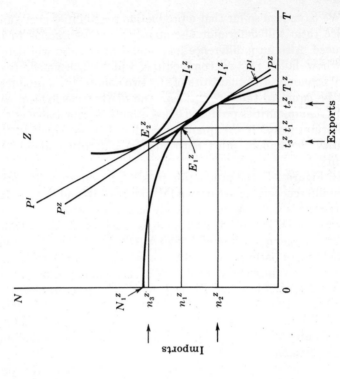

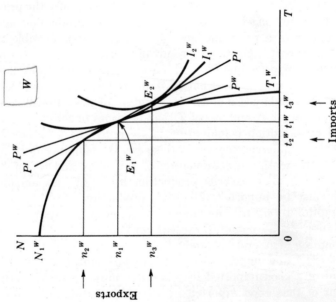

Figure 2-5

W's export of $n_3{}^W n_2{}^W$ must be equal to $n_2{}^Z n_3{}^Z$, Z's import. Also, Z's export of $t_3{}^Z t_2{}^Z$ must equal $t_2{}^W t_3{}^W$, W's imports of commodity T.

The new equilibrium position for both nations is on a higher indifference curve, and therefore both nations gain from trade. The gain is the result of each nation's expanding the output of the good it can produce more cheaply and contracting the output of the good it can produce only at a higher cost. However, neither nation specializes in the production of one commodity. Since cost is a function of output, a nation finds that there is a point beyond which it cannot produce. Likewise, the second nation finds that there is a small quantity of the good which it can supply at a competitive price.

Complete specialization comes about in models where constant costs are assumed. The reason is that factors are equally suited to both goods; increased production of one good does not require using less-suited resources which force up cost. If the international price ratio makes it profitable to produce an additional unit of N and one less of T, then it would be profitable to produce a second, third, and fourth unit of N and less of T. The increased output of N and reduced output of T do not influence the international price ratio and the costs. Thus, if it is profitable to produce one more unit of N and one less of T, there is nothing in the model to prevent the substitution from leading to complete specialization.

In the case of increasing cost, the more of a good produced, the higher the cost to produce an additional unit of N. Eventually the cost of an additional unit of N is prohibitively high.

Different Taste

We have seen how countries with different production possibilities but identical tastes gain from trade. Now we wish to see how nations with identical production possibilities but different tastes may gain from trade. The production possibilities curve in Figure 2-6 is for both countries. This means that they have the same technological knowledge and endowments. The indifference curves for the two countries show completely different tastes. Nation Z prefers commodity N; moves to higher indifference curves result in large additional units of N and small additions of T. On the other hand, W has a preference for T, with the result that moves to higher indifference curves will be accompanied by relatively large additional amounts of T and relatively small additional amounts of N. The different taste patterns bring about different demand schedules in the two countries. Nation Z will be willing to pay more for N than T, and in the absence of international trade the price of N will be relatively more than in country W, where N is not as highly prized and T is more desirable. The price ratio in Z is $P^Z P^Z$, and the amounts of N and T consumed and produced are n_1^Z and t_1^Z. The price ratio in W is $P^W P^W$, with n_1^W and t_1^W produced and consumed.

The move to international trade results in a single price ratio replacing the price ratio for each country. The international price ratio in Figure 2-6 is $P^I P^I$. Since the price ratio and the production possibilities curve are identical for both countries, the output of N and T for the two countries must be identical, namely n_2 and t_2. Nation Z has been induced to produce less N and more T and nation W more N and less T.

Figure 2-6

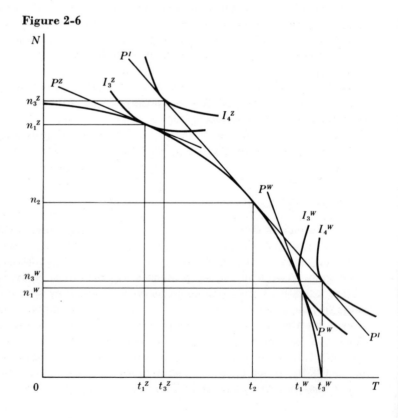

Nation W's new consumption of N and T is given by the tangency of $P^I P^I$ and indifference curve I_4, n_3^W and t_3^W. Consumption of T exceeds production by $t_3^W t_2$, the nation's imports. Production of N exceeds consumption so that $n_3^W n_2$ constitutes the nation's exports.

The tangency of the international price ratio $P^I P^I$ with Z's indifference curve yields the combination of N and T consumed by Z, namely n_3^Z and t_3^Z. $n_2 n_3^Z$ is the amount of N which must be imported, since consumption exceeds production by this amount. $t_3^Z t_2$ is the amount of home production of T not consumed and which must be exported.

As a result of international trade, each nation reached a higher indifference curve and consequently is better off. What explanation is there for both nations being better off when they have identical production possibilities curves? Essential to the explanation are their different tastes. The strong preferences of each nation for one of the goods—W for T and Z for N—resulted in the two countries in the absence of trade pushing the production of the desired commodity far along the increasing cost schedule. Z is producing N at a point where large quantities of T have to be given up for just a little N. Likewise, W is producing T at a point where large quantities of N have to be given up for little T. Clearly, the mrt (marginal rate of transformation) in the two countries is not equal. Say, for example, that Z's mrt is four of T for one of N, and W's mrt is four of N for one of T. If Z decides to produce one less unit of N, it could, with the resources, produce $4T$; and if W decided to produce one less unit of T, it could have $4N$. Now if W agreed with Z to exchange its four additional units of N for Z's four additional units of T, then Z would end up with three more units of desired N than it can produce, and W would end up with three more units of T than it can produce. Both nations have gained. The explanation of the gains for trade lies in the increasing costs.

When two nations have identical taste patterns but different production possibilities, then the nation exports the commodity in which it has a comparative advantage. If neither nation has a comparative advantage, then goods may still be traded internationally if there are different taste patterns in the two countries. When both countries have different production possibilities curves and different taste patterns, does it follow that a nation will export the commodity in which it has a comparative advantage? In Figure 2-7, we have drawn nation W's and Z's production

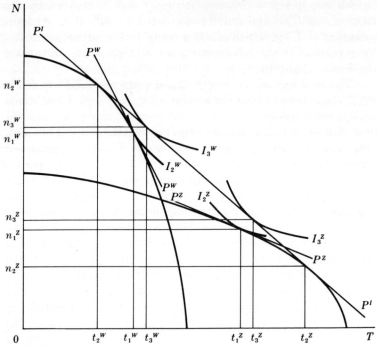

Figure 2-7

possibilities curve. With their given resources, W can produce larger quantities of N and Z can produce larger quantities of T. W has a comparative advantage in N and Z in T. Since the two countries have different tastes, the indifference maps or taste patterns for each country must also be introduced into Figure 2-7. In the absence of international trade, the domestic price ratio of $P^W P^W$ yields a consumption and production level of $n_1{}^W$ and $t_1{}^W$ in country W. Likewise the price ratio $P^Z P^Z$ in nation Z gives a consumption and production level of $n_1{}^Z$ and $t_1{}^Z$. The introduction of free trade results in one price ratio $P^I P^I$ rather than separate domestic price levels. Country W now expands its production of N to $n_2{}^W$ and contracts its production of T to $t_2{}^W$. Consumption expands to $n_3{}^W$ and $t_3{}^W$. Production of N exceeds consumption by $n_3{}^W n_2{}^W$, an amount exported. Imports are equal to the amount by which consumption exceeds production, $t_2{}^W t_3{}^W$. Country Z's production and consumption of each commodity are not equal. Production of T exceeds consumption by $t_2{}^Z t_3{}^Z$, which is exported. $n_2{}^Z n_3{}^Z$ is the amount of N by which consumption exceeds production and is imported. Nation W is exporting commodity N, in which it has a comparative advantage, and Z is exporting goods in which it has a comparative advantage. Different taste patterns, together with different production possibilities curves, need not disrupt the classical conclusion that a nation will export the commodity in which it has a comparative advantage.

Indeed, different tastes in the two countries *need not disrupt* the classical conclusion that nations will export the commodity in which they have a comparative advantage, but the question still remains as to whether this conclusion *might be disrupted.* In Figure 2-8, the production possibilities curves and the taste patterns are different for the two countries. In the absence of

Figure 2-8

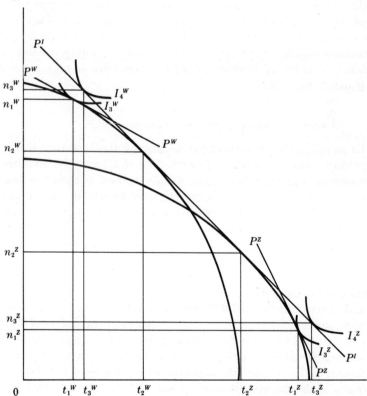

trade, nation W produces and consumes $n_1{}^W$ and $t_1{}^W$. $n_1{}^Z$ and $t_1{}^Z$ are the quantities produced and consumed by Z. The move to free trade results in the substitution of a single price ratio P^IP^I for the price ratio of each country, P^WP^W and P^ZP^Z. Country W now produces $n_2{}^W$ and $t_2{}^W$, while consuming $n_3{}^W$ and $t_3{}^W$. The consumption of N exceeds production by $n_2{}^Wn_3{}^W$; this quantity must be imported. Clearly, country W is importing commodity N, the good in which it has a comparative advantage, and is exporting commodity T, the good in which it has a comparative disadvantage.

Likewise, country Z produces $n_2{}^Z$ and $t_2{}^Z$ while consuming $n_3{}^Z$ and $t_3{}^Z$. Consumption of T exceeds production by $t_2{}^Zt_3{}^Z$, which is imported. Country Z's resources produce larger quantities of T than N, and in comparison with the productivity of W, Z has a comparative advantage in T.

Thus when two nations have different production possibilities curves and different tastes, it is not at all necessary that they export the commodity in which they have a comparative advantage. This means, then, that it is not possible to look at a nation's exports and imports and ascertain from them the commodities in which it has a comparative advantage. A nation may export goods in which it has a comparative advantage, and again, it may not.

Determination of the International Price

To simplify the exposition, let us assume that country W can produce only commodity N and does not have the required resources to produce any T. Likewise, country Z can produce only T and does not have resources required for N. In Figure 2-9, country W's total output with resources fully employed is N_1 and Z's is T_1. The indifference curves for country W have also been drawn into Figure 2-9. Alternative price ratios N_1T_1, N_1T_2, and N_1T_3 are also introduced in order to set forth the combinations of N and T which country W would consume. At a price ratio represented by the slope of N_1T_1, the amount consumed is $n_1{}^W$ and $t_1{}^W$ as determined by the tangency of the price ratio and indifference curve. The slope of N_1T_1 indicates that $N_1n_1{}^W$ must be given for $n_1{}^WE_1$. Since $n_1{}^WE_1$ is equal to $0t_1{}^W$, country W must export $N_1n_1{}^W$ and import $0t_1{}^W$ when the price ratio is N_1T_1. If the international price ratio were the slope of N_1T_2, then country W would want to consume $n_2{}^W$ and $t_2{}^W$.

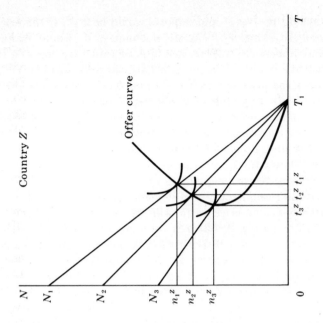

Country Z

Offer curve

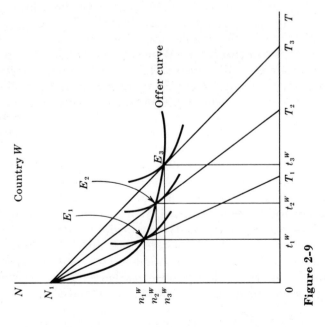

Country W

Offer curve

Figure 2-9

Exports would be $N_1 n_2{}^W$ and imports would be $0 t_2{}^W$. If the price ratio were the slope of $N_1 T_3$, then country W would export $N_1 n_3{}^W$ and import $0 t_3{}^W$. Thus it might be said that country W offers quantity $N_1 n_1{}^W$ when the international price ratio is $N_1 T_1$, $N_1 n_2{}^W$ when the price ratio is $N_1 T_2$, and $N_1 T_3{}^W$ when the price ratio is $N_1 T_3$. In this manner the amount offered can be found for any supposed price ratio. Points E_1, E_2, E_3, and all such points, of which there are an infinite number, may be connected; the resulting line, drawn in Figure 2-9, is called an *offer curve*. This curve shows the quantities of N which will be offered by country W for alternative quantities of T.

For equilibrium, supply and demand must be equal. Therefore the equilibrium price ratio will be the one at which the amount of N country W offers is the amount country Z wants to take, and the amount of T which W wishes to import must be equal to the amount Z exports. If these quantities are not equal, the international price will change until they are. It is essential then to see what quantities of N and T country Z wishes to consume.

For country Z in Figure 2-9, the price ratios $T_1 N_1$, $T_1 N_2$, and $T_1 N_3$ are drawn with the same slope as $N_1 T_1$, $N_1 T_2$, $N_1 T_3$, respectively. The tangencies of $T_1 N_1$, $T_1 N_2$, and $T_1 N_3$ will give the quantities of N and T which country Z wishes to export and import. The equilibrium price ratio is the one for which Z's export of T equals W's import, and for which Z's import of N equals W's export. The graphs are drawn such that $0 n_3{}^Z$, Z's import of N, is equal to $N_1 n_3{}^W$, W's export of N, and Z's export of $T_1 t_3{}^Z$ equals $0 t_3{}^Z$, W's import. Thus the international price ratio is $N_1 T_3$ or its equivalent $T_1 N_3$. If export and import of commodity N were not equal, then the excess supply or demand, as the case may be, would force a price adjustment. Only when the export of a commodity equals import is there no pressure on price and consequently equilibrium.

This point might better be illustrated with an *Edgeworth box diagram*. The top two diagrams which constitute illustration (a) of Figure 2-10 are a repetition of those in Figure 2-9, except that the indifference curves are omitted. With the price ratio and the offer curves, we can determine the quantities of N and T which will be exchanged at the alternative price ratios. To make an Edgeworth box diagram, we must first rotate counter-clockwise the graph of country W, illustration (b) of Figure 2-10, so that commodity N is measured along the horizontal axis and commodity T

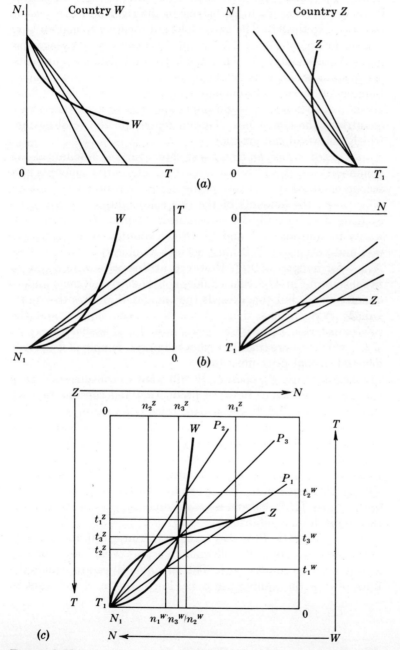

Figure 2-10

is measured vertically. The distance along the horizontal axis is $0N_1$, W's total output of N. Next, the graph for country Z must be rotated clockwise, illustration (b) of Figure 2-10, so that T is measured vertically and N horizontally. The vertical distance is limited by country Z's resources; it can produce $0T_1$. The graph for country W needs to be moved to the right and the one for country Z to the left. The two can be put together to make a box, illustration (c) of Figure 2-10; point T_1 of country Z is placed on point N_1 of country W. Thus the horizontal distance represents the maximum output of N which can be had, and the vertical distance $0T_1$ represents the maximum output of T which can be had, given a two-country world and the resources of those two countries. The closed box diagram represents the total output which the world can produce.

As noted earlier, an offer curve shows varying amounts of one commodity which will be exchanged for alternative amounts of a second commodity. For any particular price ratio which cuts an offer curve, the amounts of the two commodities which will be exchanged can readily be ascertained. At price P_1, country W wants to consume $n_1{}^W$ and $t_1{}^W$. Since country W is producing $0N_1$ and nothing of T, it must achieve its objective by exporting $N_1n_1{}^W$ for imports of $0t_1{}^W$. However, at this price ratio Z desires to consume $n_1{}^Z$ and $t_1{}^Z$. Since Z does not produce N, it must import quantity $0n_1{}^Z$, but this exceeds the amount W desires to export, namely $N_1n_1{}^W$. Thus demand for N exceeds supply, and the price must rise. Likewise at price ratio P_1, Z wishes to export $T_1t_1{}^Z$, which is more than W wishes to import. Supply of T exceeds demand so that price must fall.

At price ratio P_2, country W will want to consume $n_2{}^W$, thus leaving the difference between production and consumption for export, namely $N_1n_2{}^W$. But at this price ratio, country Z wishes to consume and import $0n_2{}^Z$. It can easily be seen that $N_1n_2{}^W$, W's exports, is greater than $0n_2{}^Z$, Z's imports. Supply exceeds demand; the price is too high. Also at this price ratio, Z will want to consume $t_2{}^Z$; the rest of the T output, $t_2{}^ZT_1$, must be exported. But at this price ratio, W wishes to consume and import $0t_2{}^W$. $0t_2{}^W$ exceeds $T_1t_2{}^Z$; demand is greater than supply, and price must rise to reach its equilibrium.

The price ratio P_3 passes through the intersection of the two offer curves. Country W will want to export $N_1n_3{}^W$, and country Z will want to import $0n_3{}^Z$. The two quantities are equal; the price of N is the equilibrium price. Furthermore, Z will want to export $t_3{}^z T_1$, and W will want to import $0t_3{}^w$. It can clearly be seen that the two vertical distances are equal; the price of T is the equilibrium price. The equilibrium price, then, is the price ratio which passes through the intersection of the two offer curves, for only here are supply and demand equal. This price ratio is also called the *barter terms of trade*.

Summary

A. Taste Patterns
  1. Illustrated by indifference curves
     a. An indifference curve shows all possible combinations of two commodities which yield a constant level of satisfaction.
     b. The slope of the indifference curve is the marginal rate of psychological substitution (mrps). The marginal rate of psychological substitution is the amount of a second commodity which must be given up for one additional unit of the first commodity so that the level of satisfaction is unchanged. For each successive unit of the first commodity, smaller amounts of the second must be given to stay on the same level of satisfaction.
     c. Indifference curves further from the origin represent higher levels of satisfaction.
     d. The consumer tries to maximize satisfaction or reach the highest indifference curve.
B. Price Ratio
  1. Barter—amount of one commodity exchanging for an amount of a second.
C. From the taste pattern and the price ratio, an amount of two commodities purchased can be ascertained.
  1. The price ratio must equal the mrps.
D. Production possibilities curve shows all possible combinations of two commodities which can be produced with the given resources of the country.
  1. The slope of the production possibilities curve is the marginal rate of transformation (mrt); the mrt is the increased amount of the first commodity which results from diverting to it the resources required to produce one unit of the second commodity.

E. From the production possibilities curve and the price ratio, the amount of two commodities produced can be ascertained.
   1. The price ratio must equal the mrt.
F. In the absence of trade, the price ratio must equate production with domestic demand for a country.
G. The price ratio for two countries must be different for international trade to be profitable.
   1. Different prices may come about as a result of different production possibilities curves in each country.
      a. Each nation exports the goods in which it has a comparative advantage.
   2. Different prices may be the result of different taste patterns in each country.
      a. Each nation imports goods according to taste.
   3. Different prices may be the result of a combination of different production possibilities curves and different taste.
      a. The nation may still export the good for which it has a comparative advantage.
      b. The nation may export the good which it likes least.
      c. It is not possible to determine from exports the commodity in which a nation has a comparative advantage.
H. With international trade, there is one price ratio for the world. The price of a good must equate production with domestic demand and exports.

Selected Readings

Books

A. E. A.: *Readings in The Theory of International Trade*, Philadelphia: Blakiston Co., 1950, items 9–14.

Caves, Richard, *Trade and Economic Structure*, Cambridge: Harvard University Press, 1960, Chap. 2.

Eastham, K. K., *Graphical Economics*, Chicago: Quadrangle Books, 1960, Chap. 14.

Ellsworth, P. T., *The International Economy*, New York: The Macmillan Co., 1964, part 2.

Graham, Frank, *The Theory of International Values*, Princeton: Princeton University Press, 1948.

Haberler, G., *Theory of International Trade*, London: William Hodge and Co., 1933, Chaps. 9–12.

——— A *Survey of International Trade Theory*, Princeton: International Finance Section of Princeton University, 1955.

Harrod, Roy, *International Economics*, Chicago: University of Chicago, 1957, Chaps. 2 and 3.

Kindleberger, C. P., *International Economics*, Homewood: Richard D. Irwin, 1963, Chaps. 5 and 6.

Majumdar, T., *Measurement of Utility*, London: Macmillan and Co., 1961.

Marsh, Donald, *World Trade and Investment*, New York: Harcourt and Brace, 1951, Chaps. 19 and 20.

Meade, J. E., *Trade and Welfare*, London: Oxford University Press, 1955, part 1.

Ohlin, Bertil, *Interregional and International Trade*, Cambridge: Harvard University Press, 1933.

Ricardo, David, *Principles of Political Economy*, Cambridge: University Press, 1951, Chaps. 22 and 25.

Robinson, Joan, *Economic Philosophy*, Chicago: Aldine Publishing Co., 1962, Chaps. 2 and 3.

Periodicals

A. E. A., *Index of Economic Journals*, classification no. 11.22.

Beckmann, M. J., "International and Interpersonal Division of Labor," *Weltwirtschaftliches Archiv.*, 1957.

Brown, A. J., "Professor Leontief and the Pattern of World Trade," *Yorkshire Bulletin of Economic and Social Research*, November, 1957.

Buchann, N. S., "Lines on the Leontief Paradox," *Economia Internazionale*, November, 1955.

Clemhout, S., "Production Function Analysis Applied to Leontief Scarce-factor Paradox of International Trade," *Manchester School of Economics and Social Studies*, May, 1963.

Ford, J. L., "The Leontief Paradox and the Heckscher-Ohlin Theory of the Basis of Commodity-trade," *Economia Internazionale*, May, 1962.

Harberger, A. C., "Some Evidence on the International Price Mechanism," *Journal of Political Economy*, December, 1957.

Harrod, R. F., "Factor-price Relations under Free Trade," *Economic Journal*, June, 1958.

Jones, R. W., "Factor Proportions and the Heckscher-Ohlin Theorem," *Review of Economic Studies*, 1956.

Leontief, W., "Factor Proportions and the Structure of American Trade: Further Theoretical and Empirical Analysis," *Review of Economics and Statistics*, November, 1956.

McKenzie, L. W., "Equality of Factor Prices in World Trade," *Econometrica*, July, 1955.

Mundell, R. A., "The Pure Theory of International Trade," *American Economic Review*, March, 1960.

Robinson, R., "Factor Proportions and Comparative Advantage," parts 1 and 2, *Quarterly Journal of Economics*, May and August, 1956.

Valavanis, S., "Factor Proportions and Structure of American Trade: Comment," *Review of Economics and Statistics*, February, 1958.

Vinar, J., "Relative Abundance of Factors and International Trade," *Indian Economic Journal*, January, 1962.

3.

Some
Qualifications

The model discussed so far has been developed under the assumption that there exist only two countries, two commodities, perfect competition, no transportation costs, and three factors of production—land, labor, and capital. Given these assumptions, price is equated for the two goods in the two countries. The supply of each resource in relation to its demand gives the price of the resource; a nation expands the production of the commodity which requires primarily its lowest-priced resource. The object of this chapter is to look further into some of these assumptions.

Number of Countries

The discussion of comparative advantage would not greatly be changed by introducing a larger number of countries all at the same stage of economic development. Each nation would import goods which would be more cheaply imported than produced at home and export those goods which could be sold at a profit on the world market. The commodities a nation would export would depend on the resources required for their production and the supply of these resources.

The real difficulty comes when the theory is projected into today's world of nations at different stages of economic development. As developing nations assert their competitive position, other nations must adjust their output. If an emerging nation increases substantially the supply of some commodity on the international market, then the world price is reduced, thereby making it unprofitable for some other nation to continue to produce the good.

Furthermore, as a nation develops, the internal prices of resources change. The cost structure at one time will allow the expansion of the production of some goods which at a later date a nation cannot continue to produce. For example, after World War II, Japan had a comparatively large labor supply and wages were low. Labor-intensive goods such as fine bone china were produced and sold competitively on the world market. However, the development of electronic and precision instruments industries forced wages up to a point where Japan is less able to compete with Great Britain in the production of fine bone china. The weakening of Japan's competitive position came not from the world price of china but rather from changes in internal costs. Heavy capital investment in Japan is making labor more scarce.

Comparative advantage is a static theory applicable to fully mature nations. It shows how nations might reallocate their resources and trade to increase economic well-being. Growth or development is not taken into account.

Changes in international prices and in the internal price structure are continually making nations adjust their output to the new economic environment. Historically, the United States has lost its comparative advantage in textiles, leather goods, and some types of heavy industry. The process will continue as other nations acquire skills and capital. This only indicates that nations at the outset were not able to determine precisely the commodities in which they had a comparative advantage. Each nation expands production and exports on present prices and expected future prices. But the prices themselves change; this is a result of growth and development. Therefore, each nation must make further adjustments in production, exports, and imports.

Technology

Comparative advantage assumes that technology is the same throughout the world, and that all nations have the same knowledge about combining capital and labor and choose the combination which suits their resources. In the real world this is, of course, not true. Underdeveloped nations have a very limited knowledge of alternative means of production, and their ignorance limits the efficient use of their resources. The methods of production used are often based on tradition rather than a choice of the best combination. This is also true in Europe today, where member countries of the Common Market have failed to reap fully the gains from mass production made possible by the large market.[1]

Furthermore, technology is not equally available to all nations. Its development is costly and undertaken only in the wealthy nations where it is protected by patents and copyrights and maintained as trade secrets. For technology to disseminate through the world takes time; by the time some new method is fully disseminated, it is often outdated.

The uneven distribution of technology not only gives some nations an advantage in world trade but also may alter a nation's ability to produce particular goods. New technology may not equally affect the production of all goods; for a particular nation, it may be biased toward export goods or import goods, or it may be neutral. In Figure 3-1a, the production possibilities curve of country W is drawn. The curve shows that W's resources will produce relatively more N than T; consequently, W will export N and import T. If new technology is biased toward exports, then a larger quantity of N can now be produced with W's resources, as shown by the new production possibilities curve in 3-1b. W will now export more; this increased supply will tend to reduce N's price. The terms of trade are said to move against W. On the other hand, if the new technology is import biased, W will be able to produce more T with its given resources, as shown in Figure 3-1c. W will have to import less

[1] J. J. Servan-Schreiber, "The American Challenge," *Harper's Magazine*, pp. 31–43, July, 1968.

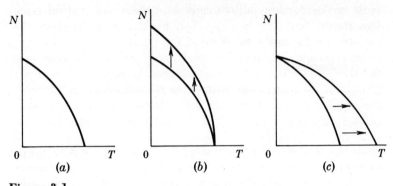

Figure 3-1

T, thereby reducing its price and the earnings of the supplying countries. It was argued that new technology after World War II was import biased in the United States, thereby explaining the United States' competitive advantage and its very favorable balance of payments.[2]

It might be clearer to look at new technology which is import biased in terms of isoquants. In Figure 3-2a, the United States cannot produce good T competitively because it requires large quantities of labor. Isoquant I_1 shows that country Z can produce the good cheaply with a relatively large amount of labor.

[2] J. R. Hicks, "The Long-Run Dollar Problem," *Essays in World Economics,* Oxford: Oxford University Press, 1957, p. 66.

Figure 3-2

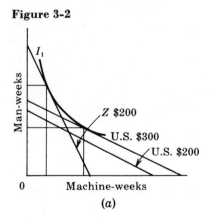
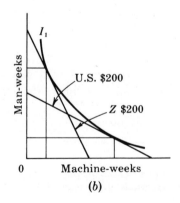

(a)   (b)

Now new technology allows capital to be substituted for labor; this means that the isoquant will be less steep to show that capital can be easily substituted for labor (Figure 3-2b). As a consequence, the United States can now produce the good competitively by producing with a relatively large amount of capital (its abundant factor) and little labor (its scarce factor).

Noncompeting Groups

According to the analysis developed, a nation with a large supply of land at low cost will tend to expand output of land-intensive goods, such as agricultural commodities. The output of a land-intensive good is explained. But there are a large number of agricultural commodities requiring extensive land for their production. The output of a particular land-intensive product must be explained. For example, Canada is an important supplier of wheat. But why does Canada place large proportions of its land into wheat rather than some other commodity requiring extensive land, such as cotton? The answer lies in the fact that all land is not homogeneous and equally suited to the production of all commodities; Canada's land is suited primarily to wheat and not particularly to cotton.

The assumption of three categories of factors of production, each consisting of homogeneous and identical units, must be modified. For example, all units of labor are not identical in skill, dexterity, and intelligence. There are, in fact, subgroups of labor, or as J. E. Cairnes[3] put it:

> What we find, in effect, is, not a whole population competing indiscriminately for all occupations, but a series of industrial layers, superimposed on one another, within each of which the various candidates for employment possess a real and effective power of selection, while those occupying the several strata are, for all purposes of effective competition, practically isolated from each other.

> No doubt the various ranks and classes fade into each other by imperceptible gradations, and individuals from all classes are constantly passing up or dropping down; but while this is so, it is nevertheless true that the average workman, from whatever rank he be taken, finds his power of competition limited for practical purposes to a certain range of occupations, so that, however high

[3] J. E. Cairnes, *Some Leading Principles of Political Economy*, New York: Harper and Brothers, 1874, pp. 66–68.

the rates of remuneration in those that lie beyond may rise, he is excluded from sharing them. We are thus compelled to recognize the existence of non-competing industrial groups as a feature of our social economy; and this is the fact which I desire here to insist upon. It remains to be considered how this organization of industry is calculated to modify the action of the principle of cost of production.

The factors of production need to be broken down into subgroups. For example, labor might be broken into unskilled, skilled, semiskilled, and managerial. Even more detailed categories might be imagined. Land might be divided by climate, fertility, terrain, or some combination of these groups. Capital might be categorized by liquid and nonliquid capital. Liquid, of course, would be money; the nonliquid would be machines and buildings. The nonliquid capital could be described by industry—agricultural, extraction, manufacturing, etc. The quantity of any of these subgroups could determine the nation's comparative advantage in static analysis.

Given identical demands for a specific factor of production in two countries, the one having the larger quantity will have the lower cost of production and comparative advantage. Thus comparative advantage is a truism. A country having more of a specific factor relative to demand has lower cost and a comparative advantage. In any situation, a larger supply for a given demand yields a lower price or cost.

With a static analysis, there is no economic explanation as to why a nation has a relatively larger supply of some factor. The explanation lies in a geographical attribute or a historical development. Upon breaking resources into subgroups, it is not very revealing to find that Latin America has more land in a tropical climate than does Russia, and commodities requiring a tropical climate are produced most cheaply by Latin America and must be imported by Russia. The enumeration and description of all subgroups to explain trade tends to reduce the significance of comparative advantage in explaining goods imported and exported. It is possible to so strictly define the subgroups that one particular nation can produce the good, since it alone has the supply.

Liquid capital is completely flexible and can enter any productive enterprise. Nonliquid capital is embodied in machinery and buildings and is comparatively inflexible. As long as this capital is earning a return, it pays to produce. The amount of a good produced will depend on the quantity of nonliquid capital and the form in which it is embodied.

The introduction of time into the analysis serves to make the noncompeting groups less rigid. Admittedly, at any given moment, it is impossible for an unskilled laborer to compete with a physician in the practice of medicine, regardless of the wage to be earned. However, over a longer time period, it is possible to train youth to be physicians rather than allow them to become unskilled laborers. The uncommitted resources, whether they be capital or labor, are fairly flexible as a group.

It was of this longer time period, the long run, that the authors of comparative advantage were thinking. Given technology and taste, each nation would direct its resources—land, labor, and capital—to produce the good in which it had a comparative advantage. This long-run analysis assumed away most of the problem of noncompeting and monopoly groups. However, it is rather difficult to assume that in the long run taste and technology are constant. Changing technology combined with nations at different stages of economic development serves to cloud true comparative advantage, especially comparative advantage in the long run.

Competition

The setting for the theory of comparative advantage is perfect competition. The large number of firms prevents any individual firm from influencing price; each is only influenced by price. Land, labor, and capital are attracted by high earnings or profits. Free trade reduces the price of some goods to so low a point that domestic producers cannot earn a profit and pay the going wages and rent. Thus the resources are attracted to the expanding industry with high earnings and profits, the export industries. Resources move out of industries where they are inefficient, into industries where they are efficient in production.

Imperfect competition, on the other hand, may forestall the redistribution of resources. For example, assume that commodity T is produced under conditions of constant returns to scale (size of firm is then of no importance), and N is produced under conditions of increasing returns to scale. Suppose also that before trade W is producing much N and little T as a result of taste patterns. Furthermore, Z is producing little N and much T. But suppose Z actually has the comparative advantage in the

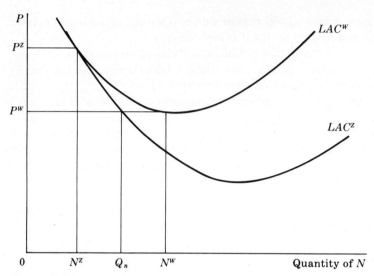

Figure 3-3

production of N and should export this good in a free trade situation. However, W is producing a larger quantity of N than is Z. As a result of economies of scale, W's large output dominates Z's comparative advantage over a substantial range of production, and this allows W to undersell Z. This is shown graphically in Figure 3-3. Z's long-run average cost curve LAC^Z lies below W's long-run average cost curve LAC^W, indicating that Z has the comparative advantage. In the absence of free trade, Z produces N^Z at a price of P^Z, and W produces the large quantity of N^W at the lower price of P^W. To compete at the price of P^W, Z must expand immediately to a minimum quantity of Q_n; a smaller quantity can be produced only at a higher price. Thus Z must grow to a large size immediately and be able to market this large quantity without disruption. Also the producers of N in country Z must have access to capital to grow to the required size. Clearly, economies of scale may make it difficult for a nation to compete even when it has the comparative advantage.

Price Difference due to Transportation Cost

The first task is to describe the effect transportation costs have on the prices in the trading countries; later the pricing of transportation costs will be discussed. The equilibrium position exclusive of transportation costs is repeated in Figure 3-4 as a point of departure. Z's supply and demand schedules take the usual form; W's supply and demand schedules are a mirror-image of the usual depiction of these schedules. Better yet, if one could imagine hinges installed on the price axis, so that the x axis could be swung on these hinges through 180 degrees, then the result would be the depiction of W's supply and demand schedules in Figure 3-4. Quantity for W increases to the left, and for Z to the right. The price axis is identical for both nations; the price in both nations is P_1. Z's production is M^z, of which C^z is consumed domestically. The amount by which production exceeds consumption, $M^z C^z$, is exported. Thus total demand—domestic consumption plus exports—equals supply, making for a stable price at P_1.

Country W produces M^W at price P_1 and consumes C^W. $M^W C^W$ represents the amount by which consumption exceeds production and is the amount imported. Thus total supply—

Figure 3-4

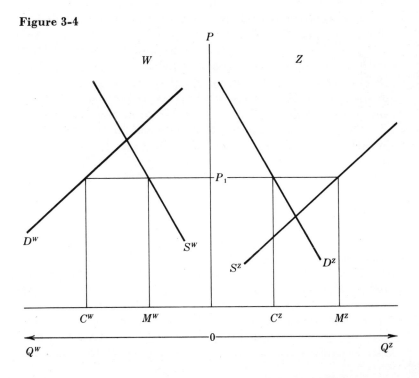

domestic production plus imports—equals demand at a stable price of P_1. In this two-country model, Z's exports $C^Z M^Z$ must equal W's imports of $M^W C^W$.

The introduction of transportation costs makes the price fall in the exporting country and rise in the importing country, until a price difference equal to the transportation costs emerges. The reason why the price difference must equal the transportation cost is rather simple. If the price in W exceeds the price in Z by more than the transportation cost, it would mean that after subtracting transportation costs, more could be earned in W than in Z. As a result, goods would flow to W, forcing down the price, and the flow from Z would force up the price there. Once the price difference equalled the transportation cost, there would be no further reason for diverting the good from one market to another. If the price difference were less than the transportation cost, then the net price received in W after paying transportation cost would be less than that received in Z. Less would be exported from Z to W, with the result that the price would rise in W and fall in Z. This would continue until the price difference equalled the transportation cost.

The consequence of introducing transportation cost is shown in Figure 3-5. The price rises in W from P_1 to P_3. As a result of a rise in price, quantity demanded falls by $C_1^W C_2^W$, and quantity supplied domestically is induced to expand $M_1^W M_2^W$. The decreased quantity demanded plus the increased domestic production yields the decreased imports. Imports were $C_1^W M_1^W$ and reduce to $C_2^W M_2^W$ as a consequence of the higher price.

The fall in Z's exports must be equal to the fall in W's imports. This reduced demand for Z's goods forces the price down to P_2. The fall in price encourages a greater domestic consumption, an increase in quantity demanded of $C_1^Z C_2^Z$, and a fall in quantity supplied of $M_1^Z M_2^Z$. Z's new level of exports $C_2^Z M_2^Z$ equals W's new level of imports $C_2^W M_2^W$.

It is important to note that the price in W did not rise by the amount of the cost of transportation. Before transportation costs were taken into consideration, the equilibrium price was P_1. The introduction of transportation costs into our supply-and-demand mechanism brought about a new equilibrium price in W of P_3. Thus the price in W rose by $P_1 P_3$, which is less than the cost of transportation. Clearly, the residents of W pay only part of the transportation cost, namely $P_1 P_3$ of $P_3 P_2$. The other part is paid by country Z. The introduction of transportation

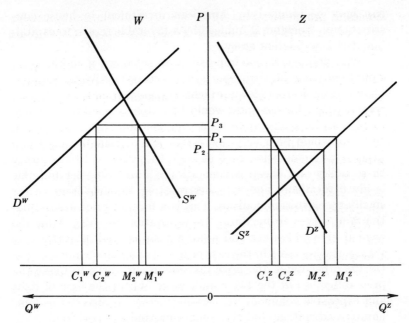

Figure 3-5

costs results in the price in Z falling by P_1P_2, the amount of
transportation costs imposed on Z.

The rise in the price in W induces an increase in domestic
output of $M_1^WM_2^W$. Simultaneously, the fall in price in Z leads
to a decrease in output of $M_2^ZM_1^Z$. The transportation costs
induce the high-cost producer to expand and the low-cost producer to contract output. The amount of the transportation
costs determines how much the prices will differ and the extent
to which production will be directed away from the low-cost
producer to the high-cost producer, given the supply and demand
schedules. The transportation cost is so great for some goods as
to preclude any international trade, with the consequence that
the price between countries will continue to exist. The price
difference between the two countries will depend on the respective costs of production and the level of demand. An extreme
example is housing; constructed houses do not move in international trade. Some of the component parts are traded, but
the house has to be built on site. There is a large difference in
the price of housing in the United States and in England. The

gap may be reduced by American investment in house construction in England, if induced by a favorable return to capital; but that is a different story.

It is difficult, if not impossible, to set down a simple principle to describe how transportation costs are derived. One rate, based on cubic footage or weight per mile, is not used for all commodities. A single rate would be a high percentage of value in the case of bulky and cheap commodities, such as coal, and this rate would be a very low percentage of value for light and expensive commodities, such as gold. In order not to discourage these bulky and cheap commodities, a lower rate per ton-mile is given for them, and a higher rate per ton-mile is given for small expensive commodities. This is a form of price discrimination and serves to maximize transportation revenue. Thus the comparative advantage and welfare position are less affected by transportation costs in the case of heavy and bulky commodities. On the other hand, the price discrimination works to make the price difference in the two countries greater in the case of light and expensive commodities, serving further to distort the comparative advantage and the welfare-maximizing position.

Variations in rates are not limited to schedules devised on the basis of weight and value of the commodity. The direction the commodity is to be shipped also plays a part. Trading routes have tended to project out from commercial centers; so that ships would not have to return in ballast, very favorable rates are given for the back haul. A small revenue is better than none. Thus comparative advantage and welfare maximization are further modified by the direction in which a nation's commodities flow in these trade routes, the development of which is a historical matter.

Localization of Industry

Land and labor are not particularly mobile internationally. National borders do get changed periodically, and a continuous stream of migration exists, but the economic significance of these changes is small. However, the third factor of production, capital, is mobile. A nation may erect plants within its borders to process raw materials into finished goods, or it may erect the plants within the country supplying raw materials.

Transportation costs play a part in determining the best geographical area for a plant. If the item loses weight through processing, then transportation costs can be reduced by processing the commodity near the raw materials. On the other hand, if the commodity gains weight through processing, then transportation costs can be reduced by shipping the raw materials and producing the good near the market. However, if the market is geographically dispersed, then a decision has to be made as to whether any economies of scale favor a single plant with a number of warehouses, or whether a number of plants in the various marketing areas is preferable.

The type of transportation which has to be used must also be taken into consideration. Water transportation is usually cheaper than land transportation. Transportation costs, then, can be reduced by locating near rivers and harbors.

The point to be made here is that although comparative advantage means that each nation produces and exports the commodity requiring its abundant factor, the rule must be modified by transportation costs, particularly in the case of capital. Whereas the production process requiring land and labor has to go to the area where supply is abundant, the production process requiring capital may go to the capital-rich country, or the capital may go to the country rich in resources. Transportation costs play an important part in determining whether the raw materials go to the capital-rich country or whether the capital goes to the country rich in natural resources.

Summary

The purpose of this chapter has been to qualify the classical conclusions of comparative advantage. The peculiar manner in which transportation costs are derived serves to distort a nation's comparative advantage. Furthermore, a dynamic world of changing taste and technology obscures the classical theorem. Finally, comparative advantage applies to nations at the same stage of economic development; a world in which nations are emerging at different rates of development adds further complications to assigning nations' production on the basis of comparative advantage.

Even though it may not be possible to determine ultimately the commodity in which a nation has a comparative advantage, the substance of classical thought remains true—each nation should export those goods which it can produce most cheaply and import those goods which it can produce only at a greater relative cost. Given the world as it is, this classical rule will guide nations to higher levels of economic well-being, even though the peak may remain unapproachable.

Selected Readings

Books
   Caves, Richard, *Trade and Economic Structure*, Cambridge: Harvard University Press, 1960, Chaps. 5 and 6.
   Ellsworth, P. T., *The International Economy*, New York: The Macmillan Co., 1964, Chaps. 7 and 8.
   Hoover, Edgar, *The Location of Economic Activity*, New York: McGraw-Hill, 1948.
   Isard, Walter, *Location and Space-Economy*, New York: John Wiley, 1956.
   Marsh, Donald, *World Trade and Investment*, New York: Harcourt and Brace, 1951, Chap. 21.
   Ohlin, B., *Interregional and International Trade*, Cambridge: Harvard University Press, 1933, Chaps. 3, 5, 6, and 10.

Periodicals
   A. E. A., *Index of Economic Journals*, classification no. 11.22.
   Bardham, P., "International Differences in Production Functions, Trade and Factor Prices," *Economic Journal*, March, 1965.
   Bhagwarti, J., "The Theory of Comparative Advantage in the Context of Underdevelopment and Growth," *Pakistan Development Review*, 1962.
   Ford, J. L., "Measures of Factor Endowments and Factor-Intensities," *Oxford Economic Papers*, November, 1963.
   Goedhuys, D. W., "Social Cost and Private Cost in the Infant Industry Argument," *South African Journal of Economics*, June, 1963.
   Kemp, M. C., and M. C. Jones, "Variable Labor Supply and Theory of International Trade," *Journal of Political Economy*, February, 1962.
   Montias, J. M., "Balanced Growth and International Specialization: A Diagrammatic Analysis," *Oxford Economic Papers*, June, 1961.

Regulating Trade

The classical theory of comparative advantage written for economies which are at the same stage of development and operating under the conditions of perfect competition does not apply without qualification in today's world. Nations at different stages of economic development do not have the same technology; economies of scale and the resulting imperfect competition impede the assignment of production according to the classical rules of comparative advantage. Nevertheless, the basic conclusions of the classical theory remain sound; each nation can improve its economic well-being by exporting the goods which it can produce cheaply and importing the goods which can be produced at home only at relatively higher costs.

Although free trade enlarges the economic well-being of the nation, some groups within the nation will suffer. Inefficient firms are not able to compete with efficient foreign firms and are consequently driven out of business. The resources now are available to the expanding export industry. However, the expanding export industry uses the scarce factor less intensively than do the contracting industries; consequently, the demand for the scarce factor is reduced, as is its real return. Tariffs are introduced with the object of protecting inefficient firms and maintaining the scarcity of some resources. Such a solution trades off the economic well-being of the nation for the well-being of a particular group. Tariffs as a source of revenue and as a means of protecting home industry are the topics of this chapter.

The Basis of the Duty

A *duty* may be imposed on the ad valorem or specific basis. An *ad valorem* basis is a percentage; the duty may be a percentage of the cost of producing the item abroad, a percentage of the cost of the competing home-produced good, or a percentage of the foreign retail price. A *specific* duty is an absolute amount and does not change with changes in cost and price.

A specific duty constitutes a larger percentage of the lower price range of a commodity; thus the protection provided to the low price range is greater. During rising prices, the specific duty becomes a diminishing percentage of price, and the protection afforded is reduced. On the other hand, at times of falling prices, the specific duty becomes a rising percentage of price, and the protection afforded increases.

An ad valorem duty provides the same percentage protection for the entire price range of a good. Furthermore, the protection afforded as measured by percentage of price does not change with rising or falling prices. However, the revenue received per unit is less for the low-priced range of a good; it increases during periods of rising prices.

The Tariff Burden

The first question to be considered is: who pays the tariff—residents of the importing country or residents of the exporting country? To answer this question, it is convenient to reintroduce Figure 3-1 as Figure 4-1. On the right side of Figure 4-1, the supply and demand schedules for W, the importing country, are drawn. The price is measured vertically, and quantity increases

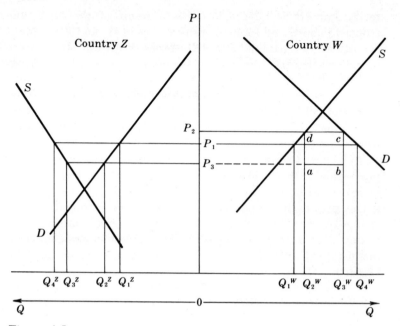

Figure 4-1

on the horizontal axis out to the right. The left side of the graph depicts the supply and demand schedules of Z, the exporting country. As indicated in Chapter 3, this graph for Z is a mirror-image of the usual depiction of supply and demand. For Z, increase in price is measured on the same vertical axis as is W's price change. However, Z's increase in quantity is measured on the horizontal axis out to the left. Z's demand schedule slopes downward from right to left to show that larger quantities are demanded only at lower prices. Furthermore, Z's supply schedule rises from right to left to show that larger quantities are supplied only at higher prices. The free trade price before the advent of tariffs is P_1. Country W demands Q_4^W and supplies Q_1^W. The difference between supply and demand is equal to imports, or $Q_1^W Q_4^W$. Nation Z supplies Q_4^Z and demands only Q_1^Z, exporting the difference between domestic supply and demand, or $Q_1^Z Q_4^Z$. Since exports equal imports, or $Q_1^W Q_4^W$ equals $Q_1^Z Q_4^Z$, the price P_1 is one of stable equilibrium.

Now suppose country W introduces a specific duty on imports. The price in W and Z must differ by the amount of the tariff. Imports will be reduced as a result of the tariff; the reduced imports will force the price to rise in W, and Z's reduced exports will force a fall in price. In terms of Figure 4-1, the price in the two countries diverges by the amount of the specific tariff, or P_2P_3.

As a result of the imposition of a tariff, price rises in W by P_1P_2 and falls in Z by P_1P_3. The tariff is equal to P_2P_3. Clearly, P_1P_3 is paid by Z and P_1P_2 is paid by W; each country pays a proportion of the tariff.

The next task is to describe the factors which determine the proportion of the tariff to be paid by each nation. This can best be explained by employing the concept of *elasticity*. Elasticity is a measure of the responsiveness of a change in quantity to a change in price. The change in quantity and price is a percentage change. The formula for elasticity is the percentage change in quantity ($\%\ dQ$) divided by the percentage change in price ($\%\ dP$).

$$\text{Coefficient of elasticity} = \frac{\%\ dQ}{\%\ dP}$$

If the coefficient of elasticity is less than 1, it means that any adjustment comes primarily through price changes, with quantity making a smaller adjustment. A coefficient of 1 indicates that quantity and price make identical adjustments. If the coefficient is greater than 1, it indicates that quantity is the primary adjustment variable with price undergoing small changes. When the coefficient of elasticity is greater than 1, i.e., the schedule is elastic, the quantity adjusts to forestall price changes. With *unitary elasticity* (a coefficient of 1), the adjustment is shared equally by price and quantity. With *inelastic schedules* (a coefficient of less than 1), quantity is rather inflexible, leaving price to do the adjusting.

If country Z's supply is inelastic, it means that output cannot readily be changed, so a smaller price will be taken to avoid a change in quantity. The more inelastic Z's supply, the more of the tariff it will pay. Furthermore, if Z's domestic demand schedule is also inelastic, larger quantities will not easily be taken up by the local market. Thus small falls in price will not induce the domestic market to absorb the good; consequently, price will fall greatly to allow the continued export to W. If its elasticity of supply and demand is small, Z will be forced to absorb a larger proportion of W's tariff.

If W's demand schedule is highly elastic, it means that W's consumers are sensitive to price and will reduce quantity to avoid paying a higher price. The quantity forced back onto Z would serve to reduce Z's price. Hence a large elasticity of demand in W will serve to shift a larger proportion of the tariff onto Z. Furthermore, if W's elasticity of supply is high, it indicates that W will readily expand output as a result of a small increase in price. W's increased production will substitute for imports from Z. Z will have to reduce price in order to compete, thereby absorbing a large proportion of the tariff. High elasticities of supply and demand in W force the larger proportion of the tariff onto Z.

Low elasticities in Z and high elasticities in W serve to place much of the tariff burden on Z. On the other hand, high elasticities in Z and low elasticities in W reserve the larger proportion of the tariff burden for the residents of W.

The Effects of Tariffs

Tariffs serve to provide revenue and to protect an import-competing industry. Thus a revenue and protection effect can be shown. Furthermore, consumption and production are influenced in both countries; a production and consumption effect can be shown for the two countries.

The protection effect is the increased output, induced by the higher price, resulting from the imposition of a tariff in the importing country. In terms of Figure 4-1, the protection effect is quantity $Q_1^W Q_2^W$; this amount is induced by the increase in price P_1 to P_2. The size of the protection effect depends on the amount by which the price rises and upon the sensitivity to price of the importing country's output. For price to rise by a large amount in W, most of the burden of the tariff must fall on W. High elasticities of supply and demand in the exporting country will serve to place most of the tariff burden on W. A high elasticity of supply indicates that quantity rather than price adjusts. Z will reduce quantity rather than let the price fall greatly; the reduced imports in W will serve to force up the price. A high elasticity of demand indicates that quantity adjusts greatly to small price changes. Z can divert a large quantity from exports to domestic consumption by reducing the price slightly if domestic demand is highly elastic. Again the reduced exports to W will force up price.

An inelastic demand schedule in W contributes to a large

protection effect. An inelastic demand schedule indicates that quantity demanded will not rapidly fall off as a result of the required large increase in price. Consequently, domestic output will be able to expand to fill the demand. Finally, a high elasticity of supply in W means that a given price rise due to the imposition of a tariff will result in a large expansion in domestic output, which constitutes the protection effect. Except for W's elasticity of supply, all those effects which force a larger proportion of the tariff onto W and thus bring about the greatest increase in W's price promote the largest protection effect.

The revenue effect is the tariff multiplied by the number of units imported. In terms of Figure 4-1, the total revenue received from the tariff is represented by the rectangle $abcd$. The amount of revenue derived from the imposition of a specific duty depends on the number of units imported. Any discouragement to imports will simultaneously reduce the revenue received from the tariff. An inelastic demand schedule in W indicates that consumers would rather pay the price than adjust quantity. The more inelastic the demand schedule, the greater the revenue effect. A highly elastic supply schedule in W indicates that, as a result of a small increase in price, output will expand and substitute for imports of the good. Thus a highly inelastic supply is conducive to a larger revenue.

Also important in determining W's revenue from the tariff is the reaction of Z's consumption and production of the goods to the change in price. If Z's supply schedule is inelastic, exports will not be greatly discouraged by the lower price. Furthermore, if Z's demand is inelastic, the goods cannot readily be diverted from exports to consumption. Inelastic supply and demand schedules in Z will contribute to a larger revenue in W.

The discussion so far presented is summarized in Table 4-1. For country W to impose a tariff which will be paid primarily by Z requires that W be very sensitive to price and willing to adjust quantity, and that Z be insensitive to price and unable to adjust quantity. For the fulfillment of the policy objective of a large revenue effect from a given specific duty, insensitivity to price in both countries is necessary. If both countries are relatively unwilling to change quantity, trade will be reduced by the least amount. Imports multiplied by the specific duty will give the greatest revenue. Finally, to have a large protection effect for home producers, W's demand should be insensitive to price change so that the higher-priced domestic production will be

Table 4-1

| | Desired Elasticities of | | | |
Policy Objective	Demand Importer	Supply Importer	Demand Exporter	Supply Exporter
Shift large proportion onto exporter	Large	Large	Small	Small
Large revenue effect	Small	Small	Small	Small
Large protection effect	Small	Large	Large	Large

purchased. Also, W's supply must be very sensitive to price so that the price rise induced by the tariff will greatly increase output. High sensitivity to price in Z means that the exporter would rather reduce output than accept the lower price necessitated by the tariff. This will make W's price rise by a great deal and provide the greatest protection to home industry.

Fulfillment of each of the three policy objectives requires completely different values for the elasticities. Thus it is not possible to have a large protection effect and a large revenue effect. A large protection effect requires the sharp curtailment of imports; a large revenue effect for a given specific duty requires that imports be reduced by the least amount.

Likewise, the objectives of shifting the tariff burden onto the exporter and obtaining a large protection effect have divergent elasticity requirements. Low elasticities in the exporting country and high elasticities in the importing country will result in the tariff burden falling on the exporter, with little increase in price in the importing country. But the small price increase in the importing country will provide little protection to import-competing countries. Thus it is not possible to have protection to home producers paid for by foreign producers. Protection to producers comes about from higher prices to the consumers; in this case, a tariff brings about a redistribution of income away from consumers to producers.

Even the objectives of obtaining a large revenue from a tariff and shifting the burden of the tariff primarily onto the exporting country are difficult to realize. Low elasticities of supply and demand in the exporting country serve the twin goals of a high tariff revenue and a large proportion of that revenue coming from the exporter. However, the fulfillment of these two goals requires two completely different values for the elasticities of supply and demand in the importing country. A large revenue requires low elasticities, and shifting the burden onto the exporter requires high elasticities.

Thus the elasticities will allow the nation to fulfill extensively one goal or partially fulfill several goals. The tariffs serve either to redistribute income from consumers in the importing country to that country's producers or to redistribute income from foreign to domestic producers. While it is possible to gain at the cost of a neighbor, it may also be possible for the neighbor to introduce a tariff to right matters. The final result, however, is that both nations are less well off.

Two other effects of tariffs may be considered, namely, consumption effect and production effect. The *consumption effect* shows the change in consumption in the two countries as a result of the imposition of the tariff in the importing country. The consumption effect in Figure 4-1 is the reduced consumption of $Q_3^W Q_4^W$ in W and expanded consumption of $Q_1^Z Q_2^Z$ in Z. The total consumption effect is $Q_3^W Q_4^W$ plus $Q_1^Z Q_2^Z$. The tariff reduces consumption in W by increasing price to induce the contraction. More will be purchased in Z only by lowering price. Reducing consumption by raising price in one country and increasing consumption in another country by reducing price do not serve to maximize economic well-being.

The *production effect* is the increased output in W, $Q_1^W Q_2^W$,

Figure 4-2

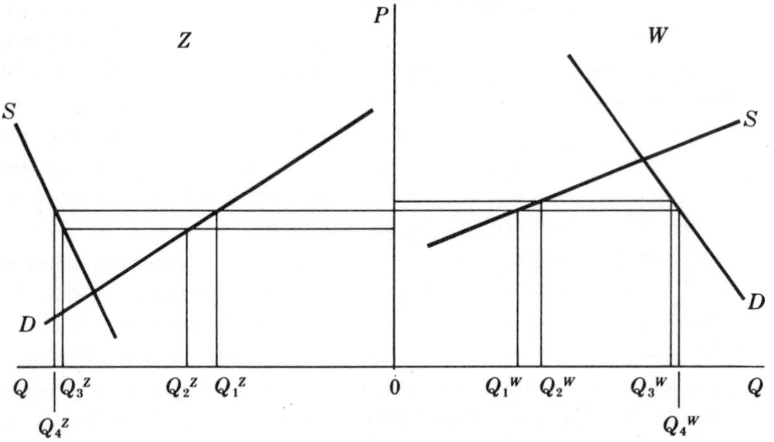

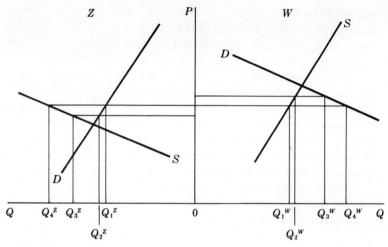

Figure 4-3

minus the reduced output in Z, $Q_3{}^Z Q_4{}^Z$. The tariff serves to expand output in W where it can increase only at higher price and to contract output in Z by forcing down the price. The efficient means of production are discouraged in Z, and the inefficient means of production are encouraged in W.

The production effect and the consumption effect of a tariff may show a net expansion. In Figure 4-2, the tariff results in a reduced consumption of $Q_3{}^W Q_4{}^W$ in W and an expansion of consumption in Z of $Q_1{}^Z Q_2{}^Z$. As may be observed, expanded consumption of $Q_1{}^Z Q_2{}^Z$ exceeds the contracted consumption of $Q_3{}^W Q_4{}^W$, so that world consumption of this commodity expands by $Q_1{}^Z Q_2{}^Z - Q_3{}^W Q_4{}^W$. If consumption expands, then production must expand by the same amount. Production in W expands by $Q_1{}^W Q_2{}^W$ and production contracts in Z by $Q_3{}^Z Q_4{}^Z$. The net increase in production is $Q_1{}^W Q_2{}^W - Q_3{}^Z Q_4{}^Z$. For equilibrium, the net increase in production must equal the net increase in consumption.

On the other hand, production and consumption of the commodity may decrease. In Figure 4-3, W's consumption falls by $Q_3{}^W Q_4{}^W$ as a result of the duty. Consumption in Z rises by $Q_1{}^Z Q_2{}^Z$. As can be seen, quantity $Q_3{}^W Q_4{}^W$ exceeds quantity $Q_1{}^Z Q_2{}^Z$, so that world consumption falls by $Q_3{}^W Q_4{}^W - Q_1{}^Z Q_2{}^Z$. For equilibrium, production must be reduced by the same amount as the consumption. Production in W expands by $Q_1{}^W Q_2{}^W$ and contracts in Z by $Q_3{}^Z Q_4{}^Z$. $Q_3{}^Z Q_4{}^Z$ is a larger quantity than is $Q_1{}^W Q_2{}^W$, so world production falls by $Q_3{}^Z Q_4{}^Z - Q_1{}^W Q_2{}^W$. Whether world production and consumption increase or decrease depends on the elasticities of supply and demand in both countries.

If full employment is assumed, then the resources required for the world expansion of the good must come from the reduced production of some other good. On the other hand, if the import duty results in a reduced output of the good, then the production of an alternative good must be increased if full employment is to be maintained. In either case, the consequences of the redistribution of world resources may be unacceptable to the exporters. Counter measures may be introduced in such a situation. Production and consumption subsidies or taxes may be introduced as the case requires.

Causes and Consequences of Price Divergences

The consequences of the import duty are depicted alternatively in Figure 4-4, which is a reproduction of Figure 2-7. The international price ratio $P^I P^I$ induces country W to produce $n_1{}^W$ and consume $n_2{}^W$ of N, with exports of $n_2{}^W n_1{}^W$. Also, country W imports $t_1{}^W t_2{}^W$, the amount by which consumption of $t_2{}^W$ exceeds production $t_1{}^W$. On the other hand, country Z produces only $n_1{}^Z$ and imports $n_1{}^Z n_2{}^Z$ to allow consumption of $n_2{}^Z$. Z produces $t_1{}^Z$ and consumes only $t_2{}^Z$, leaving $t_2{}^Z t_1{}^Z$ for exports.

As previously shown, W's import duty serves to force the price of T up in W and down in Z. T relative to N is higher priced in W; a larger quantity of N must now exchange on the market for a given quantity of T. The new price ratio in W, $P^W P^W$, is steeper than the international price ratio $P^I P^I$. In country Z the price of T falls and is relatively cheaper than good N. Thus the new price ratio $P^Z P^Z$ is flatter than the international price ratio. Producers in W receive relatively more for T than previously; consequently, they expand production of T. But producers in Z receive relatively less for T and, consequently, reduce its output. As a result of the tariff, W produces more T and less N, and country Z produces more N and less T. The new price ratios lead each country to reallocate resources to less efficient means of production. Thus our conclusion is the following rule: *Any policy instrument which makes the price ratio of two goods received by a producer different in two countries results in an inefficient pattern of world production.*

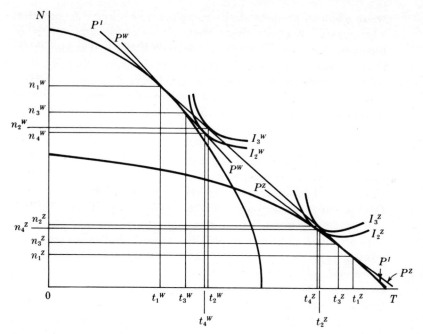

Figure 4-4

An import duty has been shown to yield different prices to producers in different countries and result in inefficient production. The higher price induces the expanded output of one good, and the low price induces the output of that good to contract. Similarly, an export subsidy on one of the two goods will lead to inefficient production. Producers of that commodity in the exporting country are receiving a subsidy which is not earned by producers in the other country. The subsidy will encourage producers in the export country to expand output of the subsidized good and contract output of the other good. Producers in the importing country will find that they cannot compete with subsidized imports and will, therefore, reduce production of that good, increasing output of the nonsubsidized good. A subsidy, like a duty, leads to inefficient world production.

An alternative to an import duty and export subsidy is a production subsidy. A production subsidy on one of the commodities encourages the increased output of that good at the expense of low-cost producers in other countries. An inefficient pattern of world production results. Efficiency requires that only those who can produce at the going price be allowed to produce. The subsidy protects firms that otherwise would go out of business. Also a production tax on one of the two commodities in one country reduces the price to producers in that country, without affecting the receipts to producers in other countries. Producers in the country where production is taxed are induced to divert resources to the nontaxed good, thereby reducing the output of one good and expanding output of the other.

Production taxes and subsidies yield different receipts to producers in the country adopting these regulations. The inducement and discouragement to these producers are different from those to which producers in other countries are responding. Production taxes are paid out of the price the producers receive, and production subsidies are receipts over the price of the good. The price the consumer pays is the same in both countries; the relative price in the two countries will be unaffected.

Anything which makes the price consumers pay in the two countries differ serves to forestall the optimization of trade. Goods induced by profits flow to the market where they earn the highest price. Goods are induced to flow until the price difference disappears. Any policy which interferes with the equalization of the price the consumer pays in the two countries also interferes with the optimization of world trade. Suppose a sales tax on one of the goods is introduced in one country; then the consumers in that country will substitute the nontaxed good for the taxed good to the extent possible. Furthermore, for the same good, price inclusive of tax will be higher than that price charged in the country not imposing a sales tax. Thus consumers in one country are paying more for the good than consumers in the other country. However, goods will not flow to equalize price in the two countries. Price cannot be the same because a tax has to be paid out of the receipts of one country; the price will always differ by the amount of the tax. If the tax were rescinded, more would flow to that country, forcing down the price, and from the other country, forcing up the price. This flow would continue until price was equal and trade pattern optimized.

A consumption subsidy likewise prohibits the optimization of world trade. A country which introduces a subsidy on a good reduces the price to its consumers. Thus the consumers in the country which subsidizes the good will pay a lower price than that paid in other countries. The goods should flow to the nation in which the consumers are willing to pay more; however,

Table 4-2

| | Forestalls | |
Measure	Optimizing Productive Efficiency	Maximizing Trade
Import tariff	Yes	Yes
Export subsidy	Yes	Yes
Production tax	Yes	
Production subsidy	Yes	
Consumption tax		Yes
Consumption subsidy		Yes

the subsidy will prohibit this flow. The amount producers will receive will be the same in the two countries; the amount consumers pay plus the subsidy will be equal to the price the consumer pays in the other country. Thus there is no further flow of goods. The subsidy prevents the good from flowing to the country where the consumers are willing to pay the higher price; optimization of world trade is prohibited.

Table 4-2 summarizes the consequences of optimizing production and maximizing trade of a number of policy instruments. Those measures which make the price diverge for two producers in different countries are checked as forestalling the optimization of production. Furthermore, those measures which make the price paid by consumers in two countries diverge are checked as forestalling the maximization of trade. Most nations have a number of taxes and subsidies in addition to tariffs. Efficiency in production and maximization of trade are greatly restrained. Many of these taxes were introduced for purposes other than influencing trade and production; for example, a progressive sales tax is a consumption tax which is employed in many countries for the purpose of obtaining revenue.

Two Arguments for Tariffs

Two arguments long recognized as being justifiable for imposing tariffs are the defense argument and infant-industry argument. Adam Smith recognized that defense was preferable to opulence.

Protection may be afforded those firms which are producing for the military or which may readily be shifted to military production. The difficulty is that most firms can show some support to an all-out military effort. For example, a button manufacturer who supplied the 13 buttons for the front of sailors' trousers argued for protection from foreign competition on the grounds that the firm was crucial to military defense. The difficulty with this argument, then, is one of establishing meaningful limits.

On the other hand, it must be recognized that trade contributes to maintaining peace. Trade creates an economic dependence which makes it difficult for any nation to pursue a divergent and separate course. To withdraw from trade means that real income will fall. From the smaller real income, greater amounts must go to military expenditure. Thus the well-being of the private sector is greatly reduced. Furthermore, a completely free trade arrangement means that all resources are available to nations willing to pay the price; consequently, it might be possible to reduce the likelihood of war resulting from the quest for resources.

The infant-industry argument pertains to a firm whose growth will be accompanied by decreasing cost. Once the firm has expanded, it will be able to compete with foreign firms without protection. The protection is recognized to be temporary; it provides the firm with a market to allow it to grow. Unfortunately, many tariffs introduced under the infant-industry argument have become permanent. The tariff allows management to be inefficient; reducing the tariff would subject a firm to some painful adjustment. To avoid such adjustment, the tariff is allowed to continue.

The Cost of Tariffs to a Nation

As shown previously, the gains from trade depend on how different the price ratios are in the two countries and also on each country's preference for the good which can be produced most cheaply abroad. The gains from trade can also be called the loss from protection.

Large nations such as the United States have large markets which allow a high degree of specialization; consequently, trade may not be as beneficial. Other nations with small markets have much more to gain from trade. Furthermore, rich nations such as the United States can more easily afford the cost of protection to avoid the adjustment process involved in moving to free trade. The welfare position of the United States is not greatly affected by free trade. The difference in the gains to be reaped by the move to free trade makes tariff negotiations more difficult.

Conclusion

United States tariffs reached an all-time high with the passage of the Smoot-Hawley Tariff Act in 1930. These high tariffs were soon understood not to be in the country's interest, and tariff reductions were undertaken even though the United States was in the midst of a severe depression. The permissive legislation was the Reciprocal Trade Agreement Act of 1934, which allowed the United States to negotiate mutual tariff reductions with other countries. Most of these reductions were negotiated on a bilateral basis.

After World War II, a multilateral approach to tariff reduction emerged through an intergovernment agreement known as the General Agreement of Tariffs and Trade (GATT). The Trade Expansion Act of 1962 allowed the United States to negotiate, through GATT, a 50 percent reduction in the tariff schedule. The act provides for adjustment assistance to firms injured by imports. These negotiations between Canada, United States, and Western Europe are known as the Kennedy Round and produced a reduction of approximately 35 percent in tariffs.

These reductions will be helpful in expanding world trade. However, in some cases the red tape involved in the tariffs serves as a more effective barrier to goods than does the level of the tariff itself. In these situations, the tariff reduction will not be particularly helpful.

Furthermore, tariffs are not the only distortion to optimizing world trade and maximizing world production. Production subsidies, export subsidies, and taxes lead to distortions. The subsidy given United States farmers allows them to produce and export more than they otherwise would. Similarly, the very high subsidies given to the United States merchant marines allow America to sell abroad considerably more shipping services than otherwise could be undertaken. Not to be overlooked, the heavy subsidies to the larger passenger planes likewise lead to distortions; Great Britain and France, for example, are subsidizing the production of the *Concorde*. Finally, the special tax allowance for depletion to the oil industry serves as a subsidy to encourage further production. A most extensive list of special subsidies and taxes could be made; but for our purposes it is sufficient to note that these, like tariffs, forestall the optimization of world trade and production.

It has been argued by the European auto industry that the safety equipment required by federal legislation serves to bar importation of foreign cars into the United States. They believe that the cost of installing this equipment is considerably greater for foreign than for American producers; consequently, a concealed tariff is introduced. This argument may be true, but can a nation decide on safety standards on this basis?

Thus while tariff barriers are being reduced, other distortions are allowed, and in some cases, expanded. Sometimes these other types of controls are introduced with the intention of influencing the level of foreign trade; in other cases, they are introduced for completely different reasons, and it is purely secondary that they have an effect on trade.

Surely, it must be seen that in a world of taxes and subsidies the full gains from trade cannot be reached.

Selected Readings

Books

Humphrey, Don D., *The United States and the Common Market*, New York: Praeger, 1962.

Meade, J. E., *Trade and Welfare*, London: Oxford University Press, 1955.

Salant, Walter S., and Beatrice N. Vaccara, *Import Liberalization and Employment*, Washington, D.C., The Brookings Institution, 1961.

Sannwald, Rolf, and Jacques Stohler, *Economic Integration*, Princeton: Princeton University Press, 1959.

Towle, Lawrence, *International Trade and Commercial Policy*, New York: Harper and Brothers, 1956.

Travis, William P., *The Theory of Trade and Protection*, Cambridge: Harvard University Press, 1964.

Periodicals

A. E. A., *Index of Economic Journals*, classification no. 11.23.

Barkin, S., "Labor's Position on Tariff Reduction," *Industrial Relations*, May, 1962.

Bieda, K., "Trade Restraints in the Western Community," *American Economic Review*, March, 1963.

Leiter, R. D., "Organized Labor and the Tariff," *Southern Economic Journal*, July, 1961.

Meade, J. E., "The Future of International Trade and Payments," *Three Banks Review*, June, 1961.

Mortensen, E., "Impact and Implications of Foreign Surplus Disposal on Developed Economies and Foreign Competitors," *Journal of Farm Economics*, December, 1960.

Thorp, W. L., "Trade Barriers and National Security," *American Economic Review*, May, 1960.

Wheeler, L. A., "The New Agricultural Protectionism and Its Effect on Trade Policy," *Journal of Farm Economics*, November, 1960.

5.

Trade and National Income

So far the discussion has centered around the functional relationship of exports and imports to national price differences. Commodities flow from the low-priced market to the high-priced market and thereby equate prices on the two markets. Ideally a single world price should emerge. In the real world, however, transportation costs, tariffs, and imperfect competition make the realization of a single world price impossible.

In discussing price, it was assumed that income was unchanged. As income increases with prices unchanged, consumption will also increase. The additional consumption expenditure will be for goods produced domestically and abroad. The value of imports is determined partly by the level of national income. For example, a higher income and standard of living for Americans would probably result in greater imports of British woolens, French wine, and German and Japanese cameras. The object of this chapter will be to establish the response of imports to changes in income, under the assumption that prices remain unchanged.

Review of National Income Determination

In a closed economy without any government activity, national income earned is equal to the expenditures on consumption goods and investment goods, or

$$Y = C + I \tag{5-1}$$

The assumption of a closed economy without any government activity limits the alternative uses of income to consumption and saving.

$$Y = C + S \tag{5-2}$$

Since the right sides of Equations (5-1) and (5-2) are both equal to Y, they must be equal to each other, as in Equation (5-3).

$$C + I = C + S \tag{5-3}$$

The C's cancel out on each side of the equation:

$$I = S \tag{5-4}$$

Equation (5-4) shows that saving and investment must be equal in the absence of foreign trade and government expenditure. Of a nation's total output, only that portion not consumed may serve investment purposes, investment being additions to plant, equipment, and inventories. However, saving is defined as not consuming, or output minus consumption. The part of total output not consumed is saving and represents all the output available for investment. Thus saving and investment are equal.

Equation (5-4) states the equilibrium condition that saving and investment must be equal, but the explanation of the values of saving and investment lies elsewhere. Saving is a function of income. At low levels of income, little can be saved, as most of the income is spent on consumption. At higher levels of income, consumption expenditure does not exhaust all the earnings; some is left for saving. Saving is some function s of income ($S = sY$), where s is the marginal propensity to save. As income rises, people save more; the fraction of additional income saved is called the *marginal propensity to save*. Thus if the marginal propensity to save is $\frac{1}{2}$, 50 cents of every additional dollar of income will be saved.

The saving schedule is drawn in Figure 5-1 to show the relation of savings to income. The schedule shows that saving rises with income; the slope of the saving schedule is the marginal propensity to save s.

The amount of investment at any particular time is assumed to be dependent on the expected rate of return to any investment outlet, together with the prevailing rate of interest. The investment will be larger, the greater the optimism about the expected rate of return and the lower the rate of interest, i.e., cost of funds. Suppose on this basis investors decide to invest an amount equal to i. This amount i is plotted on the vertical axis in Figure 5-1, and the investment schedule is drawn parallel to the horizontal axis, since it is assumed that investment is not determined by income. In this case, it is usually said that investment is autonomous, meaning that it is not determined by the independent variable—income—under study.

Since saving must equal investment, the level of national income in Figure 5-1 must be Y_1. At any level of income to the left of Y_1, investment would exceed saving, which is not possible. At any point to the right of Y_1, saving would exceed investment, which is likewise impossible. Thus Y_1 is the equilibrium level at which saving is equal to investment.

If investment increases, then saving must increase by the same amount so that the two are maintained equal. The change in investment dI must equal the change in saving dS. But the

Figure 5-1

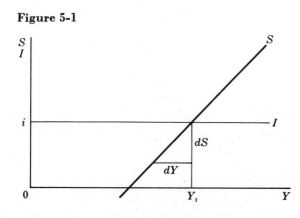

change in saving, dS, is a function s, the marginal propensity to save, of a change in income $s(dY)$. $s(dY)$ may be substituted for dS to give Equation (5-5).

$$dI = s(dY) \qquad (5\text{-}5)$$

This equation shows that if investment increases, then national income must rise until an equal amount of saving is generated.

If investment in Figure 5-2 should increase by 5 from I to I', then saving would have to increase by the same amount. Income would have to rise until $s(dY) = 5$. Suppose s is $\frac{1}{2}$, then income will have to increase by 10 so that $\frac{1}{2}(10) = 5$. If s were $\frac{1}{3}$, then income would have to expand by 15 so that $\frac{1}{3}(15) = 5$. If s were $\frac{1}{10}$, then national income would have to expand by 50 to provide the saving (5) needed to equate the additional investment. Income expands by some multiple of the increased investment. A marginal propensity to save of $\frac{1}{2}$ induces income to expand by twice the increase in investment. An s of $\frac{1}{3}$ induces income to expand by three times the increase in investment. An s of $\frac{1}{10}$ induces income to expand by ten times the increase in investment. The multiplier k is defined as the change in income from a given change in investment, or

$$k = \frac{dY}{dI}$$

The multiplier k is inversely related to the size of the marginal

Figure 5-2

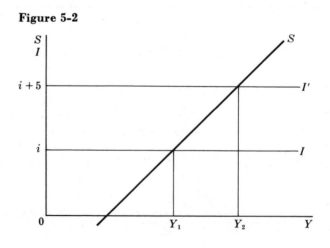

propensity to save, or

$$k = \frac{1}{s}$$

A Simple Foreign-trade Multiplier

The allowance of foreign trade in our model introduces another expenditure item, exports. Production of commodities for export yields income to the suppliers; consequently, the value of exports must be included in national income. However, expenditure on imported commodities does not create jobs and income for the importing country. The value of imports which are included in statements on expenditures of consumption and investment must be subtracted to derive the value of goods produced within the country. The equation for national income becomes

$$Y = C + I + X - M \qquad (5\text{-}6)$$

Transposing C yields

$$Y - C = I + X - M \qquad (5\text{-}7)$$

As noted earlier, income minus consumption is saving. For $Y - C$, S may be substituted.

$$S = I + X - M \qquad (5\text{-}8)$$

Transpose M:

$$S + M = I + X \qquad (5\text{-}9)$$

Equation (5-9) gives the equilibrium condition for an open economy. The sum of $S + M$ must equal the total of $I + X$, but it is no longer necessary for S to equal I. $S + M$ are leakages from the system. If an equivalent amount were not restored in the form of I and X, national income would fall. The amount going out of the system equals the amount entering the system as $X + I$; therefore the level of national income remains unchanged —at equilibrium.

The new equilibrium level of national income is presented in Figure 5-3, where the S and I schedules are taken from Figure 5-1. The amount of exports must be taken as given, since they are determined by consumption patterns in other countries. Assume that the nation has exports of X, which is added in

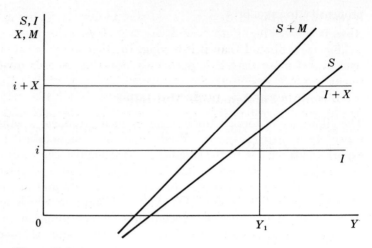

Figure 5-3

Figure 5-3 onto investment I to yield $I + X$. The $I + X$ schedule is horizontal to the y axis to indicate that these variables are autonomous, i.e., not explained by the independent variable—income—under study.

Imports are assumed to be a function of income. As income rises, people want to consume more goods, some of which must be imported. The fraction of each additional dollar of income spent on imports is called the *marginal propensity to import m*. The change in imports dM divided by the change in income dY yields the marginal propensity to import (dM/dY). The value of m is assumed[1] to be constant so that in

$$M = m(Y) \tag{5-10}$$

Figure 5-3, a linear import schedule, can be drawn on top of the saving schedule. The slope of the $M + S$ schedule is the sum of the marginal propensities to import and to save. The vertical distance between the saving schedule and the $M + S$ schedule represents imports. The equilibrium level of national income is Y_1, where

$$M + S = I + X \tag{5-11}$$

In Figure 5-3, $S + M$ equals $X + I$ at Y, but saving is not

---

[1] In this formulation, it is assumed that the marginal propensity to import and the average propensity to import are equal.

equal to investment. S_1 exceeds I_1; the country is saving more than it is investing. Furthermore, X_1 exceeds M_1; the country is selling more abroad than it is buying. In other words, a country can export more than it imports only if saving exceeds investment. Saving is output not consumed; investment is output devoted to expanding productive facilities. If all the output saved is not invested, then the remainder can be exported. Any change in the left side of Equation (5-11) must be equal to a change on the right.

$$dM + dS = dI + dX \qquad (5\text{-}12)$$

The change in imports is equal to the change in income multiplied by the marginal propensity to import.

$$dM = m(dY) \qquad (5\text{-}13)$$

The change in saving is equal to the change in income multiplied by the marginal propensity to save.

$$dS = s(dY) \qquad (5\text{-}14)$$

Substituting Equations (5-13) and (5-14) into (5-12) yields

$$s(dY) + m(dY) = dI + dX \qquad (5\text{-}15)$$

Factor out dY from the left:

$$(s + m)\, dY = dI + dX \qquad (5\text{-}16)$$

Divide both sides by $s + m$:

$$dY = \frac{1}{s + m}\, (dI + dX) \qquad (5\text{-}17)$$

An autonomous increase in X or I or both multiplied by $1/(s + m)$ yields the increase in income. $1/(s + m)$ is the multiplier; its size depends on the marginal propensity to save and the marginal propensity to import. For example, if s is 0.3 and m is 0.2, then the multiplier is 2. If exports should increase by 30, then national income will, as a result, increase by 60.

The expansion of national income can be shown through process analysis. To do so, however, requires a slight modification in the functional relationship of saving, imports, and consumption to income. The modification is a lag. Changes in income do not induce changes in consumption, imports, or saving in the same period, but rather the induced changes in these dependent variables are delayed one period. Today's consumption is a function of yesterday's income. Changes in consumption in time period t are a function of changes in income in the previous period $t - 1$, or

$$dC_t = c(dY_{t-1}) \qquad (5\text{-}18)$$

Similarly, changes in imports in time period t are a function of changes in income in the previous period $t - 1$, or

$$dM_t = m(dY_{t-1}) \qquad (5\text{-}19)$$

And changes in saving in time period t are a function of changes in income in the previous period $t - 1$.

$$dS_t = s(dY_{t-1}) \qquad (5\text{-}20)$$

Table 5-1 shows the expansion of an economy from an equilibrium level of 200 to an equilibrium level of 260. Exports in period 1 rise from 30 to 60, and national income increases by 30. In this period consumption, saving, and imports do not expand

Table 5-1

	$mpc = 0.7$		$mpm = 0.2$		$mps = 0.3$	
Period	$\dfrac{Y}{(C + I + X - M)}$	C	I	X	M	S
0	200	160	20	30	10	40
1	230	160	20	60	10	40
2	245	181	20	60	16	49
3	252.5	191.5	20	60	19	53.9
4	256.25	196.75	20	60	20.5	55.75
5	258.13	199.38	20	60	21.25	56.88
6	259.07	200.70	20	60	21.63	57.44
7	259.53	201.36	20	60	21.83	57.72
8	259.76	201.68	20	60	21.92	57.86
9	259.88	201.84	20	60	21.96	57.93
10	259.94	201.92	20	60	21.98	57.96
	260.00	202.00	20	60	22.00	58.00
			$20 + 60 = 22$		$+ 58$	

because income in the preceding period is unchanged. In period 2, consumption must increase by the value of the mpc (marginal propensity to consume) multiplied by the increased national income of period 1, $0.7 \times 30 = 21$. Also in this period, imports must increase by the marginal propensity to import multiplied by the increased income of period 1, $0.2 \times 30 = 6$. Finally, the increase in saving is equal to the increase in national income of period 1 times the mps (marginal propensity to save) $0.3 \times 30 = 9$. Exports remain at 60, and investment is assumed constant at 20. Changes in consumption, imports, and saving in period 3 are a function of the change in income in period 2. Since income increased by 15 in period 2, consumption in period 3 must increase by 0.7 of that increase in income, imports by 0.2, and saving by 0.3. National income in period 3 is 252.5.

Income increased by 30 in period 1, by 15 in period 2, and by 7.5 in period 3. The increase in national income continually gets smaller until the equilibrium level of 260 is approached. The total increase in national income is 60, which is equal to $1/(0.2 + 0.3) \times 30$. Consumption increased by 42 and saving increased by 18. Imports increased by 12 as a result of the expansion of national income. Thus an increase in expenditure forces national income to expand and with it imports increase. Commodities flow internationally in response to price differences and to changes in income.

The Foreign-trade Multiplier

The multiplier discussed above is called simple because it does not take into consideration all the repercussions of the increased autonomous exports and increased national income. As noted above, the increase in national income induces imports to expand, but these induced imports must be some other nation's exports, say nation Z. Nation Z's national income must rise by an amount equal to the induced exports times the multiplier. Furthermore, this increase in income induces Z's imports to increase. These imports are the exports of nation W. Thus there is a secondary expansionary pressure on W's national income. W's imports must also respond to this increase in national income. The circle of autonomous increase in W's exports, rise in income, induced imports, rise in Z's induced exports and national income, and induced imports is set out in the top of Figure 5-4.

The chain so set off does not continue indefinitely. The

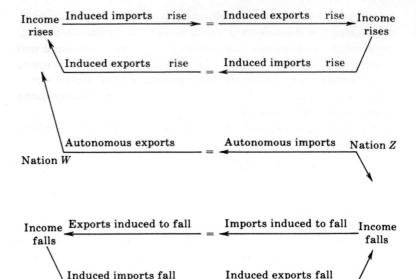

Figure 5-4

autonomous exports of 30 brought about an increase of 60 in national income and also an increase of 12 in imports. Thus country Z has an increase of 12 in exports. Now suppose Z's marginal propensity to save is 0.2 and marginal propensity to import is 0.2, then the multiplier is $2\frac{1}{2}$. The increase of 12 in Z's exports will bring an expansion of 30 in national income and an expansion of 6 in induced imports. Clearly, the induced exports of country W increase by 6, so national income rises by 12 and induced imports by 2.4. Z's income enlarges by 6 and imports rise by 1.2. The 1.2 induced exports expand W's economy by 2.4. As can be seen, the increase in income gets smaller each round and eventually goes to zero.

Simultaneous to the expansionary chain just discussed is a contractionary process. This contractionary circle is depicted in the lower part of Figure 5-4. The choice in country Z to substitute imports of 30 for an equal amount of home-produced goods brings about a contraction of national income. This reduction of 30 in home expenditure times the multiplier of $2\frac{1}{2}$ yields a reduction in national income of 75. Such a reduction in income induces a contraction of $15(75 \times 0.2 = 15)$ in imports. Clearly, induced exports of nation W fall by 15 and national income contracts by 30. The induced imports of W, or exports of Z, diminish by 6. As a result Z's income falls by 15 and its imports by 3. This contractionary process gets smaller each round and goes to zero. The autonomous exports triggered simultaneously expansionary and contractionary pressures. The foreign-trade multiplier must take into consideration all these repercussions and give the final results.

Nation W's national income is equal to consumption plus investment minus imports plus exports, or

$$Y^W = C^W + I^W - M^W + X^W \tag{5-21}$$

Combine $C + I - M$ into net domestic expenditure D^W, or:

$$Y^W = D^W + X^W \tag{5-22}$$

As noted above, the exports of country W are the imports of country Z; Z's imports are a function of its national income. For W's exports X^W, it is possible to substitute mY^Z; Z's imports are a function m of its national income. The equation then becomes

$$Y^W = D^W + mY^Z \tag{5-23}$$

The level of W's national income is dependent on the level of income in Z. This relationship is illustrated in Figure 5-5, where the

Figure 5-5

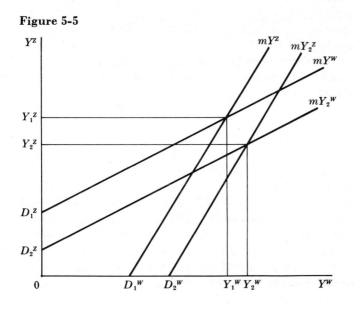

horizontal axis is W's national income and the vertical axis is Z's national income. That portion of income determined by domestic expenditure, $D_1{}^W$, is plotted on the horizontal axis. From there, W's income depends on the level of income in country Z as the mY^Z schedule shows.

Now the same analysis holds for country Z. Z's national income is equal to consumption plus investment expenditure minus imports plus exports. $C^Z + I^Z - M^Z$ are combined into net domestic expenditure D^Z, or

$$Y^Z = D^Z + X^Z \tag{5-24}$$

But Z's exports are country W's imports. These imports are a function of W's income mY^W. Thus we can substitute in Equation (5-24) mY^W for X^Z to get

$$Y^Z = D^Z + mY^W \tag{5-25}$$

The level of Z's income is partly dependent on the level of income in W. In Figure 5-5, that part of income which constitutes net domestic expenditure, $D_1{}^Z$, is plotted on the vertical axis. Additional income beyond this point is a function of income in country W, as the mY^W schedule shows. The two schedules intersect to yield the equilibrium levels of income for both countries, $Y_1{}^W$ and $Y_1{}^Z$.

To determine the level of national income for either country requires determining the level of national income for both countries. That is, the following set of simultaneous equations must be solved.

$$Y^W = C^W + I^W + X^W - M^W \tag{5-26}$$

$$Y^Z = C^Z + I^Z + X^Z - M^Z \tag{5-27}$$

In Figure 5-5, the level of income has been established for the two countries, $Y_1{}^W$ and $Y_1{}^Z$. Likewise the above set of equations with the variables so specified gives the same level for the two countries. Now we want to know what happens to the level of national income in the two countries as a result of a change in autonomous exports (autonomous imports for the other country). The question is, what is the multiplier in this situation?

It is important to note that the increase is in autonomous exports, i.e., exports not determined by income. At this stage induced exports or imports cannot change because income remains unchanged at its equilibrium level.

Induced imports are a movement along the schedule which shows the relationship of imports to income. Thus, an increase of 10 in autonomous imports means that at every level of national income, 10 more will be imported than previously. The import schedule must shift by 10.

Going back to Figure 5-5, Z's increase of autonomous imports means that the expenditure on domestic goods is decreased; people are substituting imports for domestic goods. Domestic expenditure falls from $D_1{}^Z$ to $D_2{}^Z$, and the income schedule, as a result, becomes $mY_2{}^W$. For country W, the increased exports constitute increased domestic expenditure; W's domestic expenditure increases from $D_1{}^W$ to $D_2{}^W$, and the national income schedule becomes $mY_2{}^Z$. The new level of national income in the two countries is $Y_2{}^W$ and $Y_2{}^Z$. It is necessary to calculate the multiplier in order to ascertain the size of the fall in Y^Z and the increase in Y^W.

To calculate the multiplier, we must return to our simultaneous equations. To the equation of W's national income, the autonomous exports A must be added, for the equation contained only induced exports X^W. To the equations of Z's national income, autonomous imports A (A represents autonomous imports and exports, since the two must be equal) must be subtracted, for the equation contained only induced imports M^Z.

$$Y^W = C^W + I^W + A - M^W + X^W \tag{5-28}$$

$$Y^Z = C^Z + I^Z - A - M^Z + X^Z \tag{5-29}$$

Solving[1] for dY^W yields

$$dY^W = \frac{1}{s^W + m^W + m^Z\,(s^W/s^Z)}\,(A) \tag{5-30}$$

Thus income in nation W changes by the value of the change in autonomous exports times

$$\frac{1}{s^W + m^W + m^Z\,(s^W/s^Z)}$$

which is the multiplier. Similarly the change in income in country Z is found to be

$$dY^Z = \frac{1}{s^Z + m^Z + m^W\,(s^Z/s^W)}\,(-A) \tag{5-31}$$

[1] Detailed solution is presented in the appendix (pp. 94–96).

As a consequence of an autonomous increase in the exports of country W or increase in imports of country Z, national income in W expands by A times the multiplier while income falls in Z by A times the multiplier. The expansion in W will be greater, the larger its multiplier and the smaller the multiplier in country Z. Clearly, W's multiplier times the autonomous increase yields the increase in income: a larger multiplier makes for a larger increase in national income. The decrease in Z's income is equal to Z's multiplier times the autonomous increase in imports. The decrease in Z's national income times its marginal propensity to import yields the reduction in Z's imports or W's exports. The smaller Z's multiplier, the smaller the fall in W's exports and the smaller the constraint on the expansion of W's income.

The Investment Multiplier

The autonomous increase in exports brought about an expansion in the exporting country and a contraction of national income in the importing country. Multipliers can be derived to indicate the size of the expansion or contraction. But the expansions of national income can be initiated by variables other than exports, namely consumption or investment. Furthermore, an expansion activated by an increase in consumption or investment will have quite different effects on the two countries than will an expansion triggered by exports. Unlike an increase in exports, an autonomous increase in consumption or investment will initiate only an expansionary sequence. An expansion of consumption or investment expenditure in one country does not result in a contraction in expenditure in the other country. An autonomous increase in Z's investment serves to expand its national income and imports. Since Z's imports are W's exports, the increase in W's exports will result in an increase in W's national income. The increase in W's national income will set in motion a secondary expansion through inducing W's imports to rise, or Z's exports. As a consequence, Z's national income will rise, and its increased imports will put in motion the third expansionary round. To determine the total increase in income of nations Z and W, it is necessary to derive the investment multiplier.

The *investment multiplier* is derived from the national income equations of the two countries. A change in W's income dY^W must be equal to a change in consumption dC plus a change in exports

dX^W minus a change in imports dM^W. Investment is assumed unchanged in country W. But a change in investment is introduced in country Z. Therefore the change in Z's national income is equal to the change in Z's consumption dC^Z plus the change in investment dI^W plus the change in exports dX^W minus the change in imports dM^Z. The level of national income in W and Z can be found by solving the following simultaneous equations.

$$dY^W = dC^W + dX^W - dM^W \tag{5-32}$$

$$dY^Z = dC^Z + dI^Z + dX^Z - dM^Z \tag{5-33}$$

Solving[2] for dY^Z yields

$$dY^Z = \frac{1 + (m^W/s^W)}{s^Z + m^Z + m^W(s^Z/s^W)}\,(dI^Z) \tag{5-34}$$

As a result of an increase in investment of I^Z in country Z, national income increased by

$$\frac{1 + (m^W/s^W)}{s^Z + m^Z + m^W(s^Z/s^W)}$$

times the increased investment. Clearly

$$\frac{1 + (m^W/s^W)}{s^Z + m^Z + m^W(s^Z/s^W)}$$

is the investment multiplier for a nation experiencing increased investment. The smaller Z's marginal propensities to save and to import, the larger its multiplier. Also, the smaller W's marginal propensity to save and the larger its marginal propensity to import, the greater Z's multiplier.

The increased income in country Z induces imports to expand. Accordingly, the exports of country W will increase, as will its income. There must be a multiplier which shows the increase in W's income as a result of the increased investment in Z. Solving for dY^W gives

$$dY^W = \frac{(m^Z/s^Z)}{s^W + m^W + m^Z(s^W/s^Z)}\,(dI^Z) \tag{5-35}$$

W's national income will increase by

$$\frac{(m^Z/s^Z)}{s^W + m^W + m^Z(s^W/s^Z)}$$

[2] Detailed solution is presented in the appendix (pp. 96–98).

times the amount of the increased investment in Z.

$$\frac{(m^Z/s^Z)}{s^W + m^W + m^Z(s^W/s^Z)}$$

is the multiplier which shows the rate of increase in W as a result of increased investment in Z. W's income will expand more from a given increase in Z's investment, the smaller the marginal propensities to save in both countries, the smaller W's marginal propensity to import, and the larger Z's marginal propensity to import.

In Table 5-2, the importance of small propensities for the multiplier are shown. A large value for the investment multiplier in both countries is seen to be dependent on small values for the saving propensities in both countries. However, a small m^W makes for a larger multiplier in country W and a small multiplier in country Z. Similarly, a small value of m^Z makes for a small multiplier in W and a large multiplier in Z.

In the real world, the value of the mpm varies considerably from country to country. The mpm of the United States is very small—in the order of 6 or 7 percent. In contrast, Norway's is very large—in the vicinity of 40 percent. Japan's mpm is somewhat more intermediate—around 12 percent. These values contribute to making the United States' multiplier larger and Norway's smaller, although it cannot be said that the United States' multiplier is larger than Norway's without knowing the values of all other propensities. For a given change in income, Norway's imports will increase by more than the United States'. However, the changes in income in the two countries tend not

Table 5-2

	Size of			
Small Value of These Propensities	Foreign-trade Multipliers $-dY^z$	$+dY^w$	Investment Multipliers $+dY^z$	$+dY^w$
s^z	Large	Small	Large	Large
s^w	Small	Large	Large	Large
m^z	Large	Large	Large	Small
m^w	Large	Large	Small	Large

to be the same; the sizes of the two economies are quite different. For example, in 1965, United States national income rose by $46 billion with an increase in imports of $2.6 billion. Norway's greatest increase in imports during the period 1961–1967 was only $0.35 billion. Even though the United States' mpm is very small, the value of its imports is large due to the size of the economy.

Conclusion

What we have shown is that exports which may be induced by, say, price difference, cause income in the trading countries to change. If, because of inflation in Great Britain, the price of British goods rises in relation to American goods, then British consumers will choose to buy the American goods rather than the more expensive British goods. Diverting expenditure from domestic output to imports could cause a contraction in British income. This will serve to slow down Great Britain's rate of inflation. Simultaneously, the increased exports will result in United States income rising. The increase in American productivity which reduces its prices relative to British prices will also induce British consumers to divert expenditure from domestic output to American goods. Again income in Great Britain will fall and rise in the United States. Or if the United States produces what is considered a better product, exports to Great Britain will rise with a fall in British national income and a rise in American income.

The attempts of one country to invest in another influence the levels of income and trade. Direct American investment in British industry will tend to expand British national income and reduce United States income, unless corrective action is taken by the governments.

International trade serves to equalize the price of goods and to relate functionally the levels of national income in all trading countries. A change in prices, income, or trade in one country sets in motion an adjustment process which involves these variables in all the trading countries. The economies of the world are bound together by trade.

It is the resulting high degree of economic interdependence which has made nations reluctant to participate fully in international trade. The depression of the 1930s spread throughout the world through reduced trade. In the post-World War II period, nations have been unwilling to become heavily involved in trade with the United States in fear of further uncontrolled depression in the United States which would become transmitted throughout the world. The Employment Act of 1948 states clearly the U.S. government's obligation to maintain full employment. This act, together with fair success in overcoming prolonged recession, has served to mitigate some of the fears of recessions being transmitted from the United States. New confidence is in part reflected in the Kennedy Round of tariff cutting.

Selected Readings

Books
Hicks, J. R., *Essays in World Economics*, Oxford: Clarendon Press, 1959.
Kindleberger, C. P., *International Economics*, Homewood: Richard D. Irwin, 1963, Chap. 10.
Machlup, Fritz, *International Trade and the National Income Multiplier*, New York: August M. Kelly, 1943.
Marsh, Donald, *World Trade and Investment*, New York: Harcourt, Brace and Co., 1951, Chaps. 10 and 11.
Salant, Jarlav, *International Trade: Theory and Economic Policy*, Homewood: Richard D. Irwin, 1962, Chaps. 6 and 7.

Periodicals
A. E. A., *Index of Economic Journals*, classification nos. 11.322 and 11.323.
Collery, A., "A Full Employment, Keynesian Theory of International Trade," *Quarterly Journal of Economics*, August, 1963.
Dosser, D., "National-income and Domestic-income Multipliers and Their Application to Foreign-aid Transfers," *Economica*, n.s. February, 1963.
Frumkin, A., "The Bourgeois Theory of the Foreign Trade Multiplier," *Problems of Economics*, October, 1960.
Gehrels, F., "The Unit Terms-of-Trade Multiplier," *Zeitschrift für Nationalokonomie*, May, 1960.
Ikemoto, K., "The Foreign Trade Multiplier, Devaluation, and Transfer Problem," *Kobe University Economic Review*, 1963.

Appendix Algebraic Derivation of Multipliers

Foreign-trade Multiplier
Start with Equations (5-28) and (5-29) or

$$Y^W = C^W + I^W + A - M^W + X^W \qquad \text{(5-A1)}$$

$$Y^Z = C^Z + I^Z - A - M^Z + X^Z \qquad \text{(5-A2)}$$

Transposing C in both equations yields

$$Y^w - C^w = I^w + A + X^w - M^w \tag{5-A3}$$

$$Y^z - C^z = I^z + X^z - A - M^z \tag{5-A4}$$

Income minus consumption equals saving. S is substituted for $Y - C$.

$$S^w = I^w + A + X^w - M^w \tag{5-A5}$$

$$S^z = I^z + X^z - A - M^z \tag{5-A6}$$

Transpose all items with a minus sign to obtain the following equations:

$$S^w + M^w = I^w + A + X^w \tag{5-A7}$$

$$S^z + A + M^z = I^z + X^z \tag{5-A8}$$

Any change in the value of the right side of the equation must be equal to any change in the left. However, in both equations I is assumed to be constant. Therefore, any change in $S^w + M^w$ must be equal to a change in $X^w + A$. Likewise, any change in $S^z + A + M^z$ must be equal to the change in X^z, or

$$dS^w + dM^w = A + dX^w \tag{5-A9}$$

$$dS^z + A + dM^z = dX^z \tag{5-A10}$$

It has already been pointed out that one nation's exports are the other country's imports, which are determined by the level of national income in the importing country. Thus

$$dX^w = dM^z \tag{5-A11}$$

$$dM^z = m^z(dY^z) \tag{5-A12}$$

And

$$dX^z = dM^w \tag{5-A13}$$

$$dM^w = m^w(dY^w) \tag{5-A14}$$

Also

$$dS^w = s^w(dY^w) \tag{5-A15}$$

$$dS^z = s^z(dY^z) \tag{5-A16}$$

Substituting Equations (5-A13) through (5-A16) into Equations (5-A11) and (5-A12) yields

$$s^w(dY^w) + m^w(dY^w) = A + m^z(dY^z) \tag{5-A17}$$

$$s^z(dY^z) + A + m^z(dY^z) = m^w(dY^w) \tag{5-A18}$$

Reorder the two equations to get

$$s^w(dY^w) + m^w(dy^w) - m^z(dY^z) = A \tag{5-A19}$$

$$-m^w(dY^w) + m^z(dY^z) + s^z(dY^z) = -A \tag{5-A20}$$

Add the two equations to get

$$s^W(dY^W) + s^Z(dY^Z) = 0 \qquad (5\text{-}A21)$$

Or

$$s^W(dY^W) = -s^Z(dY^Z) \qquad (5\text{-}A22)$$

Or

$$-\frac{s^W}{s^Z} dY^W = dY^Z \qquad (5\text{-}A23)$$

In Equation (5-A19) substitute for (dY^Z), $-(s^W/s^Z)(dY^W)$ to get

$$s^W(dY^W) + m^W(dy^W) + m^Z\left(\frac{s^W}{s^Z} dY^W\right) = A \qquad (5\text{-}A24)$$

Factor out dY^W:

$$\left[s^W + m^W + m^Z\left(\frac{s^W}{s^Z}\right)\right] dY^W = A \qquad (5\text{-}A25)$$

Divide both sides by $[s^W + m^W + m^Z(s^W/s^Z)]$:

$$dY^W = \frac{1}{s^W + m^W + m^Z(s^W/s^Z)} \text{ (A)} \qquad (5\text{-}A26)$$

Investment Multiplier

The investment multipliers can be derived by solving Equations (5-32) and (5-33), which are reintroduced here as

$$dY^W = dC^W + dX^W - dM^W \qquad (5\text{-}A27)$$

$$dY^Z = dC^Z + dI^Z - dM^Z + dX^Z \qquad (5\text{-}A28)$$

Since Z's imports are W's exports in a two-country model, dM^Z can be substituted for dX^W. Likewise dM^W can be substituted for dX^Z. The equations now become

$$dY^W = dC^W + dM^Z - dM^W \qquad (5\text{-}A29)$$

$$dY^Z = dC^Z + dI^Z - dM^Z + dM^W \qquad (5\text{-}A30)$$

Transpose dC in both equations and substitute dS for $dY - dC$ to get

$$dS^W = dM^Z - dM^W \qquad (5\text{-}A31)$$

$$dS^Z = dI^Z - dM^Z + dM^W \qquad (5\text{-}A32)$$

For the respective countries, $m\,dY$ can be substituted for dM and $s\,dY$ for dS.

$$s^W\,dY^W = m^Z\,dY^Z - m^W\,dY^W \qquad (5\text{-}A33)$$

$$s^Z\,dY^Z = dI^Z - m^Z\,dY^Z + m^W\,dY^W \qquad (5\text{-}A34)$$

Adding the two equations yields

$$s^W \, dY^W + s^Z \, dY^Z = dI^Z \tag{5-A35}$$

Transposing

$$s^W \, dY^W = dI^Z - s^Z \, dY^Z \tag{5-A36}$$

Divide by s^W

$$dY^W = \frac{dI^Z - s^Z}{s^W} \tag{5-A37}$$

Substituting for dY^W in Equation (5-A33) to get

$$dI^Z - s^Z \, dY^Z = m^Z \, dY^Z - m^W \left(\frac{dI^Z - s^Z \, dY^Z}{s^W} \right) \tag{5-A38}$$

$$dI^Z - s^Z \, dY^Z = m^Z \, dY^Z - \frac{m^W}{s^W} \, dI^Z + m^W \frac{s^Z}{s^W} \, dY^Z \tag{5-A39}$$

Transposing

$$dI^Z + \frac{m^W}{s^W} \, dI^Z = s^Z \, dY^Z + m^Z \, dY^Z + \frac{m^W s^Z}{s^W} \, dY^Z \tag{5-A40}$$

Factoring

$$\left(1 + \frac{m^W}{s^W} \right) dI^Z = \left(s^Z + m^Z + \frac{m^W S^Z}{s^W} \right) dY^Z \tag{5-A41}$$

Divide by $[s^Z + m^Z + m^W(s^Z/s^W)]$:

$$\frac{1 + (m^W/s^W)}{s^Z + m^Z + m^W(s^Z/s^W)} \, dI^Z = dY^Z \tag{5-A42}$$

The increased income in country Z induces imports to expand. Accordingly, the exports of country W will increase, as will its income. There must be a multiplier which shows the increase in W's income as a result of the increased investment in Z. Repeating Equation (5-A35)

$$s^W \, dY^W + s^Z \, dY^Z = dI^Z \tag{5-A43}$$

Transposing to solve for dY^Z

$$s^Z \, dY^Z = dI^Z - s^W \, dY^W \tag{5-A44}$$

Divide by s^Z:

$$dY^Z = \frac{dI^Z - s^W \, dY^W}{s^Z} \tag{5-A45}$$

Substituting for dY^Z in Equation (5-A34) to get

$$dI^Z - s^W \, dY^W = dI^Z - m^Z \left(\frac{dI^Z - s^W \, dY^W}{s^Z} \right) + m^W \, dY^W \quad (5\text{-A}46)$$

Transposing

$$dI^Z - dI^Z + \frac{m^Z}{s^Z} \, dI^Z = s^W \, dY^W + m^W \, dY^W + \frac{m^Z s^W}{s^Z} \, dY^W \quad (5\text{-A}47)$$

Factoring

$$\frac{m^Z}{s^Z} \, dI^Z = \left(s^W + m^W + \frac{m^Z s^W}{s^Z} \right) dY^W \quad\quad\quad (5\text{-A}48)$$

Divide by $[s^W + m^W + m^Z(s^W/s^Z)]$

$$\frac{(m^Z/s^Z)}{s^W + m^W + m^Z(s^W/s^Z)} \, dI^Z = dY^W \quad\quad\quad (5\text{-A}49)$$

Capital

The discussion so far has centered around the transaction of goods. First the gains from trade were discussed, and then the consequences of trade for price and income were analyzed. International commercial transactions are not limited to goods or services; capital moves internationally for investment purposes and as aid to underdeveloped countries. The purpose, then, of this chapter is to discuss the reasons for capital movement and also the consequences of capital flow.

Definitions

Capital involved in international transactions can be divided into three subheadings: short-term capital, long-term capital, and transfer payments. *Short-term capital* is any financial instrument which is redeemable within a year. For example, a saving deposit is short term, since funds can be withdrawn upon short notice. Checking accounts constitute short-term capital, along with notes and bonds of any duration which mature within a year.

Long-term capital is any financial instrument which is not refundable within a year. Bonds and stocks of duration greater than a year fit into this category, as does direct investment, such as purchase of title to property.

Transfer payments are unilateral gifts for aid. The receiver is not required to provide goods or services, or to make repayment. The aid may be for military purposes or for economic development. Usually transfer payments are given for specific purposes and have conditions which the receiver must fulfill.

Short-term Capital Flow

A firm doing business in a foreign country will inevitably have to hold short-term balance in the form of demand deposits in that foreign country. Sales will be deposited to that account, and business expenses incurred in the foreign country will be paid out of the account. Periodically, the excess over what is required for doing business will be converted into the home currency. These balances might be called the transactions demand for foreign currency.

Short-term capital may also flow from country to country as a result of speculation. The basis of the speculation may be anticipated change in the interest rate or an expected change in the exchange rate. If interest rates are expected to rise, one does not want to buy bonds and securities at the low rate of interest, or, what is the same thing, at high bond prices. It is more profitable to wait for the interest rate to rise so as to get the higher rate or the lower bond price. One might invest short term abroad while waiting for a change in the interest rate at home.

On the other hand, if one expects interest rates abroad to fall, it pays to buy bonds and securities at their low price and sell later at a high price. Thus a country which is expected to have a fall in its interest rates may experience an inflow of capital.

If one expects the country to devalue, i.e., to lower the price of its currency in terms of all other currencies, then it pays to move out of that currency and buy back after devaluation at a lower price. Residents of a country expected to devalue will try to convert their currency into foreign balances. Likewise, non-residents will try to reduce balances held in that country.

If, on the other hand, a country is expected to appreciate its currency, i.e., increase the foreign price of its currency, then people will want to buy that currency while it is cheap and sell it later at the higher price.

Long-term Capital

Whereas short-term capital is usually for either transactions or speculative purposes, long-term capital is most often used for investment. The investor's objective is to obtain assets which will yield income over time or appreciate in value allowing for a profit in an eventual sale. But either way the object is primarily earnings.

In choosing an area in which to invest, one usually compares the expected rate of return from a particular investment with the expected rate of return from alternative investments. So it is with international investment. The investor evaluates in terms of his currency the expected rate of return to be had by investing abroad. In evaluating an investment in a foreign country, one must consider the political climate, the economic climate, and the likelihood of devaluation both in his own and in the foreign country.

By *political climate*, we mean the nation's ability to maintain order so that economic and social progress will not be disrupted by riots and civil war. The political attitude toward nationalization of foreign-owned assets must also be considered; and not only the nation's attitude toward nationalization, but in addition, its commitment toward compensation for assets nationalized. Surely a strong preference for nationalization of foreign-owned assets with little real concern for compensation will do little to induce foreign capital. Even though capital may be very profitable in that country, an investor fearing nationalization may see a very low expected rate of return to his investment in that country.

Success in maintaining full employment and the growth record of the economy are important aspects of the economic climate. An economy which has maintained full employment and a vigorous growth rate will be particularly appealing to capital. On the other hand, an economy with a consistently low level of employment will not be particularly attractive to capital.

The rate of return one expects to earn from his capital will be lower.

If the foreign country under consideration is likely to have to devalue in the near future, then the expected rate of return is lower. A given investment earning a certain amount of foreign currency will convert into a smaller number of home-currency units after devaluation, thereby making the earning on the initial investment smaller. For example, a $10,000 investment in a foreign country earning, say, 5,000 pesos a year will earn a rate of return of 10 percent at an exchange rate of 5 pesos per $1. But after the currency is devalued to 10 pesos per $1, the investment is earning a rate of return of only 5 percent. On the other hand, appreciation will serve to increase the rate of return.

Investment may flow to a country in order to jump that country's tariff barrier. If tariff barriers prohibit the export of goods to a particular country, then it might be profitable to erect a plant within that country so that the good can be produced or finished there. The development of a common market where tariffs are removed for member nations but retained for nonmember nations may serve to induce the inflow of capital. A nonmember in competition with a member of the common market is put at a distinct disadvantage by the tariff. Businessmen of the nonmember country may establish a subsidiary company within the common market to produce the good and avoid the tariff. If within the common market there are no restrictions on the repatriation of profits of nonmember countries, then the investment in the common market will serve as a means for nonmember countries to continue to compete without suffering the disadvantage of a tariff barrier.

Consequence of Capital Flow

Reasons for capital flowing from one country to another have been outlined. The next task is to determine the effect the capital flow has on the level of exports and imports. The capital flow itself has no direct effect on income. What is important is the effect the capital flow has on investment expenditure in each country. Capital flowing from one country to another may affect the incomes of those two countries by inducing changes in investment expenditures and, concomitantly, the level of imports and exports, which are a function of income.

Suppose investors in W divert capital of amount A from

country W to Z, with the result that investment expenditure falls in W by amount A and investment expenditure rises by amount A in Z. The reduction of investment in W will cause national income and imports to fall. But if W's imports fall, then Z's exports and national income must also fall. The fall in Z's national income and imports will induce a further fall in W's national income and imports. Thus a whole sequence of reductions in imports and national income is set off by the reduced investment in W. The total consequence for the two countries can be determined by using the investment multiplier set forth in Chapter 5. W's national income will change by

$$dY^W = \frac{1 + (m^Z/s^Z)}{s^W + m^W + m^Z(s^W/s^Z)} (-A)$$ (6-1)

National income in Z will fall by

$$dY^Z = \frac{(m^W/s^W)}{s^Z + m^Z + m^W(s^Z/s^W)} (-A)$$ (6-2)

However, W's investors place the capital in country Z. As a result of the investment of A in country Z, national income and imports rise. W's exports and thus national income rise. An expansionary sequence is set off in the two countries. The increase in Z's national income as a result of the increased investment is given by

$$dY^Z = \frac{1 + (m^W/s^W)}{s^Z + m^Z + m^W(s^Z/s^W)} (A)$$ (6-3)

The increase in W's income as a result of the rise in investment in Z is

$$dY^W = \frac{(m^Z/s^Z)}{s^W + m^W + m^Z(s^W/s^Z)} (A)$$ (6-4)

Clearly, both countries are subjected to contractionary pressures as a result of decreased investment in W and to expansionary pressures as a result of the increased investment in Z. To determine the net effect for W, it is necessary to add Equations (6-1) and (6-4):

$$dY^W = \frac{1 + (m^Z/s^Z)}{s^W + m^W + m^Z(s^W/s^Z)} (-A)$$
$$+ \frac{(m^Z/s^Z)}{s^W + m^W + m^Z(s^W/s^Z)} (A) \quad (6-5)$$

which is equal to

$$dY^W = \frac{-1}{s^W + m^W + m^Z(s^W/s^Z)} (A) \qquad (6\text{-}6)$$

The contractionary and expansionary pressure on Z is the sum of Equations (6-2) and (6-3).

$$dY^Z = \frac{(m^W/s^W)}{s^Z + m^Z + m^W(s^Z/s^W)} (-A)$$

$$+ \frac{1 + (m^W/s^W)}{s^Z + m^Z + m^W(s^Z/s^W)} (A) \qquad (6\text{-}7)$$

or $\quad dY^Z = \dfrac{1}{s^Z + m^Z + m^W(s^Z/s^W)} (A) \qquad (6\text{-}8)$

Assigning values to A and to the marginal propensities to import and to save will help to clarify what is happening. Suppose investors in country W reduce investment expenditure in their own country by 10 and employ the capital so as to bring about a net increase in investment expenditure of 10 in Z. Suppose also that the propensities have the following values:

$$s^W = 0.2$$

$$m^W = 0.1$$

$$s^Z = 0.2$$

$$m^Z = 0.1$$

Plugging these values into Equation (6-6) yields

$$dY^W = \frac{-1}{0.2 + 0.1 + 0.1(0.2/0.2)} (10) = -25$$

Plugging into country Z's Equation (6-8):

$$dY^Z = \frac{1}{0.2 + 0.1 + 0.1(0.2/0.2)} (10) = 25$$

National income in country W falls by 25 and rises by 25 in country Z.

To determine the change in imports in the country, it is necessary only to multiply its marginal propensity to import by the change in income. Thus the change in W's imports is

$$dM^{\overline{w}} = 0.1(-25) = -2.5$$

Change in Z's imports is

$$dM^z = 0.1(25) = 2.5$$

Since one country's imports are the other country's exports, the change in each country can be shown:

$$dM^W = -2.5 \qquad dX^W = 2.5$$

$$dM^Z = 2.5 \qquad dX^Z = -2.5$$

The flow of capital, for whatever reason, definitely influences the level of trade. The magnitude of the change in the imports of the two countries depends on their marginal propensities to save and to import. In Table 6-1 different propensities are given in order to ascertain the resulting multiplier change in income for the two countries and the change in imports. Row A repeats the results we have derived above. In row B, the marginal propensity to save of country W is changed from 0.2 to 0.3; all other marginal propensities in row B are the same as in A. The result of increasing the marginal propensity to save of country W while keeping all other propensities constant is a reduced multiplier for country W and a smaller fall in income and imports. The larger marginal propensity to save also influences the multiplier in country Z. A larger marginal propensity to save in country W contributes to a larger multiplier in Z, resulting in larger income and imports. The larger marginal propensity to save in country W brings about a net expansion of trade; Z's imports increase by an amount greater than the decreased imports of W.

In row C, country W's marginal propensity to import is

Table 6-1

Row	s^W	m^W	s^Z	m^Z	Mult.^{W}	dY^W	dM^W	Mult.^{Z}	dY^Z	dM^Z
A	0.2	0.1	0.2	0.1	2.5	−25	−2.5	2.5	+25	+2.5
B	0.3	0.1	0.2	0.1	1.8	−18	−1.8	2.8	+28	+2.8
C	0.2	0.2	0.2	0.1	2	−20	−4.0	2	+20	+2.0
D	0.2	0.1	0.3	0.1	2.8	−28	−2.8	1.8	+18	+1.8
E	0.2	0.1	0.2	0.2	2	−20	−2.0	2	+20	+4.0

increased; all other propensities are of the same value as given in row A. The result is a smaller multiplier and, consequently, a smaller decrease in income and a larger decrease in imports. This change has repercussions on Z. Z's multiplier is smaller and, as a result, imports and income increase by a smaller amount. The net result for trade is a contraction; the decrease in W's imports exceeds the expansion of Z's imports.

The result of a larger marginal propensity to save in country Z, the nation receiving the capital, is a smaller multiplier in Z together with a smaller increase in income and imports, row D. The consequence for country W, the nation giving the capital, is a larger multiplier with a greater decrease in imports and income. Net trade is adversely affected. The contraction in W's imports is greater than the expansion in Z's.

Finally, the result of a larger marginal propensity to import in Z, with all the other propensities of the same value as in row A, is set forth in row E. Z's multiplier is smaller and its income increases by a smaller amount, but imports increase by a larger amount. For country W, the multiplier is smaller, and imports and income fall by less. The net effect for the two countries is an expansion of trade.

To summarize, capital flows from W to Z, with the result that income falls in W as a result of reduced investment and rises in Z as a result of increased investment. Since imports are a function of income, both nations' imports must adjust to the changes in income. It is found that a larger marginal propensity to save in a country experiencing the outflow of capital promotes an expansion of net trade. Also a larger marginal propensity to import in the country receiving the capital serves to expand net trade. But either a larger marginal propensity to import in the country with the capital outflow or a larger marginal propensity to save in the recipient country serves to reduce the net amount of trade.

It is not necessarily the case that nations will allow their national income to rise or fall in response to capital flow. Corrective action might be taken. Suppose the authorities in country W through fiscal or monetary policy just replace the capital outflow but do nothing to counter the repercussions from the expansion in country Z. Thus the direct effects of the capital flow will be increased investment in Z and no change in W. The consequence for trade may now be analyzed.

This is simply the case of increased investment in the one country for which the investment multiplier was derived. The multiplier of the country Z experiencing the increased investment of amount A is

$$dY^Z = \frac{1 + (m^W/s^W)}{s^Z + m^Z + m^W(s^Z/s^W)} \quad (A)$$

The repercussions for the other country, W, are

$$dY^W = \frac{(m^Z/s^Z)}{s^W + m^W + m^Z(s^W/s^Z)} \quad (A)$$

Suppose that A is 10 and the values of the propensities are

$s^W = 0.2$

$m^W = 0.1$

$s^Z = 0.2$

$m = 0.1$

The results for nation Z would be

$$dY^Z = \frac{1 + 1/2}{0.2 + 0.1 + 0.1(0.2/0.2)} \quad (10)$$

or $dY^Z = 37.5$

The results for country W are

$$dY^W = \frac{(0.1/0.2)}{0.2 + 0.1 + 0.1(0.2/0.2)} \quad (10)$$

or $dY^W = 12.5$

Both countries have a marginal propensity to import of 0.1. Thus imports in each country will expand as follows:

$dM^Z = 0.1(37.5) = 3.75$

$dM^W = 0.1(12.5) = 1.25$

Since imports are expanding in both countries, the effect on net trade is the sum of the increase in each country, or $3.75 + 1.25 = 5$. World trade increases by 5.

The consequences of assuming alternative values for the propensities are shown in Table 6-2. In row A, the values established above are repeated. In row B, country W's marginal propensity to save is increased, while the value of all other variables is the same as in row A. A larger marginal propensity to

Table 6-2

Row	s^W	m^W	s^Z	m^Z	Mult.^{W}	dY^W	dM^W	Mult.^{Z}	dY^Z	dM^Z
A	0.2	0.1	0.2	0.1	1.25	12.5	1.25	3.75	37.5	3.75
B	0.3	0.1	0.2	0.1	0.9	9	0.9	3.6	36	3.6
C	0.2	0.2	0.2	0.1	1.0	10	2	4	40	4.
D	0.2	0.1	0.3	0.1	0.92	9.2	0.92	2.72	27.2	2.72
E	0.2	0.1	0.2	0.2	2	20	2	3	30	6

save in W yields a smaller multiplier, a smaller increase in income, and a smaller increase in imports for country W. Simultaneously, W's larger marginal propensity to save makes for a smaller multiplier, an increase in income, and increase in imports for country Z. The total increase in imports is 4.5, a smaller increase than occurred with the value of the propensities given in row A.

The results of a larger marginal propensity to import for W are considered next in row C. As can be seen, the size of the multiplier, increase in income, and increase in imports in country W are smaller than the situation described in row A. However, W's larger marginal propensity to import yields a larger multiplier, increase in income, and imports for country Z. The total increase in imports in the two countries, nevertheless, is larger than it is with the values of the propensities assumed in row A.

A larger marginal propensity to save for country Z, the country receiving the capital flow, yields a smaller multiplier and a smaller expansion of country Z's income and imports, row D. Also country W has a smaller multiplier and increase in income and imports. The net effect is to reduce the size of the net increase in total imports of the two countries.

The final case to be looked at is the one in which the marginal propensity to import in Z is larger than in row A. Row E shows that country Z has a smaller multiplier, increase in income, and imports. However, country W, as a result of the larger marginal propensity to import in Z, has the largest multiplier, increase in income, and imports. The total increase in imports is again larger than it is in row A.

The level of trade between two countries is influenced even in the case where the capital flow brings about an expansion of expenditure only in the receiving country. The increase in the imports of both nations will be larger, the greater the marginal propensities to import and the smaller their marginal propensities to save.

Suppose the context of the capital flow is different from that above. The nation from which the capital flows allows its expenditure and income to fall. But the nation receiving the capital employs monetary and fiscal measures to prevent its expenditure and national income from rising as a result of the capital flow.

Again the investment multipliers are needed. Country W has a fall in domestic investment of A, while Z has no change in investment. The change in W's national income will be given by

$$dY^W = \frac{1 + (m^Z/s^Z)}{s^W + m^W + m^Z(s^W/s^Z)}(-A)$$

The repercussions of these changes in W's income will have the following effects on Z's national income:

$$dY^Z = \frac{(m^W/s^W)}{s^Z + m^Z + m^W(s^Z/s^W)}(-A)$$

Again, let A be 10 and the propensities be $s^W = 0.2$, $m^W = 0.1$, $s^Z = 0.2$, and $m^Z = 0.1$. Plugging these values into the multiplier for W yields

$$dY^W = \frac{1 + (0.1/0.2)}{0.2 + 0.1 + 0.1(0.2/0.2)}(-10)$$

or $dY^W = -37.5$

The repercussions for country Z are

$$dY^Z = \frac{(0.1/0.2)}{0.2 + 0.1 + 0.1(0.2/0.2)}(-10)$$

or $dY^Z = 12.5$

The fall in income in the two countries will bring about a fall in both countries' imports.

$$dM^W = 0.1(-37.5) = -3.75$$

$$dM^Z = 0.1(-12.5) = -1.25$$

Imports fall by a total of 5.

Row A of Table 6-3 repeats the results just discussed. Rows B through E have one of the propensities different from that in row A so that the consequence of changing that propensity can be shown. In all situations total imports fall. The greatest decrease

Table 6-3

Row	s^W	m^W	s^Z	m^Z	$Mult.^W$	dY^W	dM^W	$Mult.^Z$	dY^Z	dM^Z
A	0.2	0.1	0.2	0.1	3.75	−37.5	−3.75	1.25	−12.5	−1.25
B	0.3	0.1	0.2	0.1	2.7	−27	−2.7	0.9	−9	−0.9
C	0.2	0.2	0.2	0.1	3	−30	−6	2	−20	−2
D	0.2	0.1	0.3	0.1	3.3	−33	−3.3	0.9	−9	−0.9
E	0.2	0.1	0.2	0.2	4	−40	−4	1	−10	−2

in imports occurs when the marginal propensities to save in both countries are small and the marginal propensities to import are large.

Conclusion

To give some sense of the magnitude of capital flow, it might be useful to look at the flow of capital from developed economies and the capital flow for a particular country, for example, the United States. At least half of the capital flowing from developed countries to underdeveloped countries takes the form of grants.

Table 6-4   *Capital flow to underdeveloped economies (millions of U.S. dollars)*

	1961	1962	1963	1964	1965
From market economies and multilateral institutions					
Official bilateral transactions	4,695	4,963	5,272	5,186	5,449
Grants	3,585	3,741	3,727	3,795	3,728
Gov. long-term capital	1,110	1,223	1,545	1,391	1,721
Private long-term capital	2,362	1,600	1,808	2,009	2,703
Direct	1,744	1,381	1,557	1,566	2,210
Portfolio	618	219	251	443	493
Multilateral agencies	952	881	370	642	840
Official contributions	840	634	401	471	531
Private portfolio investments	112	247	−31	171	309
From centrally planned economies					
Total reported	27	238	112	187	
Total	8,036	7,682	7,571	8,024	8,992

Source: United Nations, *Statistical Yearbook*, 1966.

The next largest amount is long-term investment, of which the greatest proportion is direct investment. The international organizations, such as the International Bank for Reconstruction and Development, constitute the smallest source of capital for economic development. Furthermore, capital provided by centrally planned economies never exceeds an amount equal to half the grants of the market economies. The total capital flow to underdeveloped countries listed in Table 6-4 is equivalent to less than 2 percent of the United States' gross national product.

The United States' capital outflow, sum of government and private, ranged between $10 and $7.1 billion for the period 1963–1967. This is equivalent to less than 25 percent of the value of exports. The foreign capital flow to the United States

Table 6-5 *Capital flow of the United States (millions of dollars)*

Item	1963	1964	1965	1966	1967
U.S. Govt. grants and capital flow, net	−3,581	−3,560	−3,375	−3,446	−4,127
Grants, loans and net change in foreign currency holdings and short-term claims	−4,551	−4,263	−4,277	−4,680	−5,128
Scheduled repayments on U.S. Govt. loans	644	580	681	806	996
Nonscheduled repayments and selloffs	326	123	221	428	5
U.S. private capital flow, net	−4,456	−6,523	−3,743	−4,213	−5,446
Direct investments	−1,976	−2,416	−3,418	−3,543	−3,027
Foreign securities	−1,104	−677	−758	−482	−1,252
Other long-term claims:					
Reported by banks	−754	−941	−232	337	284
Reported by others	163	−343	−88	−112	−301
Short-term claims:					
Reported by banks	−781	−1,523	325	−84	−739
Reported by others	−4	−623	428	−329	−411
Foreign capital flow, net, excluding change in liquid assets in U.S.	689	685	278	2,512	3,077
Long-term investments	326	109	−68	2,176	2,235
Short-term claims	−23	113	149	269	390
Nonliquid claims on U.S. Govt. associated with:					
Military contracts	347	228	314	341	68
U.S. Govt. grants and capital	94	50	−85	−213	−85
Other specific transactions	1	208	−25	−12	−1
Other nonconvertible, nonmarketable, medium-term U.S. Govt. securities	−56	−23	−7	−49	470

ranged from $0.2 to $3 billion. This is less than 10 percent of the value of imports. In international commerce, the trade in commodities is considerably greater in value than the capital flows. This is not at all surprising, since commodities flow as a result of price difference and as a result of capital flow.

Capital flows have a direct effect on commodity trade. If the outflow of capital is allowed to reduce a country's expenditure and increase the expenditure of a receiving country, then the level of imports will expand or contract, depending on the size of the propensities. However, an expansion in the receiving country combined with monetary and fiscal measures to compensate for the outflow in the paying country will be marked by an increase in the level of imports in the two countries. The size of the increase will depend on the propensities. If the receiving country offsets capital inflows while the paying country allows its income to fall, then total imports will fall; the amount of the fall will depend on the propensities. In all cases, imports made some adjustments to the capital flow.

Selected Readings

Books
Fellner, William, et al., *Maintaining and Restoring Balance in International Payments*, Princeton: Princeton University Press, 1966, no. 14.
Harrod, Roy, and D. C. Hague, *International Trade Theory in a Developing World*, London: Macmillan and Co., 1963, no. 5.
Machlup, Fritz, *International Payments, Debts, and Gold*, New York: Charles Scribner's Sons, 1964, part 5.
Nurkse, Ragnar, *Problems of Capital Formation in Underdeveloped Countries and Patterns of Trade and Development*, New York: Oxford University Press, 1967, part 6.
Ward, Richard, *International Finance*, Englewood Cliffs: Prentice-Hall, 1965.

Periodicals
A. E. A., *Index of Economic Journals*, classification no. 11.35.
Ball, R. J., "Capital Imports and Economic Development: Paradox or Orthodoxy," *Kyklos*, 1962.
Bruton, H. J., "The Theory of Foreign Aid," *Indian Economic Journal*, January, 1961.
Jasay, A. E., "The Social Choice between Home and Overseas Investment," *Economic Journal*, March, 1960.

Kreinin, M. E., "International Lending as a Countercyclical Measure," *Review of Economics and Statistics*, February, 61.

Meek, P., "The Revival of International Capital Markets," *American Economic Review*, May, 1960.

Murphy, J. C., "International Investment and the National Interest," *Southern Economic Journal*, July, 1960.

Rothwell, K. J., "The Extra Borrowing Costs of Fixed-Return Over Equity Foreign Capital," *Indian Economic Journal*, January–March, 1964.

Schmidt, W. E., "The Economics of Charity: Loans versus Grants," *Journal of Political Economy*, August, 1964.

Stein, J. L., "International Short-Term Capital Movements," *American Economic Review*, March, 1965.

7.

The Balance of Payments

It has been shown that commodities flow as a result of price differences in two countries. Furthermore, goods are induced to flow from country to country as a result of changes in national income. Capital which flows in search of high returns and as aid induces commodities to move internationally. These expenditures for the purchase and sale of commodities and investment result in the international flow of currency. The receipt and expenditure of foreign earnings during a year are recorded in order to ascertain a nation's economic position with the rest of the world. The *balance of payments* is a summary statement of all such receipts and payments.

Accounting

The balance of payments is a record of the foreign transactions of the residents of a country with the rest of the world during a year. This means, then, that all goods, services, and capital flowing from one country to another are included in the record of foreign transactions. Furthermore, expenditures by tourists are included as imports of the tourist's country and exports of the visited country. But, after a person resides in a country for some legally specified time, he is considered a resident of that country, even though he is not a citizen, and his expenditures and earnings are no longer considered foreign transactions.

Corporations and companies are residents of the country in which they are incorporated. Since a foreign subsidiary is incorporated in the country in which it resides, its purchases or sales on the domestic market are not considered foreign transactions; but any transaction with the parent company is a foreign transaction. On the other hand, a branch office is not incorporated in the country in which it is situated; therefore, its transactions on the domestic market are considered foreign and are included in the balance of payments. In this case, transactions with the home office are not considered foreign transactions.

The accounting of the balance of payments is double entry and must therefore balance. The value of anything received from abroad is placed in the column entitled "debit" and the value of anything given up to foreigners is listed in the column marked "credit." Since a commercial transaction has something received,

Table 7-1 *Balance of payments of country W (millions of dollars)*

Debit		Credit	
A Goods from Z	$100	Cash to Z	$100
B Cash from Z	250	Goods sold to Z	250
C Meals, lodging in		Cash to Z	75
Z by W tourists	75		
D Cash from Z	30	Meals, lodging, and	
		transportation	
		sold to Z tourist	30
E Shipping from Z	25	Cash to Z	25
F Cash from Z	40	Shipping to Z	40
G Ten-year bonds from Z	100	Cash to Z	100
H Cash from Z	175	Stocks sold to Z	175
I Gift to Z	125	Cash to Z	125
	920		920

goods or money, and something given up, money or goods, a debit and a credit of equal value are entered for each transaction. Hence the sum of credits and sum of debits are equal, and the payments balance within this accounting framework. In Table 7-1, a list of credit and debit entries is given for W's balance of payments. Row A shows that goods of value of $100 were purchased and debited, and cash of $100 was given and credited. The value of credits and debits is equal; this is double-entry bookkeeping. Rows B through F show entries for goods and services and the resulting cash flow. Rows G through I show capital flows. Country W buys $100 of bonds and receives securities for which $100 of cash is paid, the credit entry. Finally, row I shows the entry of a transfer payment or gift. Since nothing is received in return for a gift, the debit entry is just the word "gift" to show that nothing is received and the value of the gift is credited.

Current Account

The balance of payments is broken down into two subcategories, the *current account* and the *capital account*. The current account contains a summary statement of all commodities and services imported and exported, together with all transfer payments, both official and private. All commodity imports are summed and debited, while all commodity exports are summed and credited. Services imported are debited and services exported are credited; W's gift is debited. The credits show a nation's earnings of foreign exchange from goods and services; the debits indicate the amount of foreign exchange used for the purchase of foreign goods and services. As can be seen in Table 7-2, the nation's purchases exceed its sales by $5.

Table 7-2 *Current account of balance of payments of country W (millions of dollars)*

Debit		Credit	
Commodity imports	100	Commodity exports	250
Services	100	Services	70
Transfer payments	125		
	325		320

Capital Account

The capital account summarizes the net change in a nation's capital position. This account contains short- and long-term capital and gold. Short-term capital is any financial asset which is cash or which will mature and be redeemed for cash within a year; long-term capital is any financial asset which will not mature within a year. Thus in Table 7-1, the bonds of row G and the stocks of row H are long term. The long-term capital purchased by W is debited and the stocks sold to Z are credited as long-term capital of $175.

Now all the cash payments received by W are summed; from this all cash payments made to Z are subtracted. If this figure is negative, it means that country W gave more cash than it received. The net cash outflow must be credited under the title of short-term capital. If the difference is positive, then country W received more cash than it paid out to Z. The positive difference represents an inflow and must be debited. In Table 7-1, country W received cash of $495 and paid $425, leaving a net receipt of $70. This net addition of $70 of short-term capital may have been deposited in banks abroad; therefore the capital account would have a debit entry against "increase in balance held abroad." Alternatively, Z may have reduced its balances in W by the $70 of short-term capital, in which case W's capital account would show a debit entry against "decrease in balance due to foreigners." Thus W's net receipts may take the form of an increased balance held abroad, a reduced balance due to foreigners, or a combination of the two, as shown in Table 7-3.

Actually Table 7-3 does not cover all cases, as it is possible for an increase in the balance due to foreigners to occur while

Table 7-3

Debit		Credit	
Long-term capital	$100	Long-term capital	$175
Increase in balances held abroad	50		
Decrease in balances due to foreigners	20		
	170		175

Table 7-4

Debit		Credit	
Long-term capital	$100	Long-term capital	$175
Increase in balances		Increase in balances	
held abroad	100	due to foreigners	30
	200		205

country W has a net receipt of currency. The net receipt will have to be larger. Suppose, for example, the balance due to foreigners increased by $30, as credited in Table 7-4. Now if country W's receipts are to be a net increase of $70, the balances held abroad must be $100, so that balances held abroad minus balances due to foreigners equal $70. This is not an unlikely situation. Firms doing business abroad must maintain checking accounts to receive and make payments. The size of these accounts is a function of business decisions.

The long- and short-term capital in Table 7-4 is the result of private transactions. However, governments borrow long and short term from other countries. It is customary to indicate whether the capital is private or official, as shown in Table 7-5.

Gold

Although both governments and private businessmen hold foreign currencies, there is a limit to these holdings. Once the

Table 7-5

Debit		Credit	
Long-term capital		Long-term capital	
Private	$80	Private	$120
Official	20	Official	55
Increase in balances		Increase in balances	
held abroad		due abroad	
Private	60	Private	10
Official	40	Official	20
	200		205

Table 7-6

Debit		Credit	
Long-term capital		Long-term capital	
Private	$80	Private	$120
Official	20	Official	55
Increase in balances		Increase in balances	
held abroad		due foreigners	
Private	60	Private	10
Official	20	Official	20
Gold	20		
	200		205

official holdings have gone beyond some agreed amount, the excess currency is exchanged for gold. Suppose the authorities do not wish to hold the $40 of nation Z's currency. $20 is turned in for gold; then the capital sector will appear as in Table 7-6.

The Complete Balance of Payments

Table 7-7 gives one form in which the balance of payments may be presented. The credits show earnings or receipts, and the total credits indicate the total value of foreign currency received. The debits indicate how the currency is dispersed. As can be seen, the currency was used to pay for imports, services, and gifts; some was invested abroad and the residual of $20 was converted into gold. Since the balance of payments shows how foreign currency was acquired and how disbursed, the balance of payments must always balance. This is the result of double-entry bookkeeping; the meaning of imbalance in the balance of payments will be discussed later.

Capital Transfer

Note that in Table 7-7 debits exceed credits by $5 in the current account, and, conversely, the credits exceed debits by $5 in the capital account. Since total debits and credits in the overall balance of payments must be equal, then any excess in one column must be matched by an equal excess in the other column in the capital account. This means, then, that if a country spends

$5 more on commodities, services, and transfers than it sells on current account, the country must have a net inflow of capital equal to $5; or in other words, a country cannot receive net investment funds in excess of the amount by which the current account is in deficit. Similarly, a nation can invest abroad a net amount just equal to the excess receipts over expenditure for commodities, services, and transfers. Thus just as an individual must earn more than he spends in order to be able to invest, so a nation must earn more abroad than it spends in order to make net investments abroad. A nation receiving investment funds is one that is spending more than it earns on foreign account.

Assume that the long-term capital being invested in country W is not $120 as given in Table 7-7 but rather $150. The question arises as to what use is made of the extra receipts of $30. If the $30 is spent on commodities, services, or even transfers, then net investment rises by the $30. But suppose only $20 of the extra $30 is spent on commodities, services, or transfer payments. The other $10 is retained as a balance, which means that the

Table 7-7 *Balance of payments of country W*
(*millions of dollars*)

Debit		Credit	
Current account			
Commodity imports	$100	Commodity exports	$250
Services	100	Services	70
Transfer payments	125		
Total	325		320
Capital account			
Long-term capital		Long-term capital	
Private	$80	Private	$120
Official	20	Official	55
Increase in balances		Increase in balances	
held abroad		due foreigners	
Private	60	Private	10
Official	20	Official	20
Gold	20		
Total capital	200		205
Total balance of			
payments	525		525

account entitled "balance held abroad" increases by $10, as shown in Table 7-8. As can be seen, the debits in the current account exceed credits by $25, an increase of $20 over that in Table 7-7. Simultaneously, the credits in the capital account exceed the debits by $25, also an increase of $20. Thus the net increase in credits in the capital account is equal to the increase in debits in the current account. The net increase of $20 in the capital account shows that country W has received only $20 of net additional capital. What has happened to the other $10?

The long-term capital received by country W has increased by $30, and the short-term capital extended by this country has increased by $10, as indicated by the account entitled "balances held abroad officially." Thus if a country does not spend all the capital received, it keeps some in the form of balances and is in fact extending short-term credit. Clearly then, a country can have an increase in net capital receipts only equal to the amount by which debits exceed credits on current account.

Likewise a country can loan a net amount equal to the excess credits over debits on current account. This excess rep-

Table 7-8 *Balance of payments of country* W *(millions of dollars)*

Debit		Credit	
Current account			
Commodity imports	$120	Commodity exports	$250
Services	100	Services	70
Transfer payments	125		
Total	345		320
Capital account			
Long-term capital		Long-term capital	
Private	$80	Private	$150
Official	20	Official	55
Increase in balance		Increase in balances	
held abroad		due foreigners	
Private	60	Private	10
Official	30	Official	20
Gold	20		
Total capital	210		235
Total debit	555	Total credit	555

resents the amount by which earnings exceed expenditures. If a country made a loan of $40, its expansion of exports would transfer the value of $40 to the receiving country. However, if the borrowing country placed the $40 in a bank in country W, then the balance of payments would show that country W loaned $40 on long term and received a short-term loan (balances due to foreigners) of $40. No net investment has taken place; nations making loans must have an excess of exports over imports, and nations receiving loans must have an excess of imports over exports. A loan in money must be transferred into goods for investment to occur.

In the previous chapter, we used the international-investment multiplier to show the consequences of a nation trying to invest $10 in the other country. This problem was looked at under the various conditions of expansion and contraction in the paying and receiving country. In most cases the full $10 was not transferred. This was because the imports and exports together could not be made to change by a total of $10. If the difference between imports and exports increases by less than $10, say $5, then the net investment is $5, and a counter short-term loan absorbs the remaining $5. Although the capital flow is $10, the real transfer of capital is said to be $5.

Imbalance

If the balance of payments is always balanced in total, what does it mean to say that a nation has a deficit or surplus in its balance of payments? In the balance of payments all foreign transactions are included, both those for commercial purposes and those which come into being only to bring balance into the foreign account. If we could delete from the balance of payments those items which serve to balance the account, we would have some idea of the imbalance in foreign transactions. For example, if as a result of commercial transactions a nation receives more foreign exchange than it wishes to use, it may convert the excess into gold. The gold is included, as in Table 7-8, and brings about the balance. But the gold flow is the result of the imbalance, i.e., excess receipts over desired expenditures. Thus while the gold is itemized in the balance of payments, its presence suggests the existence of a surplus.

Clearly then, all items which occur as a result of the surplus must be subtracted in order to reveal the imbalance. Such items are called "accommodating," as they reconcile the value of credits and debits. Accommodating items may be official, such as gold, or they may be private, such as short-term balances which cannot be converted. Furthermore, accommodating items may be short-term balances held abroad either privately or officially, or long-term loans given to help a nation through a balance-of-payments crisis. The only criterion, then, for an accommodating entry is that its existence is a function of the surplus or deficit. All other entries are called "autonomous," meaning that they are not determined by the status of the balance of payments; autonomous items come about for reasons other than balancing deficits or surpluses.

The difficulty with this dichotomy is that it requires knowledge of the motives behind the transactions. Was the transaction undertaken for commercial purposes, in which the transaction is autonomous, or was the transaction necessitated by an imbalance in the foreign transaction, in which case the item is accommodating? Since it would be extremely difficult, if not impossible, to determine the motive for each transaction, it is necessary to take entire categories as accommodating or autonomous. All the items

Table 7-9   *Autonomous items of balance of payments of country W (millions of dollars)*

Debit		Credit	
Current account			
Commodity imports	$120	Commodity exports	$250
Services	100	Services	70
Transfer payments	125		
Total	345		320
Capital account			
Long-term capital		Long-term capital	
Private	$80	Private	$150
Official	20	Official	55
Increase in balances		Increase in balances	
held abroad		due abroad	
Private	60	Private	10
Total	160		215
Total debit	505	Total credit	535

which constitute the current account are assumed to be autonomous; also long-term capital, aid, and private short-term capital. Gold and official short-term capital are considered to be accommodating entries. In Table 7-9, the autonomous items are listed. The credits (receipt of foreign exchange) exceed the debits (disbursement of foreign exchange); the excess of credits over debits is called a *surplus* in the balance of payments. As can be seen, the current account is in deficit; debits exceed credits. However, country *W* purchased $160 of foreign-held capital while selling $215 of its own capital to foreigners; the capital account is in surplus by $55. The surplus on capital account of $55 minus the deficit on current account of $25 leaves an overall surplus of $30. This $30 must be matched by an equal amount of accommodating capital.

Balance on Basis of Official Reserve Transactions

If autonomous supply of a currency exceeds autonomous demand, the difference must be purchased, accommodating demand. For the monetary authorities to purchase the excess supply, they must make use of their gold reserves, reserves of other currencies, and increasing indebtedness to other countries. When the balance of payments is devised exclusive of these reserve transactions, the resulting surplus or deficit which emerges is called in the United States' balance of payments the "balance on basis of official reserve transactions." This balance is equal to the change which occurs in the official reserves.

In Table 7-10, all autonomous supply and demand transactions are·presented to get the balance on basis of official reserve transactions. As can be seen, the United States ran a deficit of $3,398 million during 1967. Autonomous supply exceeded autonomous demand; the excess must be purchased through "official reserve transactions." Under this title it can be seen that the United States used $52 million of its "official reserve assets," increased its debt to "foreign central banks and governments and IMF" by $2,072 million, and increased "certain nonliquid liabilities" by $1,274 million. The deficit plus the reserve transactions, of course, brings the overall account into balance.

In 1966, the United States acquired a surplus of $225 million in all nonliquid reserve transactions. A surplus means that

Table 7-10 *United States balance of payments (millions of dollars)*

Item	1963	1964	1965	1966	1967
Exports of goods and services—Total	32,339	36,958	39,147	43,039	45,693
Merchandise	22,071	25,297	26,244	29,168	30,463
Military sales	657	747	844	847	1,272
Transportation	2,115	2,324	2,390	2,589	2,701
Travel	934	1,095	1,380	1,573	1,641
Investment income receipts, private	4,156	4,932	5,376	5,650	6,163
Investment income receipts, Govt.	498	460	512	595	622
Other services	1,908	2,103	2,401	2,617	2,831
Imports of goods and services—Total	−26,442	−28,468	−32,203	−37,937	−40,893
Merchandise	−16,992	−18,621	−21,472	−25,510	−26,980
Military expenditures	−2,936	−2,834	−2,921	−3,694	−4,319
Transportation	−2,316	−2,462	−2,674	−2,914	−2,965
Travel	−2,090	−2,201	−2,438	−2,657	−3,170
Investment income payments	−1,271	−1,404	−1,729	−2,074	−2,277
Other services	−837	−946	−969	−1,088	−1,182
Balance on goods and services	5,897	8,490	6,944	5,102	4,800
Remittances and pensions	−867	−879	−1,024	−1,010	−1,284
1. Balance on goods, services, remittances and pensions	5,030	7,611	5,920	4,092	3,516
2. U.S. Govt. grants and capital flow, net	−3,581	−3,560	−3,375	−3,446	−4,127
Grants, loans and net change in foreign currency holdings and short-term claims	−4,551	−4,263	−4,277	−4,680	−5,128
Scheduled repayments on U.S. Govt. loans	644	580	681	806	996
Nonscheduled repayments and selloffs	326	123	221	428	5
3. U.S. private capital flow, net	−4,456	−6,523	−3,743	−4,213	−5,446
Direct investments	−1,976	−2,416	−3,418	−3,543	−3,027
Foreign securities	−1,104	−677	−758	−482	−1,252
Other long-term claims:					
Reported by banks	−754	−941	−232	337	284
Reported by others	163	−343	−88	−112	−301
Short-term claims:					
Reported by banks	−781	−1,523	325	−84	−739
Reported by others	−4	−623	428	−329	−411

Table 7-10 *United States balance of payments (millions of dollars)*
(Continued)

Item	1963	1964	1965	1966	1967
4. Foreign capital flow, net, excluding change in liquid assets in U.S.	689	685	278	2,512	3,077
Long-term investments	326	109	−68	2,176	2,235
Short-term claims	−23	113	149	269	390
Nonliquid claims on U.S. Govt. associated with:					
Military contracts	347	228	314	341	68
U.S. Govt. grants and capital	94	50	−85	−213	−85
Other specific transactions	1	208	−25	−12	−1
Other nonconvertible, nonmarketable, medium-term U.S. Govt. securities	−56	−23	−7	−49	470
5. Errors and unrecorded transactions	−352	−1,011	−415	−302	−595
6. Change in liquid liabilities to nonofficial holders					
Commercial banks abroad	470	1,454	116	2,697	1,265
Other private residents of foreign countries	385	345	306	212	394
International and regional organizations other than IMF	−236	−245	−291	−525	−208
Less: Change in certain nonliquid liabilities to foreign central banks and govts	−7	302	100	802	1,274
Balance on basis of official reserve transactions	−2,044	−1,546	−1,304	225	−3,398
Official reserve transactions	2,044	1,546	1,304	−225	3,398
Change in U.S. official reserve assets (increase, −)	378	171	1,222	568	52
Change in liquid liabilities to foreign central banks and govts. and IMF	1,673	1,073	−18	−1,595	2,072
Change in certain nonliquid liabilities to foreign central banks and govts:					
Of U.S. private organizations	9	148	−38	788	820
Of U.S. Govt.	−16	154	138	14	454

autonomous demand exceeds autonomous supply. The United States must have acquired reserves in the form of gold, reduced liabilities to foreign central banks and governments and IMF, and reduced nonliquid liabilities. As can be seen, the United States reduced its liquid liabilities to foreign central banks and governments and IMF by $1,595 million—an amount $1,370 million in excess of the surplus. Consequently, United States official reserve assets were reduced by $568 million and nonliquid liabilities increased by $788 million to bring balance. The surplus of $225 million plus the sale of official reserve assets of $568 million plus the increase in nonliquid liabilities of $802 million equals the reduction in liquid liabilities to foreign central banks and governments and IMF of $1,595 million.

The liquid liabilities held by "commercial banks abroad" and "other private residents of foreign countries" are being demanded for reasons known only to the holders. These holdings constitute part of the autonomous demand. However, liquid holdings can be presented for conversion at any time as a result of any whim. These holdings represent a potential threat. Thus for analytical purposes, it is useful on occasion to recognize fully the possibility and consider these liquid liabilities as the means of financing the deficit, accommodating demand. This approach is taken in Table 7-11, where the "balance on liquidity basis" is presented. All liquid liabilities are removed from the autonomous-demand category. The resulting deficits are in every case greater than those listed in the balance on the basis of official reserve transactions. The deficit of $3,575 million for 1967 is settled by using $52 million of official reserve assets plus an increased liquid indebtedness to all foreign accounts of $3,523 million.

Conclusion

The balance of payments is the record of all expenditures and receipts of residents of a country with the rest of the world for a year. The system is one of double-entry accounting. The sum of credits and debits is equal; the overall account balances.

The data can be broken down in different ways to determine a surplus or deficit. For example, one can strike a balance on the current account, called "balance on goods and services, remittances and pensions" in Table 7-10. Furthermore, one can

Table 7-11   *United States balance of payments (millions of dollars)*

Item	1963	1964	1965	1966	1967
Exports of goods and services—Total	32,339	36,958	39,147	43,039	45,693
Merchandise	22,071	25,297	26,244	29,168	30,463
Military sales	657	747	844	847	1,272
Transportation	2,115	2,324	2,390	2,589	2,701
Travel	934	1,095	1,380	1,573	1,641
Investment income receipts, private	4,156	4,932	5,376	5,650	6,163
Investment income receipts, Govt.	498	460	512	595	622
Other services	1,908	2,103	2,401	2,617	2,831
Imports of goods and services—Total	−26,442	−28,468	−32,203	−37,937	−40,893
Merchandise	−16,992	−18,621	−21,472	−25,510	−26,980
Military expenditures	−2,936	−2,834	−2,921	−3,694	−4,319
Transportation	−2,316	−2,462	−2,674	−2,914	−2,965
Travel	−2,090	−2,201	−2,438	−2,657	−3,170
Investment income payments	−1,271	−1,404	−1,729	−2,074	−2,277
Other services	−837	−946	−969	−1,088	−1,182
Balance on goods and services	5,897	8,490	6,944	5,102	4,800
Remittances and pensions	−867	−879	−1,024	−1,010	−1,284
1. Balance on goods, services, remittances and pensions	5,030	7,611	5,920	4,092	3,516
2. U.S. Govt. grants and capital flow, net	−3,581	−3,560	−3,375	−3,446	−4,127
Grants, loans and net change in foreign currency holdings and short-term claims	−4,551	−4,263	−4,277	−4,680	−5,128
Scheduled repayments on U.S. Govt. loans	644	580	681	806	996
Nonscheduled repayments and selloffs	326	123	221	428	5
3. U.S. private capital flow, net	−4,456	−6,523	−3,743	−4,213	−5,446
Direct investments	−1,976	−2,416	−3,418	−3,543	−3,027
Foreign securities	−1,104	−677	−758	−482	−1,252
Other long-term claims:					
Reported by banks	−754	−941	−232	337	284
Reported by others	163	−343	−88	−112	−301
Short-term claims:					
Reported by banks	−781	−1,523	325	−84	−739
Reported by others	−4	−623	428	−329	−411

Table 7-11 *United States balance of payments (millions of dollars)*
(Continued)

Item	1963	1964	1965	1966	1967
4. Foreign capital flow, net, excluding change in liquid assets in U.S.	689	685	278	2,512	3,077
Long-term investments	326	109	−68	2,176	2,235
Short-term claims	−23	113	149	269	390
Nonliquid claims on U.S. Govt. associated with:					
Military contracts	347	228	314	341	68
U.S. Govt. grants and capital	94	50	−85	−213	−85
Other specific transactions	1	208	−25	−12	−1
Other nonconvertible, nonmarketable, medium-term U.S. Govt. securities	−56	−23	−7	−49	470
5. Errors and unrecorded transactions	−352	−1,011	−415	−302	−595
Balance on liquidity basis	−2,670	−2,798	−1,335	−1,357	−3,575
6. To settle balance on liquidity basis	2,670	2,798	1,335	1,357	3,575
Change in U.S. official reserve assets (increase, −)	*378*	*171*	*1,222*	*568*	*52*
Gold	461	125	1,665	571	1,170
Convertible currencies	−113	−220	−349	−540	−1,024
IMF gold tranche position	30	266	−94	537	−94
Change in liquid liabilities to all foreign accounts	*2,292*	*2,627*	*113*	*789*	*3,523*
Foreign central banks and govts.:					
Convertible nonmarketable U.S. Govt. securities	703	375	122	−945	455
Marketable U.S. Govt. bonds and notes	466	−59	−20	−245	48
Deposits, short-term U.S. Govt. securities, etc.	504	757	−154	−582	1,547
IMF (gold deposits)			34	177	22
Commercial banks abroad	470	1,454	116	2,697	1,265
Other private residents of foreign countries	385	345	306	212	394
International and regional organizations other than IMF	−236	−245	−291	−525	−208

obtain a balance on basis of official reserve transactions or a balance on liquidity basis. One is usually trying to separate continuing items from those which cannot go on.

The temptation in analyzing deficits in the balance of payments is to look for some item of similar magnitude and make that item responsible for the deficit. For example, the United States' deficit has often been blamed on "grants and loans" given by the United States. These grants are of a similar magnitude to the deficit. Thus it is often said that the problem with the United States' balance of payments is the result of trying to give too much away. However, the amount spent on transportation is also of similar magnitude. If we did not pay transportation charges to foreigners, we could reduce the deficit. Cutting out travel expenditures would likewise remove the deficit. These items only happen to be of similar magnitude and do not necessarily cause the deficit.

Assigning the exact causes of the deficit is not easy without looking further into the economies. For example, the United States' deficit could be corrected by exporting more or importing less. Exports and imports are functions of price, income, and other factors. The deficit could be the result of United States' prices rising faster than those in the rest of the world. A study of price trends in the United States and in other countries would be needed to determine this. The United States could be having a faster increase in income, inducing a more rapid growth in imports. The interest-rate structure might be out of line and need correcting to bring capital flows to a level more consistent with balance. Or the exchange rate might be too high. A combination of these items could be the cause of the deficit; the items in the balance of payments are only the manifestation of the disequilibrium, not the cause. One needs to look further.

The remainder of this book will be concerned with the adjusting mechanism for maintaining equilibrium in the balance of payments. It must be remembered, however, that policies devised to correct deficits often do not deal with the causes, but only the symptoms. The President's recent attempt to restrict travel to correct the deficit is a case in point. Travel expenditures are not the likely cause of the deficit, but reducing travel expenditures will reduce the deficit; the symptom is being treated rather than the cause. Tariff barriers and trade controls usually treat the symptoms rather than the cause. France's use of these barriers at this time to correct a deficit is a good example.

Selected Readings

Books

A. E. A., *Readings in the Theory of International Trade*, Philadelphia: The Blakiston Co., 1950.

Allen, William, and Clark Allen, *Foreign Trade and Finance*, New York: The Macmillan Co., 1959.

Baldwin et al., *Trade, Growth and the Balance of Payments*, Chicago: Rand McNally, 1965.

Fellner, William, and others, *Maintaining and Restoring Balance in International Payments*, Princeton: Princeton University Press, 1966.

Machlup, Fritz, *International Payments, Debts and Gold*, New York: Charles Scribner's Sons, 1964.

Meade, J. E., *The Balance of Payments*, London: Oxford University Press, 1951.

Salant and Associates, *The United States Balance of Payments in 1968*, Washington: The Brookings Institution, 1963.

Ward, Richard, *International Finance*, Englewood Cliffs: Prentice-Hall, 1965.

Wasserman, Max, and Charles Hultman, *Modern International Economics*, New York: Simmons-Boardman, 1962.

Periodicals

A. E. A., *Index of Economic Journals*, classification no. 11.3.

Allen, W. R., "Another Balance of Payments Pitfall: 'Dollar Use' and 'Dollar Supply,' " *Review of Economics and Statistics*, November, 1962.

Gemmill, R. R., "Notes on the Measurement of International Liquidity," *Journal of Finance*, March, 1960.

Gordon, W., "The Criterion for an Adverse Balance of Payments," *American Economic Review*, March, 1963.

Høst-Madsen, P., "Asymmetries between Balance of Payments Surpluses and Deficits," *International Monetary Fund Staff Papers*, July, 1962.

Kenen, P., "Measuring the United States' Balance of Payments," *Review of Economics and Statistics*, May, 1964.

Klein, T. M., "The United Kingdom Balance-of-Payments Accounts," *Economic Journal*, December, 1964.

LaBarge, R. A., "The Imputation of Values to Intra-Company Exports: The Case of Bananas," *Social and Economic Studies*, June, 1961.

Leighton, Richard I., "Balance of Payments of Israel, 1950–1959," *Artha-Vikas*, July, 1966.

Pal, S., "Basis of Modern Balance of Payments Statistics and Analysis," *Indian Journal of Economics*, April, 1964.

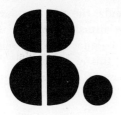

The Gold
Standard

The development of this book began by showing why trade takes place and the gains from trade. It has been shown that goods move internationally as a result of price difference, changes in national income, and capital movements. The autonomous supply and demand of foreign currency will not necessarily be equal. If the demand exceeds supply, the nation is said to have a surplus in its balance of payments; and if supply exceeds demand, the nation is said to have a deficit. The question to be considered now is this: how can a deficit or surplus in the balance of payments be corrected, or how can equilibrium be restored? There are three basic attacks.

1. Allow domestic prices and income to change until the balance is restored in the foreign account. Corrections in the balance of

payments come about primarily this way under the gold standard. 2. Allow the price of foreign exchange to adjust to equate the supply and demand, thereby maintaining balance in the foreign account. A flexible exchange rate works in this manner. 3. Finance the deficits or surpluses up to some specified magnitude and then adjust the exchange rate. This is the system of fixed exchange rates with adjustable pegs.

Supply and Demand for Currency

In order to undertake commercial transactions in a foreign nation, it is essential to obtain the nation's currency with which to make payment. The demand for a currency is derived from the demand for the nation's goods and investment outlets. The price of a foreign nation's goods depends, in part, on the price of that nation's currency. For example, suppose a resident of country W wishes to buy a lamp in country Z which costs 400 pesos. If the price of the peso in terms of W's currency is 10 cents, then the lamp costs $40, but if the peso is 5 cents, the lamp costs only $20 to a resident of country W. The price of Z's goods to W residents, then, depends on the price to W of Z's pesos. The cheaper Z's pesos in terms of W's dollars, the cheaper all Z's goods will be to W residents and, for this reason, larger quantities of Z's pesos will be demanded at lower dollar prices, as depicted in Figure 8-1.

Figure 8-1

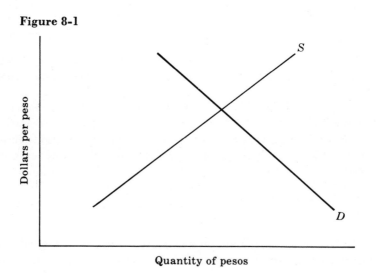

Quantity of pesos

The number of pesos supplied will depend on the dollar price. The more dollars given per peso, the cheaper all goods in W will be to residents of Z. A higher dollar price induces residents of Z to supply pesos for a larger number of dollars to buy goods in W, which in terms of pesos are cheaper. The supply schedule, then, is the usual upward sloping schedule, showing a larger quantity of pesos offered at a higher price for pesos.

Adjustment Mechanism of Gold Standard

The *gold standard* is a fixed-exchange-rate system; the forces of supply and demand are constrained so that they have only limited effect in determining the exchange rate. Each country fixes the price of its currency in terms of gold. The nation must be willing to supply any amount of its own currency for gold at the fixed rate, thereby preventing the price of its currency from rising above this fixed rate. Similarly, the nation must be willing to demand any amount of its currency for gold at the fixed rate, thereby prohibiting the rate from falling. Hence, a nation fixes the price of its currency in terms of gold by selling or buying any amount of its currency required to make supply and demand equal at the fixed rate.

Any two currencies fixed in terms of gold are simultaneously fixed in the price for which they exchange. For example, suppose country W fixes the price of its currency at $35 an ounce of gold and country Z fixes it at a price of 70 pesos per ounce of gold. $35 must be equal to ₱70, since both of these values are equal to one ounce of gold. Clearly, $1 exchanges for ₱2, or 50 cents equals ₱1.

The market price cannot depart from 50 cents for ₱1. No one would pay 70 cents for ₱1; instead, one would take his 50 cents to W's treasury and turn it in for $\frac{1}{70}$ ounce of gold. The $\frac{1}{70}$th of an ounce of gold can be exchanged for ₱1 at Z's treasury. As long as currency can be exchanged for gold, one need not pay more than 50 cents for ₱1. Similarly, one would not need to sell a peso for 40 cents. ₱1 in country Z can be exchanged for $\frac{1}{70}$th of an ounce of gold which can be exchanged for 50 cents in country W. Since 50 cents can be converted into ₱1 by gold movements, the market price of dollars for pesos cannot depart from the 1 to 2 ratio.

The shipping of gold from one treasury to another does entail a cost; this cost alters the rate at which dollars exchange

for pesos through gold shipments. Suppose, for example, that
all costs incurred for shipping $\frac{1}{70}$th of an ounce of gold between
treasuries amount to 5 cents. The price of obtaining a peso by gold
shipment would be 55 cents, 50 cents for the gold and 5 cents for
the shipping costs. Similarly, the ₱1 can be converted into $\frac{1}{70}$th
of an ounce of gold which can be sold for 50 cents; but out of the
money received, 5 cents must be used to pay the shipping costs.
Thus through gold shipments, ₱1 will bring a net amount of
45 cents.

Obviously, one would prefer to buy pesos on the exchange market at any price below 55 cents, the opportunity cost of obtaining
gold and shipping it. No one would pay more than 55 cents, because
for this amount one could get gold and pay all shipping charges to
obtain ₱1 from Z's treasury. Similarly, one would accept for ₱1
on the exchange market anything over 45 cents. An offer below
45 cents would not be accepted, for the conversion of ₱1 into
gold and gold into dollars would bring 45 cents. The free market
price for pesos may fluctuate between 45 cents and 55 cents
but not outside this range. The price which induces gold to flow
in, 45 cents in this case, is called the *gold import point*. The price

Figure 8-2

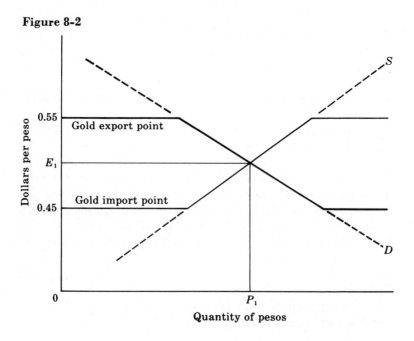

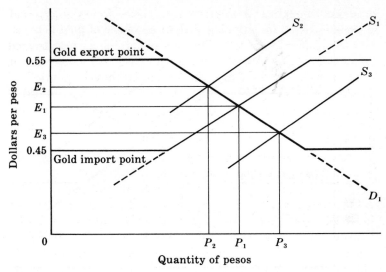

Figure 8-3

which induces gold to flow out, 55 cents in this example, is called the *gold export point.**The gold export and import points set the limits within which the forces of supply and demand determine the exchange rate. In Figure 8-2, the market sets a price of E_1 with the quantity of pesos sold as P_1. Since the autonomous supply and demand for pesos are equal, the balance of payments is said to be in equilibrium.

A decrease in supply from S_1 to S_2 in Figure 8-3 results in the exchange rate rising to E_2, and the quantity of pesos sold falls to P_2. At the exchange rate E_2, the autonomous supply and demand for pesos are equal; the nation is not confronted with a balance-of-payments problem. Similarly, an increase in the supply of pesos to S_3 forces down the exchange rate to E_3 and increases the number sold to P_3. Again, autonomous supply and demand are equal, and the foreign account balances.

An increase in the demand for pesos from D_1 to D_2 in Figure 8-4 results in a new exchange rate of E_2 and quantity of pesos sold of P_2. Since the autonomous supply and demand are equal, there is neither deficit nor surplus in the balance of payments. A decrease in demand to D_3 brings about a lower exchange rate of E_3 and a smaller quantity of pesos bought and sold, but the balance remains in the foreign account. Thus the forces

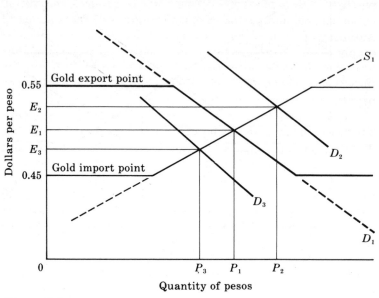

Figure 8-4

of supply and demand determine the exchange rates within the limits of the gold export and import points, and any exchange rate within these limits is accompanied by balance in the foreign account.

It has been shown that supply and demand determine the exchange rate within the limits of the gold export and import points, and it has also been shown that at these rates the balance in the foreign account is maintained. The question as to what happens outside of these limits must now be considered. Suppose the supply of pesos in Figure 8-5 falls from S_1 to S_2; then the exchange rate is under pressure to rise to E_2. However, E_2 is above the price at which pesos can be obtained through gold shipments. Rather than pay E_2 per peso, one would obtain pesos through the cheaper means of shipping gold. At the gold export point of 55 cents, the autonomous supply of pesos is quantity P_2 and the autonomous demand is P_3. Of the quantity P_3 demanded, P_2 can be purchased on the free market at a price of 55 cents, as supply schedule S_2 shows. The remainder of the quantity demanded, namely P_2P_3, will not be forthcoming on the free market at a price of 55 cents. Gold in sufficient quantity to purchase P_2P_3 pesos at Z's treasury will be shipped; the cost of obtaining gold and paying shipping charges is 55 cents per peso. Autonomous demand for pesos of P_3 exceeds the autonomous supply of P_2; the inequality reveals a balance-of-payments problem equal to P_2P_3 pesos. Gold of value equal to P_2P_3 pesos is the accommodating item and reveals the surplus in Z's balance of payments.

Now suppose the demand for pesos increases to D_2 in Figure 8-6. The exchange rate which would be determined by supply and demand lies above the gold export point. Rather than buy currency on the exchange market at E_2, people will buy gold and export it to Z's treasury for pesos. At the gold export point, the free market will supply P_3 pesos at a price of 55 cents, as indicated by the autonomous supply schedule. The autonomous demand for pesos at 55 cents is P_2. Autonomous demand exceeds supply by P_3P_2; the value of gold will be exported to Z's treasury to be exchanged for pesos. The flow of gold to Z is an accommodating item and reveals the surplus in Z's balance of payments.

In the two cases studied, demand has exceeded the supply

Figure 8-5

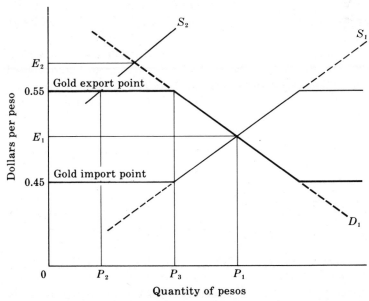

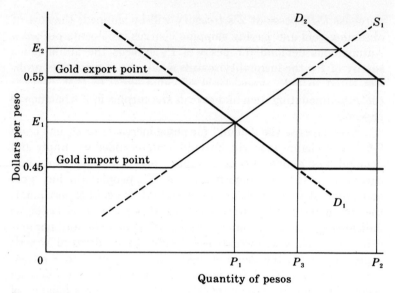

Figure 8-6

Figure 8-7

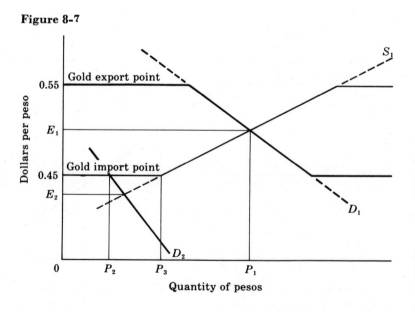

of foreign exchange, and the demanding nation has exported gold with which to acquire foreign currency. Two more cases need to be considered; both show the consequence of supply exceeding demand. Suppose demand should fall to D_2 in Figure 8-7; the free market rate of E_2 lies below the gold import point. However, no supplier of pesos will accept less than 45 cents; instead one would convert the pesos into gold and sell the gold for dollars at W's treasury, realizing 45 cents per peso. P_1 pesos will be demanded and P_2 supplied at the gold import point of 45 cents. Autonomous supply exceeds demand, gold is imported into country W (which has a surplus), and gold flows out of country Z (which has a deficit). The value of the gold flow is P_2P_3.

Finally, suppose the autonomous supply of pesos increases to S_2, so that the market equilibrium price is below 45 cents, as shown in Figure 8-8. At 45 cents per peso, quantity P_3 is demanded and P_2 supplied. Since autonomous supply exceeds demand by P_2P_3, this excess supply of pesos must be converted into gold and imported into country W. Again country W has a surplus and country Z has a deficit equal in value to P_2P_3 pesos.

Thus we have seen that when country W's demand for pesos exceeds Z's supply, gold equal to the value by which demand exceeds the supply of pesos is exported by W to Z.

Figure 8-8

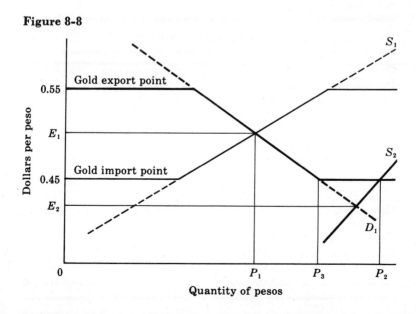

When supply exceeds demand for pesos, gold by the amount of the inequality is imported by W from Z. The next question to be considered is whether this gold flow will continue indefinitely or until the gold sources are depleted. To consider this question, the consequences on the domestic economy of the flow of gold must be considered.

Correcting Imbalance through Gold Flows

If, as a result of a surplus in W's balance of payments, gold flows from Z to W, then the quantity of the two currencies in circulation must change. The gold imported by W is converted at the treasury for dollars; the inflow of gold expands dollars at the rate of \$1 for every $\frac{1}{35}$ ounce of gold received. Likewise in Z currency is turned in for gold; the outflow of gold reduces the currency by ₱2 for every $\frac{1}{35}$ ounce of gold. If these countries have a fractional reserve banking system, then the expansion of money in W and contraction in Z will be greater than the monetary value of the gold flow.

For illustration purposes, assume that both W and Z have fractional reserve systems and that each country has a single monopoly bank which serves the whole country. The monopoly

Table 8-1

Monopoly bank of country W			
Cash	. . . .	Demand deposits	$1,000,000
Deposits			
(with central bank)	$200,000		
Government bonds	300,000		
Loans	900,000	Capital	400,000
	$1,400,000		$1,400,000

Monopoly bank of country Z			
Cash	. . . .	Demand deposits	₱2,000,000
Deposits			
(with central bank)	₱400,000		
Government bonds	800,000		
Loans	1,200,000	Capital	400,000
	₱2,400,000		₱2,400,000

bank of each country must keep on deposit with its central bank an amount equal to one-fifth of demand deposits (i.e., checking accounts). Each country's balance sheet is given in Table 8-1. Each country's bank is assumed to be fully loaned (i.e., deposits with central banks are equal to one-fifth of demand deposits), and it is assumed that neither bank need hold cash. If the autonomous supply of pesos exceeds the demand by ₱700, these pesos will be exchanged for 10 ounces of gold. A check for ₱700 for the 10 ounces of gold will be presented to Z's central bank, which acts for the treasury. The central bank draws the ₱700 from the deposits of the bank against which the check is drawn, in this case the monopoly bank. Thus the monopoly bank deposits with the central bank are reduced by ₱700. The cancelled check is given to the monopoly bank. In turn, the monopoly bank draws the pesos from the individuals' accounts, so demand deposits are down by ₱700. The monopoly bank's demand deposits are ₱1,999,300, and its deposits with the central bank amount to ₱399,300.

However, to fulfill the reserve requirement of one-fifth, the monopoly bank's demand deposits must not exceed ₱1,996,500 for deposits with the central bank of ₱399,300. The monopoly bank must reduce its demand deposits by ₱2,800. The only way the demand deposits can be reduced is by calling in loans of ₱2,800; individuals will repay their loans by drawing upon their demand deposits by the required amount. The monopoly bank of Z will now have the balance sheet presented in Table 8-2. The bank is once again in a position of being fully loaned, but demand deposits have contracted by ₱3,500. The outflow of 10 ounces of gold has brought a contraction of ₱3,500 to a country with a

Table 8-2

	Monopoly bank of country Z		
Cash	. . . .	Demand deposits	₱1,996,500
Deposits			
(with central bank)	₱399,300		
Government bonds	800,000		
Loans	1,197,200	Capital	400,000
	₱2,396,500		₱2,396,500

reserve requirement of one-fifth. If the reserve requirement had been smaller, the contraction would have been larger.

The 10 ounces of gold are imported into country W and exchanged for $350. The money is deposited with the monopoly bank of country W, and the monopoly bank in turn deposits the cash with the central bank, so that both demand deposits and deposits with the central bank rise by $350. Now the deposits with the central bank of $200,350 allow the monopoly bank to have demand deposits equal to $1,001,750, with a reserve requirement of one-fifth. Therefore the bank may expand its loans and demand deposits by $1,400 and arrive at the position shown in Table 8-3. The importation of 10 ounces of gold brought about an expansion of $1,750 in country W. Again, had the reserve requirement been smaller, the expansion would have been larger.

To determine the consequences of the increase in money in country W and decrease in Z, it is necessary to introduce the *quantity theory of money*, which was the "classical school's" explanation of the consequence of the gold flow. The quantity theory of money states that money multiplied by the velocity of money must be equal to the average price of all output multiplied by the number of units of output, or

$$MV = PO$$

where M is the quantity of money, V is the number of times money changes hands during the year, P is the average price of output, and O is the number of units of output. Clearly, if the total amount of money in the economy is $2,000,000 and this money changes hands five times in a year, then the total value of sales must be $2,000,000 × 5 or $10,000,000, which must be equal to the value of the output sold. This is a truism. The "classical economist" assumed that V and O were constant. Thus

Table 8-3

		Monopoly bank of country W	
Cash	. . . .	Demand deposits	$1,001,750
Deposits			
(with central bank)	$200,350		
Government bonds	300,000		
Loans	901,400	Capital	400,000
	$1,401,750		$1,401,000

changes in the quantity of money had proportionate changes in prices. The flow of gold, then, would reduce the prices in country Z and increase them in W.

W's prices would increase relative to Z. The result would be: (1) Z would substitute home-produced goods for imports from W, resulting in a reduced supply of pesos, and (2) W would substitute cheaper imports for high-priced goods produced at home, resulting in an increased demand for pesos. The gold would continue to flow, increasing the demand for pesos and reducing the supply, until autonomous supply and demand were equal, at which point gold would no longer flow and the imbalance would have been corrected. Thus the correction to the balance of payments comes through the inflation of the surplus economy and deflation of the deficit country. The domestic economies are made to adjust until equilibrium is restored in the balance of payments.

Furthermore, the increased gold and money supply in W and reduced gold and money supply in Z would reduce W's interest rate relative to Z's. Consequently, capital would start to flow from W's low-interest market to Z's high-interest market. The capital flow would increase the autonomous demand for Z's currency and increase the supply of W's currency, thereby serving to restore equilibrium to the balance of payments.

If prices are inflexible downward, as Keynesians assume, then changes in M will not affect P but instead O. Thus Z's reduction in money will bring about a fall in output and employment. A nation with a deficit must accept unemployment in order to correct the deficit.

But there are monetary policies which can be used to correct inflation and deflation. For example, a nation going through inflation could increase the reserve requirement in order to reduce the quantity of money; the central banks could sell securities or change the rediscount rate, i.e., the interest rate at which the central bank loans to member banks. If these monetary policies were successful in combating inflation, there would be no increase in P and no increased demand for the other country's currency. Furthermore, if monetary policy in the deficit country were successful in prohibiting deflation, there would be no reduction in the supply of its currency. Thus the correction mechanism would be foiled. For the gold standard to maintain equilibrium, nations could not forestall indefinitely the necessary inflation or deflation. To be fully effective, nations must passively accept inflation, deflation, or unemployment.

Gold discovery in any country induces worldwide inflation. Newly mined gold sold to the treasury results in an expansion of money and then increase in prices. The increase in prices results in a reduction in exports and increase in imports, which are relatively cheaper. A deficit is introduced in the balance of payments with gold flowing out. The gold flows out to inflate prices in other countries and thereby eradicates the deficits.

Conclusion

What has been described is a pure gold standard where the currency is left unmanaged by the monetary authorities. Such a system has never existed in reality; throughout history nations have managed their currencies to varying degrees. The gold standard which emerged and existed during the period 1840 to 1920 probably came closest to the pure gold standard, but even here the currency was not left unmanaged. For example, the Bank Act of 1844 placed Great Britain on what was conceived to be a rather pure gold standard; however, this act provided for departures under emergency conditions. The government's intervention took the form of "Chancellor's letters," which in effect allowed banks to lend beyond the maximum in order to relieve pressures in the money market. These emergency conditions were employed in 1847, 1857, and 1866. On occasions the bank rate, which influenced all interest rates, was raised in reaction to the outflow of gold. The higher interest rate would attract capital and increase the demand for sterling, thereby reducing the outflow of gold. This action is consistent with the purposes of the gold flow, except more of the adjustment tends to be through changes in the interest rate and capital flow than through changes in prices and commodity flow. This assistance is a definite attempt to manage the currency so as to reduce the burden on gold; the outflow of gold is not as great and reserves are maintained.

Other devices, such as offering a price above the gold import point, were used to intervene into the currency system. What is important is the fact that the concept of an unmanaged currency system, in which the money was tied to gold and changes in the quantity of money were purely the result of gold flows, was never accepted.

This gold standard expired during World War I and was never reinstituted. There was strong sentiment to return to the gold standard after the war, but prices had risen greatly, serving to increase the value of trade in relation to gold. Gold was scarce, relatively speaking. To overcome what were considered inadequate gold supplies, the gold-bullion system was inaugurated. In general, gold coins were not minted, and the currency could be converted for gold for export only. The gold-bullion system became, by and large, a reserve system by which foreign-held currency units could be converted for gold at the issuing country's treasury. The quantity of money was not tied strictly to the quantity of gold held in reserves.

The gold-bullion system was not successful; most nations gave it up in the late twenties or early thirties. The failure might be attributed to four factors: (1) the maldistribution of gold after the war, (2) inflation, which created a problem in determining the appropriate exchange rate in terms of gold, (3) high protectionism, (4) lack of international cooperation.

During the war, gold tended to flow to the United States, the Netherlands, Sweden, Denmark, and Norway. The Netherlands and Sweden ceased buying gold as large quantities started to flow in. The gold flow was the result of inflation, surplus in the balance of payments, and capital in search of security. Immediately after the war, the reparations and war debts tended to accentuate the maldistribution. Thus the gold-bullion system was inaugurated at a time when some nations had more than adequate reserves while others had insufficient reserves.

The inflation during the war reduced the value of currency in terms of gold. Since the rate of inflation varied from country to country, the amount by which each country's money was depreciated varied. Some nations' currency had fallen a great deal, and these nations reduced the price of the currency in terms of gold from the prewar par value. For example, France fixed its par value at one-fifth the prewar par value; Belgium at approximately one-eighth, and Italy at approximately one-fourth. The new par value tended to undervalue the French franc. Other countries, whose currency fell in value but not by as much as those listed above, felt the prestige of going back to the prewar rate worth the inconvenience of the required deflation. Such countries were the United Kingdom, Australia, Union of South Africa, the Netherlands, Norway, and Denmark. For Great Britain, this tended to overvalue the currency in terms of gold. The United States currency had fallen by little and was able to go back to the prewar par value without difficulty. Gold tends to flow from overvalued currency to undervalued currency. Consequently, gold tended to flow from Great Britain to France and the United States, furthering the maldistribution.

This was also a period of high protectionism. For example, France had not only high tariffs but also legal restrictions and high taxes on the export of capital. Since it was so difficult to create a French demand for one's currency for either imports or investment, it was necessary to pay gold for a large proportion of French goods. France was not the only country to have high tariffs; as noted earlier, United States tariffs reached their all-time high in 1930. These tariffs placed further strains on gold reserves.

The gold acquired by France and the United States was not used to expand credit. Therefore, prices did not rise to correct the outflow of gold. Furthermore, a large portion of the gold flowing to the United States was used to buy securities on the stock market. There prices did indeed rise, but the expectation was for further increases. Gold tended to continue to flow to purchase securities which were expected to continue to increase in price. Rising price expectations prevented the gold flow from bringing about a correction.

Given the bullion standard in a world in which gold was maldistributed, protectionism extensive, exchange rates departing from their market value, and prices inflexible, a very high degree of cooperation and mutual assistance in the form of loans was necessary to maintain the system. Unfortunately, this mutual assistance was not sufficient to meet the needs. Until 1928, the United States had been using its surplus to give large loans abroad. The boom in 1928 required large sums of capital and reduced the amount available to foreign countries. Thus the surplus in the United States balance of payments had to be paid in gold; most foreign nations did not have the gold with which to make the payment, i.e., redeem their excess currency. Some nations were forced off the gold-bullion system—Argentine and Uruguay in 1929 and Canada shortly after.

Great Britain was borrowing short to make long-term loans. As the market grew weak, the Bank of England tried unsuccessfully to obtain foreign credits. Without the credits, England would have to use gold reserves in order to meet the short-term debt. However, in 1931, Great Britain discontinued the sale of gold in order to protect its reserves. Although large reserves are rationalized to redeem the currency held by foreigners, the gold reserves often become important for their own sake. Rather than allow the gold reserves to sink, the country refuses to redeem its currency.

With the depression of the 1930s the United States went off the gold-bullion standard. The gold-bullion system had thus come to an end.

A fully automatic system can maintain equilibrium in the balance of payments, as discussed above. However, it is clear that nations are unwilling to accept the conditions required for bringing balance to the foreign account. Most nations are unwilling to allow external forces to dictate inflation and deflation and will avoid, if at all possible, surrendering control over the domestic economy to external determinants. This is particularly true in a world where politicians are sensitive to inflation and unemployment. Another mechanism which allows delay and alternative correctives will be adopted.

Selected Readings

Books

Cassell, G., *The Downfall of the Gold Standard*, New York: Kelley, 1936.

Ellsworth, P. T., *The International Economy*, New York: Macmillan Co., 1964, Chap. 19.

Haberler, G., *The Theory of International Trade*, London: William Hodge, 1936, Chap. 3.

Kemmerer, E. W., *Gold and the Gold Standard*, New York: McGraw-Hill, 1944.

Marsh, Donald, *World Trade and Investment*, New York: Harcourt, Brace and Co., 1951, Chap. 14.

Ohlin, Bertil, *Interregional and International Trade*, Cambridge: Harvard University Press, 1957, Chap. 18.

Viner, Jacob, *Studies in the Theory of International Trade*, New York: Harper and Brothers, 1937.

Wasserman, Max, and Charles Hultman, *Modern International Economics*, New York: Simmons-Boardman, 1962, Chap. 7.

Yeager, Leland, *International Monetary Relations*, New York: Harper and Row, 1966, Chap. 6.

Periodicals

A. E. A., *Index of Economic Journals*, classification no. 11.3321.

Altman, O., "Russian Gold and the Ruble," *International Monetary Fund Staff Papers*, April, 1960.

Ford, A. G., "The Truth about Gold," *Lloyd's Bank Review*, July, 1965.

Friedman, M., "Real and Pseudo Gold Standards," *Journal of Law and Economics*, October, 1961.

Heilperin, M. A., "The Triumph of Gold," *South African Journal of Economics*, September, 1961.

Kenen, P. B., "International Liquidity and the Balance of Payments of a Reserve-Currency Country," *Quarterly Journal of Economics*, November, 1960.

Wonnacott, P. A., "A Suggestion for the Revaluation of Gold," *Journal of Finance*, March, 1963.

9.

Flexible Exchange Rates

Under the gold standard, the exchange rate is fixed. Equilibrium between supply and demand is maintained by income or price changes pressuring the schedules into shifting, so that their intersection is consistent with the fixed rate. Rather than force the supply and demand schedules for foreign exchange to find their intersection at some predetermined and fixed price, the price of foreign exchange may be allowed to fluctuate and be determined by the free forces of supply and demand. If the price is allowed to fluctuate to maintain an equilibrium of supply and demand, then balance-of-payments problems cannot exist. This equilibrating mechanism is variously called *freely fluctuating exchange rates* and *flexible exchange rates*.

Autonomous Supply and Demand

In order fully to explain the workings of a flexible-exchange-rate system, it will be necessary further to define the supply and demand for foreign currency. Rather than limit the discussion to the total demand for foreign currency, consideration will be given to the demand for currency for goods and the demand for currency for purposes of foreign investment. Likewise, the supply of currency is divided into the supply for imports and the supply for investing abroad. We shall be concerned with the supply and demand schedules for Z's pesos expressed in W's dollar prices.

In a fluctuating-exchange-rate system, the exchange rate is determined by the free forces of supply and demand for a currency. However, we have already seen that the demand for foreign goods is determined by the relative prices of the good in the two countries and by changes in income. Given the relative prices and income in the two countries, the demand for a currency for purposes of buying that country's exports is determined by the exchange rate. The lower the price of the peso, the more of Z's goods and, concomitantly, the more of Z's currency, will be demanded. The lower the dollar price of the peso, the cheaper the price of Z's exports in country W, given Z's and W's domestic prices. Thus the demand for pesos with which to buy Z's exports D_X will slope downward, showing that a larger quantity will be demanded at a lower dollar price, as drawn in Figure 9-1.

Similarly, the number of pesos supplied depends on the dollar price. At high dollar prices, residents of Z can import goods more cheaply from W. For example, at \$2 per peso, a good selling for \$4 in W will cost a resident of Z 2 pesos. However, at \$4 per peso, the resident of Z need give only ₱1 to import the goods. W's goods are cheaper to Z at a higher dollar price; i.e., a larger number of dollars are given per peso. Thus more pesos will be supplied for the purpose of importing W's goods (S_M) at a higher dollar price per peso, as shown in Figure 9-1.

To these supply and demand schedules we must add the supply and demand for B's currency for investment purposes. What we have in mind here is capital which moves for long-term investment, as opposed to speculative capital, which may flow for political reasons, expectations about changes in bond prices, or expected changes in exchange rates.

Investment, regardless of whether it is to be made in the home or in the foreign country, is assumed to be a function of the

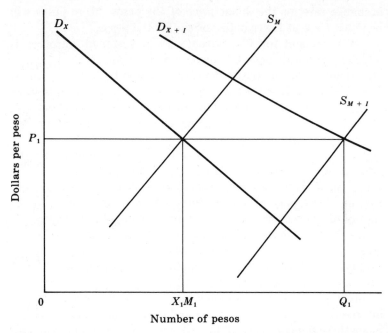

Figure 9-1

rate of return. In deciding on the amount to invest at home and abroad, the investor is interested in comparing the expected rate of return which his domestic monetary outlay will earn at home with what it will earn abroad. Given the expected rate of return to investment at home and abroad, the investor is able to determine the amount he wishes to invest in a foreign country; this amount earmarked for foreign investment is converted into the foreign currency at the going rate of exchange. Consequently, the number of units of foreign currency received depends on the exchange rate.

The amount investors of country W wish to invest in Z depends on the interest rates in the two countries. The greater the interest rate in Z relative to that in W, the larger the amounts of capital which will flow from W to Z. Given the interest rates in the two countries, suppose W's investors decide to invest I dollars.

In order to invest in Z, the I dollars must be converted into pesos. The number of pesos given for I dollars will depend on the exchange rate, or the dollar price of the pesos. More pesos will be given for I at lower dollar prices for the pesos.

W's demand for Z's currency for investment purposes is added horizontally onto W's demand for Z's currency for exports D_X, yielding the composite demand schedule D_{X+I} in Figure 9-1. The horizontal distance between the D_X and the D_{X+I} schedules increases down the x axis. This distance is W's investment in terms of Z's currency, the size of which is dependent on the dollar price of the peso.

The amount Z desires to invest in W also depends on the interest rates in the two countries. Given these interest rates, the supply of Z's currency for investment in W can be determined. Adding the supply of Z's currency for investment in Z to the supply of Z's currency for the purpose of imports in Figure 9-1 yields the total supply schedule S_{M+I}. The total supply schedule must be parallel to Z's supply of currency for imports, since the supply of Z's currency for investment is a function of the interest rate, not the exchange rate.[1]

In Figure 9-1, the exchange rate of P_1 is determined by the intersection of the total demand and supply schedules for pesos. Since these schedules are all for autonomous supply and demand, their equality determines the exchange rate and guarantees equilibrium in the balance of payments. Also in Figure 9-1 exports equal imports, with the demand and supply of currency for investment equal. An equilibrium at which exports and imports are equal is one of a number of possible equilibrium positions. Changes in supply or demand bring about a new exchange rate, at which a balance in the foreign account is maintained.

Increased Demand for Exports

Suppose, for example, that the demand for exports shifts to $D_X{}^2$. The total demand schedule must shift by the same amount to D_{X+I}^2, since the demand for investment is added to the demand for exports. The increased demand in Figure 9-2 raises the price

---

[1] If an alternative assumption were made that investors wish to purchase foreign assets, then they must obtain foreign currency in amount equal to the price of the asset. The demand for the currency will not now be affected by the exchange rate, and the two demand schedules will be parallel. However, at higher exchange rates, the investor will have to offer more of his currency to purchase the determined amount of foreign currency. This assumption will make the supply schedules nonparallel.

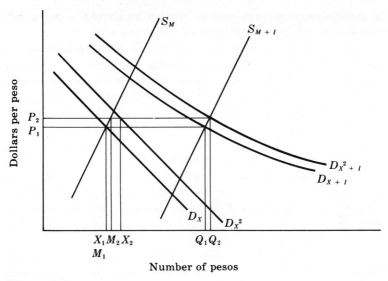

Figure 9-2

to P_2, at which price total supply and demand are again equal at Q_2. Imports increase by M_1M_2 and exports by X_1X_2. Since M_1 equals X_1, it can be seen that the increase in exports exceeds the increase in imports by M_2X_2. The amount by which exports exceed imports represents the net increase in expenditure in country Z; this increase times the multiplier is the income-expansionary pressure being exerted on Z by forces external to the domestic economy. Part of the adjustment comes through income changes.

It can also be seen in Figure 9-2 that the increase in imports M_1M_2 is exactly equal to the increase in the number of pesos supplied Q_1Q_2. The rise in the exchange rate induces an increase in total currency supplied only through inducing an increase in the supply of currency for imports. The increase of M_1M_2 provides some of the pesos required by the increased demand. The number of additional pesos which will be supplied depends on the coefficient of elasticity of the S_M schedule. A large coefficient of elasticity indicates that a small increase in price serves to induce a large increase in the quantity of pesos supplied; thus a large portion of the increased demand for pesos will be provided by the increased supply. If the schedule tends to be inelastic, then a large change in price will be needed to bring about a small increase in the quantity supplied.

On the other hand, the increase in price reduces the quantity of exports demanded and, concurrently, the quantity of pesos[2]. The higher the coefficient of elasticity of the schedule, the greater the reduction in the quantity of exports demanded as a result of a given increase in price. Accordingly, the coefficients of elasticity play a part in determining the amount by which the value of exports may exceed imports.

The extent to which autonomous increase in the demand for exports brings about a net expenditure increase in Z's economy depends on the price mechanism. The increase in price encourages imports to expand and discourages exports, thereby helping to determine the net increase in expenditure and expansionary pressure to which Z's economy is subjected. But this is not the full story. Currency equal to the amount by which exports exceed imports must be provided. The exchange rate, as we have seen, does not influence the supply of pesos for investment in W; this amount is determined solely by the relative rates of interest in the two countries. Hence the number of pesos equal to the difference in the values of exports and imports can be provided only by reducing the quantity of this currency demanded for investment in Z. As the price rises, fewer pesos at the higher price are needed to convert the constant amount of dollar investment. Consequently, at the higher dollar price, less pesos are required by investors and, therefore, they are made available to exporters.

The amount by which exports can exceed imports depends on the number of pesos released from investment demand as a result of an increase in the dollar price. Accordingly, the slope

[2] An increase in demand refers to a shift of the demand schedule. A decrease in *quantity demanded* refers to a movement along the schedule as a result of price change. Thus an increase in demand forces price up, but the increase in price brings about a decrease in *quantity demanded*. *ab* is the increase in demand; *bc* is the decrease in quantity demanded.

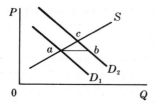

of the total demand schedule is the crucial factor here. If the schedule is steep, a large increase in price will release few pesos from investors to exporters and, simultaneously, the large increase in price will encourage imports to expand and reduce the increase in exports. Therefore, the value of imports will approximate the value of exports, with little net expenditure change arising in the foreign account. On the other hand, if the total demand schedule is flat, a small rise in price will release a large amount of this currency from investment to those wishing to buy exports. The small increase in price will induce little change in imports, so that exports will be able to exceed imports by a large amount.

At the point where the D_{X+I} schedule becomes nearly parallel to the x axis, exports increase fully, imports remain nearly unchanged, and the exchange rate also remains virtually unchanged. The net expenditure change—exports minus imports—is at a maximum, and the full burden of adjustment is placed on the national income.

Increased Supply for Imports

Now suppose an autonomous increase in imports such that the S_M schedule shifts to $S_M{}^2$ and, concomitantly, the S_{M+I} shifts to S^2_{M+I}, as shown in Figure 9-3. The dollar price of the peso falls to P_2, and the quantity of pesos supplied and demanded is Q_2. These changes have retained balance in the foreign account. Imports increase to M_2 while exports increase to X_2. Imports exceed exports by X_2M_2, an amount which, multiplied by the appropriate multiplier, gives the change in the level of Z's national income. The extent to which Z's national income is under pressure to change depends on the degree of success the fall in the exchange rate has in inducing exports to expand to offset the increased imports. Z's expenditure is diverted from domestic production to imports; if these released domestic goods can be exported, production and national income are not adversely affected. But if only some part of these domestic goods is exported, production and national income must fall.

The fall in the exchange rate means that dollars cost more in terms of pesos; as a result, there is a decrease in quantity of pesos supplied (a movement along the schedule) for imports. The fall in the exchange rate serves to divert demand back from imports to home-produced goods. Concurrently, the reduced exchange rate serves to induce an expansion of exports. The

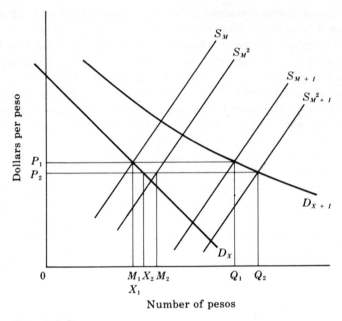

Figure 9-3

magnitude of the difference in imports and exports is dependent
upon the coefficients of elasticity of the demand for currency for
exports and the supply of currency for imports, together with
the slope of the total demand schedule for currency. If the
coefficient of elasticity of demand for exports is large, then a
small reduction in the exchange rate will bring about a large
increase in the total value of exports. Simultaneously, the
increase in imports will be restricted by the reduced exchange
rate; the greater the coefficient of elasticity of supply, the
smaller the increase in imports. The larger the coefficients of
elasticity of the supply and demand schedules, the more nearly
the value of exports will approximate the value of imports.
Correspondingly, the difference in the increase in imports and
exports will be greater, the more inelastic these two schedules.

The increased supply of currency for imports can exceed the
increased demand for exports only as long as the excess currency
is demanded. This excess supply of currency may be absorbed by
the increased demand for currency for investment. As the
exchange rate falls, more pesos must be given for the constant

amount of dollar investment. The exchange rate falls until the excess supply of currency is demanded.

The responsiveness of the demand for pesos for investment to a fall in the exchange rate is central in determining the amount by which imports may exceed exports. A relatively flat total demand schedule indicates that investors will readily increase the quantity of pesos demanded upon a small fall in the exchange rate. A small decrease in the exchange rate will do little to expand exports or limit the increase in imports; consequently, imports will greatly exceed exports with the excess supply of currency being demanded by investors. Accordingly, the domestic economy will be under maximum deflationary pressure. A relatively steep total demand schedule indicates that the investor will not greatly increase the number of pesos demanded in response to a fall in the exchange rate. In such situations, the total supply of currency and the total demand can be equated only by allowing the value of imports to increase by an amount equal to the increase in exports.

In Figure 9-3, the slope of the total demand schedule is smaller at lower points. The progression terminates at zero slope where the price moves imperceptibly to bring about large changes in quantity of currency demanded, and the difference in the value of imports is at a maximum.

Increased Demand for Investment

With the interest rates and all other independent variables unchanged, suppose W's investors decide to increase their investment in Z by some specific dollar amount. This increased investment will have two effects on Z's economy. Firstly, the increased investment times the appropriate multiplier brings about an expansion in Z. Secondly, the transfer of capital influences the balance of payments, resulting in another expenditure change which influences Z's level of income. This section is concerned only with the second effect. To forestall the change in the first effect, it is assumed that Z's government through fiscal and monetary policy maintains the total investment at a constant level.

The increased foreign investment in Z shifts the D_{X+I} schedule in Figure 9-4 by the amount of additional investment to D_{X+I}^2. However, the schedule does not shift in a parallel manner, since the increased investment is constant only in terms of dollars. The peso value of additional investment depends on the exchange rate; a high exchange rate converts a given dollar investment into a small number of pesos. At lower exchange rates the peso value is larger; therefore, the distance between D_{X+I} and D_{X+I}^2 must widen down toward the x axis.

The increased demand for Z's currency forces up the exchange rate to P_2, the point of intersection of S_{M+I} and D_{X+I}^2 schedules. As a result of the greater dollar price of Z's exports, the quantity demanded falls to X_2. Simultaneously, the larger number of dollars given per peso induces imports to expand to M_2. The net result is a current-account deficit of X_2M_2. The substitution of imports for home-produced goods, together with reduced exports, subjects Z's economy to deflationary pressures equal to X_2M_2 times the multiplier.

The decrease in exports of X_1X_2 and increase in imports of M_1M_2 constitute the current-account deficit of X_2M_2. Therefore, the responsiveness of imports and exports to a variation in the exchange rate is of central importance in ascertaining the magni-

Figure 9-4

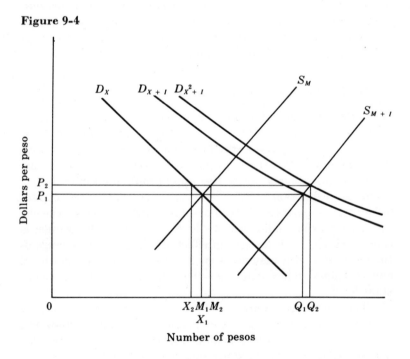

tude of the resulting current-account deficit. A small increase in the exchange rate will reduce considerably the number of pesos demanded for exports, when the coefficient of elasticity is large. Simultaneously, the rise in the exchange rate induces a large increase in the supply for imports, when the coefficient of elasticity of supply is large. Clearly, the larger these two coefficients of elasticity, the larger is the amount of currency which will be made available to investors from a given increase in the exchange rate.

If the coefficients are so low that large changes in the exchange rate are required, then such changes will alter the peso value of the capital being transferred. Therefore, the responsiveness of capital to variations in the exchange rate, together with the coefficients of elasticity, determines the size of the deficit. If the peso value of capital is very responsive, then a rise in the exchange rate will limit the peso value of the capital transferred, thereby resulting in a small current-account deficit. Or in other words, for a given degree of responsiveness of capital to changes in the exchange rate, low coefficients for imports and exports will require large changes in the exchange rate. But these large changes will reduce the peso value of capital and, concurrently, the peso value of the current-account deficit. High coefficients of elasticity will require small changes in the exchange rate and in the peso value of capital transferred. Therefore, the current-account deficit will be large. Clearly then, the more inelastic the import and export schedules, the smaller the peso value of the current-account deficit required to transfer a given dollar investment.

Starting from a point, such as P_1 in Figure 9-4, an increase in investment (an outward movement of the investment schedule) will force up the exchange rate. A secondary reduction in investment (a movement along the investment schedule) is induced by the rise in the exchange rate. The net increase in investment, or the enlargement of the current-account deficit, depends on the responsiveness of investment to changes in the exchange rate. If the initial equilibrium position in Figure 9-4 is down the total demand schedule where it is relatively flat, then a given increase in the exchange rate greatly reduces the peso value of investment. Thus the net peso value of additional investment is smaller, requiring a smaller current-account deficit to transfer the capital. If the initial equilibrium is on the upper section of the total demand schedule where it is steep, a large increase in the exchange rate reduces the demand for pesos by little. Therefore, the increased currency must be supplied to investors by directing currency from exports and increasing supply through enlarged imports. The difference between imports and exports will be greatest in this region.

The slope of the total demand schedule at the point of initial equilibrium, together with the coefficients of elasticity, determines the peso value by which imports must exceed exports, in order to transfer a given increased dollar investment. While determining the amount by which imports must exceed exports, these factors establish simultaneously the size of the deflationary pressure on Z's economy. The larger the difference in imports and exports with a given multiplier, the greater the deflationary pressure exerted on Z.

Increased Supply for Investment

The next question to arise is that of what happens if Z's investors decide to invest more in W. An increase in investment means that the S_{M+I} schedule moves to S_{M+I}^2 in Figure 9-5.

Figure 9-5

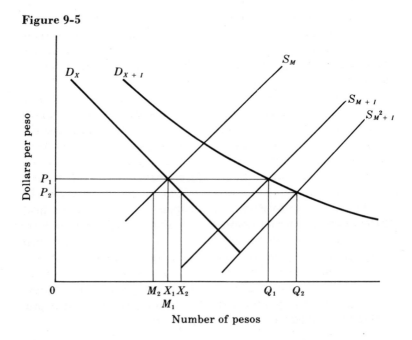

Number of pesos

Since the amount of the investment is determined in terms of pesos, the level of the exchange rate does not affect the value of the investment in pesos. The S_{M+I} schedule shifts in a parallel manner. The exchange rate P_2 is determined by the intersection of the S^2_{M+I} and the D_{X+I} schedules.

The fall in the exchange rates induces exports to expand and imports to contract. Exports exceed imports by M_2X_2, which must be equal to the net increase in capital transferred from Z to W. However, this current-account surplus is not necessarily equal to the increased investment represented by the horizontal distance between S_{M+I} and S^2_{M+I}. The increased investment and the additional net investment are made unequal by the fall in the exchange rate, which serves to induce an expansion of Z's peso investment in W.

The important factors in explaining the effect of increased outflow of investment on Z's economy are the coefficients of elasticity of the S_M and the D_X schedules, together with the slope of the D_{X+I} schedule. With large coefficients of elasticity of the D_X and S_M schedules, small falls in the exchange rate are required to induce the current-account surplus needed to transfer the increased investment. Of equal importance is the slope of the D_{X+I} schedule; the flatter the schedule, the larger the amount by which W's investment increases as a result of a small fall in the exchange rate. In other words, the flatter the D_{X+I} schedule, the larger the proportion of the increased supply of pesos for investment which will be absorbed by W's investors, thereby reducing Z's investment in W. Near the x axis, the D_{X+I} schedule becomes nearly horizontal to the x axis. If the initial equilibrium is in this area, an increase in Z's investment will be almost entirely absorbed by W's increased investment in Z, with the consequence that the value of imports and exports will have changed by little.

For a given increase in Z's investment, the additional net investment equal to X_2M_2 depends on the elasticity of S_M and D_X and the slope of D_{X+I}. It is this additional net investment times the multiplier which represents the expansionary pressure on Z's national economy. If Z's investors are to increase their investment in W, while maintaining the same level of investment in the domestic economy, savings must expand to equal the increased foreign investment. The export surplus of M_2X_2 forces the national economy into expanding and, thereby, into providing the greater savings.

Conclusion

A flexible exchange-rate system has been described in which the free market determines the exchange rate without official intervention. In the post-World War II period, a number of countries have experimented with flexible exchange rates— Argentina, Brazil, Canada, Chile, Colombia, Indonesia, and Uruguay, but none of these systems were completely free of official intervention. The Canadian exchange rate, free to fluctuate during the period 1951 to 1961, makes an interesting example.

As can be seen in Table 9-1, the Canadian exchange rate fluctuated within a range of 95.97 Canadian cents per United

Table 9-1 *Exchange rates and balance of payments of Canada, 1948–1964*

	1948	1949	1950	1951	1952	1953	1954
Exchange rates			*Canadian Dollars per Currency Unit:*				
U.S. dollar: Spot rate	1.0025	1.1025	1.0600	1.0169	.9706	.9744	.9663
Balance of payments			*Millions of Canadian Dollars:*				
Goods and services	440	174	−325	−515	189	−418	−416
Exports-imports fob	432	293	10	−147	489	−58	13
Nonmonetary gold	119	139	163	150	150	144	155
Travel receipts	279	285	275	274	275	302	305
Travel payments	−134	−193	−226	−280	−341	−365	−389
Investment income	−255	−307	−384	−335	−268	−239	−276
Other services	−1	−43	−163	−177	−116	−202	−224
Transfers:							
Private	34	9	−4	7	−9	.....	−5
Central government	−23	−6	−5	−9	−16	−25	−11
Capital, n.i.e.	41	−49	1,056	573	−127	405	556
Direct investment in Canada	71	94	222	309	346	426	392
Outstanding Canadian stocks	......	......	......	......	72	21	129
Canadian bonds:							
new issues	150	105	210	411	316	335	331
retirements	−114	−147	−284	−184	−89	−146	−203
outstandings	3	8	329	38	−166	−52	−66
Other long-term	−69	−109	579	−1	−606	−179	−27
Short-term							
Monetary authorities	−492	−128	−722	−56	−37	38	−124
IMF accounts	......	......	......	......	.....	.....	.....
Special short-term borrowing	......	......	......	......	.....	.....	.....
Foreign assets	−492	−128	−722	−56	−37	38	−124

Source: International Monetary Fund, *International Financial Statistics*

States dollar and 99.91 cents per United States dollar during the period 1952–1960. Indeed the range of the fluctuation has been rather small. However, the rate was not allowed to fluctuate freely. As can be seen at the bottom of Table 9-1, the Canadian monetary authority was buying foreign assets during 1951, 1952, 1954, 1956, 1958, and 1961. Buying foreign assets increased the supply of Canadian dollars; the consequence was either a devaluation of the Canadian exchange rate, more Canadian cents exchange for the United States dollar, or an unchanged exchange rate, with increased supply forestalling an appreciation of the currency. The amount of foreign assets purchased by the monetary authority represents the surplus in Canadian balance of payments for those years, and the surplus was the result of official intervention.

1955	1956	1957	1958	1959	1960	1961	1962	1963	1964
End of Period									
.9991	.9597	.9847	.9641	.9528	.9962	1.0431	1.0778	1.0809	1.0741
Minus Sign Indicates Debit									
−655	−1,320	−1,382	−1,030	−1,376	−1,103	−855	−787	−463	−343
−211	−728	−594	−179	−422	−148	173	177	503	700
155	150	147	160	148	162	162	155	154	145
328	337	363	349	391	420	482	562	609	662
−449	−498	−525	−542	−598	−627	−642	−605	−589	−712
−323	−381	−435	−444	−489	−480	−561	−592	−646	−665
−155	−200	−338	−374	−406	−430	−469	−484	−494	−473
−19	−16	−33	−48	−56	−79	−71	−51	−33	−21
−24	−30	−40	−53	−72	−61	−56	−36	−61	−69
654	1,414	1,350	1,240	1,493	1,204	1,272	1,029	703	796
417	583	514	420	550	650	520	495	240	255
138	188	137	88	110	51	39	−116	−169	−97
166	667	798	677	707	421	493	708	952	1,102
−184	−141	−133	−158	−258	−256	−245	−290	−259	−306
−165	11	−45	.....	91	3	61	64	39	77
282{	113	31	84	−49	42	42	−193	−190	−178
	−7	48	129	342	293	362	361	90	−57
44	−48	105	−109	11	39	−290	−155	−146	−363
.....	−15	.....	.....	−59	.....	−61	378	−86	−277
.....	.....	.....	.....	.....	.....	....	4	......	......
44	−33	105	−109	70	39	−229	−537	−60	−86

During 1953, 1955, 1957, and 1960, Canada sold some of its foreign assets. The purpose of selling these securities was to increase the demand for Canadian dollars. This increased demand served either to pressure an appreciation of the currency or fewer Canadian cents exchange for United States dollars, or to negate downward market pressures.

From 1951 to 1961 Canada incurred deficits in the current account for every year except 1952. These deficits exceeded those incurred in the years 1962–1964, for which the exchange rate was fixed. During 1956 to 1961 large amounts of capital flowed into Canada, equal to twice the level which flowed during 1951 through 1955. This large flow tended to pressure the exchange rate upward; an appreciation of the exchange rate without a fall in the price of exports served to make Canadian exports more expensive to foreigners and imports cheaper to Canadians. The decreased demand for Canadian goods contributed to the unemployment rate, which reached a high of approximately 10 percent. Unsuccessful attempts were made to reduce the interest rate to discourage the inflow of foreign capital and restore the competitiveness of Canadian goods.

For a given exchange rate there is a combination of interest rate, price level, and level of national income consistent with domestic equilibrium, i.e., full employment, and equilibrium in the balance of payments. A fluctuating exchange rate maintains equilibrium in the balance of payments, but changes in the exchange rate require that the combination of interest rate, price level, and level of national income accommodate itself to the new exchange rate if domestic equilibrium is to be maintained. If interest rates cannot readily be made to move downward, as appears to have been the case in Canada, then prices and the level of national income will have to do the adjusting to changes in the exchange rate. It appears that the level of national income and employment took the brunt of the adjustment. Had wages and prices fallen as the exchange rate appreciated, Canadian exports might have remained at an unchanged price to foreigners. However, if prices do not fall as the currency appreciates, the high price to foreigners will result in a decrease in demand for exports, bringing about unemployment.

For flexible exchange rates to maintain equilibrium in the balance of payments without creating domestic disequilibrium in employment, it is necessary that internal prices, wages, and interest rates are sufficiently flexible to adjust to the changes in demand originating in the foreign account. Wages and prices are considered to be rather rigid as to downward movements; thus appreciations in the exchange rate resulting from increased capital inflows can be expected to create unemployment. Only if the interest rate can be lowered to forestall the increased capital inflow from appreciating the exchange rate can full employment be maintained. If the interest rate cannot readily be reduced, then the nation must choose between equilibrium in the balance of payments maintained by flexible exchange rates and full employment. We can expect most nations to choose full employment, with the resulting disequilibrium in the balance of payments.

Selected Readings

Books
Allen G. & Allen G., *Foreign Trade and Finance*, New York: The Macmillan Co., 1959, essay no. 15.
American Enterprise Institute, *International Payments Problems*, Washington: American Enterprise Institute, part 2.
Friedman, M. Hon, and Robert Roosa, *The Balance of Payments: Free versus Fixed Exchange Rates*, Washington, D.C.: American Enterprise Institute, 1967.
Harrod, Roy, *Reforming the World's Money*, New York: St. Martin's Press, 1965, Chap. 2.
Sohmen, Egon, *Flexible Exchange Rates*, Chicago: University of Chicago, 1961.
Williams, John Burr, *International Trade under Flexible Exchange Rates*, Amsterdam: North-Holland, 1954.
Yeager, Leland, *International Monetary Relations*, New York: Harper & Row, 1966.

Periodicals
A. E. A., *Index of Economic Journals*, classification no. 11.3311.
Caves, R. E., "Flexible Exchange Rates," *American Economic Review*, May, 1963.
Eastham, H. C., "French and Canadian Exchange Rate Policy," *Journal of Economic History*, December, 1955.
Ford, A. G., "Flexible Exchange Rates and Argentina," *Oxford Economic Papers*, October, 1958.
Ingram, J. C., "The Canadian Exchange Rate," *Southern Economic Journal*, January, 1960.
Leighton, R. I., "Flexible Exchange Rates, Investment and National Income," *South African Journal of Economics*, December, 1966.

Meade, J. E., "The Case for Flexible Exchange Rates," *The Three Banks Review*, September, 1955.

Morgan, E. V., "The Theory of Flexible Exchange Rates," *American Economic Review*, June, 1955.

Mundell, R. A., "Flexible Exchange Rates and Employment Policy," *Canadian Journal of Economics*, November, 1961.

Yeager, L. B., "Exchange Rates within a Common Market," *Social Research*, January, 1959.

10.

The Dollar-Exchange Standard

Two mechanisms for maintaining balance in the foreign account have been discussed, namely, the gold standard and flexible exchange rates. With flexible exchange rates, supply and demand for currency yield an exchange rate which maintains balance in the foreign account; the exchange rates adjust to ensure balance. The gold standard is a fixed-exchange-rate system in which gold flows to shift the supply and demand schedules, so that balance in the foreign account is consistent with the fixed rate.

The writing of the Articles of Agreement of the International Monetary Fund was concluded at Bretton Woods in 1944. The nations participating in the International Monetary Fund Agreement have erected what is sometimes called the "dollar-exchange standard." The currencies of most noncommunist countries are bound together by the dollar-exchange standard. Some Western nations, such as Switzerland, have not agreed to the standard but behave as though they had. A few other nations are linked to sterling, and with the exception of Yugoslavia, Communist nations have remained aloof from the dollar-exchange standard. Below is a somewhat general discussion of the mechanism of the dollar-exchange standard.

Dollar-exchange Standard

Under the gold standard, the price of a currency is fixed in terms of gold by each country being willing to buy or sell gold at some fixed price. A currency is fixed under the dollar-exchange standard by a nation's willingness to buy or sell its currency for dollars at some specified dollar price. For example, nation Z fixes the price of the peso at $1 and will buy or sell any number of pesos required to maintain that rate. Now the United States does not fix its currency in terms of any other currency. It fixes its currency in terms of gold—$35 an ounce—and the dollar is convertible into gold by any central bank.

The price of a currency in terms of gold may fluctuate under the gold standard by the amount of the cost of transporting and insuring the gold. The free market may determine the price of the currency within the range of the gold export point and the gold import point. Under the dollar-exchange standard, a nation is not required to maintain the currency at the fixed rate, called par. Instead, a nation must intervene to prevent the value of its currency from moving outside the so-called support points. The nation is free to set the upper support point within $+1$ percent of par value and the lower support point within -1 percent of par value. Once these support points are set, the nation must buy or sell its currency for dollars as required to keep the exchange rate within the support points. So far the system is different from the gold standard only in that dollars are being used instead of gold.

Suppose nation Z fixes its currency at the rate of $1 per peso, and sets the support points at the full 1 percent interval above and below par value. The upper support point would be $1.01, a price per peso which cannot be exceeded; the lower support point is $0.99, the lowest possible price for which the peso can be sold. The free interplay of supply and demand may determine the exchange rate within the points $1.01–$0.99. The central bank of Z must intervene in the market to prevent the exchange rate from moving outside these support points.

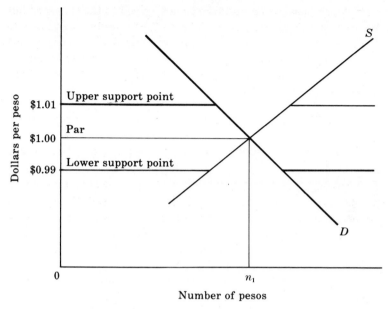

Figure 10-1

The supply and demand for pesos are presented in Figure 10-1. The par value of $1, together with the upper support point of $1.01 and lower support point of $0.99, is indicated. The supply and demand schedules determine an exchange rate of $1 with n_1 pesos traded. Since the market has determined the exchange rate within the support points, there is no need for official intervention in the market to support the currency.

Suppose demand increases from D to D_2 in Figure 10-2 (ignore S_2 for the time being). The free market, if allowed, would determine a rate of $1.02. However, $1.02 per peso is beyond the support point, and the central bank of Z must intervene to prevent the rate from rising over $1.01. At $1.01 the demand for pesos is n_3 and the supply is n_2; demand exceeds supply, producing an upward pressure on price. To maintain the price at $1.01, supply equal to the excess demand at this price must be forthcoming. Z's central bank must sell n_2n_3 pesos at a price of $1.01 per peso; it sells pesos and gains dollars.

The consequences of a decreased supply of pesos is also shown in Figure 10-2 (disregarding D_2 now). Supply decreases from S to S_2, resulting in pressure for a market price of $1.025.

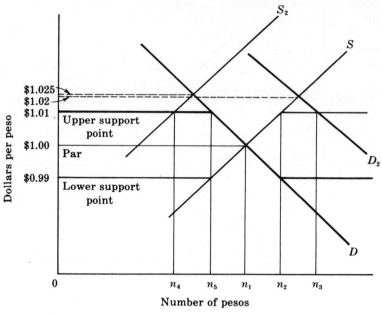

Figure 10-2

At the upper support point of $1.01, demand for pesos is n_5 and supply is n_4. To prevent the exchange rate from exceeding $1.01, Z's central bank must sell pesos for $1.01 in a quantity equal to the excess demand of $n_4 n_5$, so that supply and demand are equal at $1.01. Z has increased its holdings of dollars.

As long as there is pressure for the exchange rate to rise above the support point due to decreased supply or increased demand, Z's central bank must sell pesos for dollars to stabilize the exchange rate at the upper support point. Z's central bank will not want to accumulate dollars indefinitely; it may exchange dollars for gold at the rate of $35 per ounce of gold. The United States does not fix its currency in terms of any currency, only in terms of gold. The United States will buy or sell any quantity of gold at $35 an ounce.

Suppose, now, the supply of pesos increases from S to S_2 in Figure 10-3 (ignore demand schedule D_2). As a result of the increased supply, the exchange rate is under pressure to fall to $0.97, a price below the lower support point. However, Z's central bank must act to prevent the exchange rate from falling below the lower support point of $0.99. It does this by purchasing the excess supply of pesos, namely n_2n_3, for dollars.

Similarly, allow the demand schedule in Figure 10-3 to fall from D to D_2 (ignore S_2). The equilibrium exchange rate is now $0.98 per peso, which is below the lower support point. At the lower support point, demand is n_4 and supply is n_5; supply exceeds demand by n_4n_5. This excess supply of pesos must be purchased with dollars to make total demand and supply equal at $0.99 per peso.

Where does Z's central bank get the dollars with which to buy its own currency to prevent its price from falling below the lower support point? First, it might use any dollars which it may have acquired during a previous period. Secondly, it may sell gold for dollars with which to buy pesos in order to prevent the exchange rate from falling below the lower support point.

When demand exceeds supply at the upper support point, pesos have to be supplied by Z's central bank. The excess demand for pesos represents the surplus in the balance of payments. Similarly, when supply exceeds demand at the lower support point, the central bank has to demand pesos to equal the excess supply. This excess supply represents the deficit in the balance

Figure 10-3

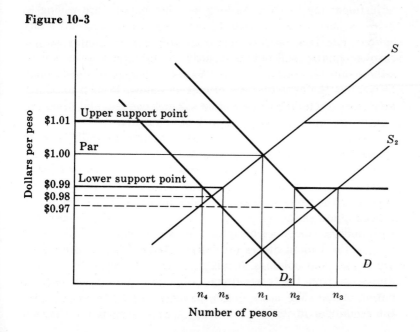

of payments. In other words, there is equilibrium in the balance of payments only where the supply and demand for currency are equal within the support points. Furthermore, deficits and surpluses exist only because the exchange rate is prohibited from adjusting to correct the imbalance. The imbalance means that nations gain or lose dollars and gold depending on whether a surplus or deficit exists in the balance of payments.

The Adjustment Mechanism

Under the gold standard, a surplus nation gains gold and a deficit nation loses gold. The inflow of gold into the surplus country forces prices up and the outflow of gold from the deficit country forces prices down. The price changes result in increased demand for goods from the deficit country and reduced demand for goods from the surplus country. Demand for the deficit country's goods continues to increase, and demand for the surplus country's goods continues to fall as a result of gold movements and price changes until the surplus and deficit are wiped out. Nations abiding by the rules of the gold standard have an automatic device for maintaining balance in the foreign account.

The dollar-exchange standard does not contain an automatic adjustment mechanism. As long as other nations are willing to hold its currency, a nation with a deficit need not take any action. The flow of currency from the deficit country to the surplus country will not necessarily change prices or income in either country. Nations are free to use monetary or fiscal policy to counter the consequences of currency flow. If such measures are taken, then income and price will not change, and disequilibrium will continue in the balance of payments.

If the flow of currency does not automatically restore equilibrium in the balance of payments, then what happens when the surplus country is no longer willing to hold the currency of the deficit country? Once nations are no longer willing to hold Z's currency, the exchange rate is under pressure to fall below the lower support point. Thus Z must intervene and buy its currency with dollars. Once its supply of dollars is exhausted, it may sell gold to the United States for dollars. After Z has exhausted its dollar and gold holdings, it might obtain loans from the United States and from the International Monetary Fund. Each member nation of the IMF has a quota, payable 25 percent in gold and the remainder in its own currency; against this quota a nation may borrow any other member's currency, subject to the limitation that the Fund's holding of the borrowing nation's currency will neither increase by more than 25 percent per annum nor exceed 200 percent of its quota. Nations are expected, as a general rule, to repay within three to five years.

Access to the IMF's facilities is not automatic, with one exception. Nations may borrow virtually automatically an amount equal to the "gold tranche," the 25 percent of the quota paid in gold. A nation may borrow another 25 percent, not in the same year, under fairly liberal IMF procedures; this is called the "first credit tranche." Since, with the exception of the gold tranche, loans are not automatic, a nation needs some advanced knowledge as to the IMF funds available. Standby arrangements may be negotiated by a deficit country with the IMF for specified amounts for a definite period. Thus a nation knows what is available and need not negotiate at the actual time of borrowing.

Z may also change the par value of its currency. Over time, a country may devalue the currency by 10 percent of the original par value without permission of the Fund. Devaluations which will reduce the currency below 90 percent of the original par value must have the approval of the Fund before being undertaken. The Fund requires that devaluation be undertaken only to correct "fundamental disequilibrium," although the conditions required are not spelled out.

Credit facilities provide short-run financing for balance-of-payments deficits. However, after all credit facilities are exhausted, the remedy becomes devaluation, i.e., reducing the price of the currency in terms of the dollar. The credit facilities provide a nation the time needed to introduce monetary and fiscal policies to correct the deficit, as will be discussed in the next chapter. If the internal measures will not restore equilibrium to the balance of payments, then a more suitable par value for the currency must be found.

Devaluation

As discussed in Chapter 7, for stable equilibrium in the balance of payments, autonomous receipts must equal autonomous payments. Devaluation improves a nation's balance of payments by increasing the autonomous demand for its currency and decreasing its autonomous supply, thereby reducing the downward pressure on the exchange rate and the excess supply of currency. Autonomous supply and demand include all items exchanged for commercial purposes. Both commodity and financial transactions constitute the autonomous categories. The question, then, is one of how commodity trade and capital flow respond to devaluation. First the response of commodity trade to devaluation will be considered.

Suppose, for example, the authorities in Z reduce the par value of the peso from \$1 to \$0.90, with the upper support point being \$0.909 and the lower support point being \$0.891. All of Z's exports are now cheaper in the United States. An item which sells for ₱5 costs United States residents \$5 before devaluation and \$4.50 after devaluation. Thus there will be increased demand for Z's exports. Furthermore, United States exports will now be more expensive in Z; an item selling for \$10 in the United States costs Z's residents ₱10 before devaluation and ₱11.11 after devaluation. There will be, consequently, a reduced supply of Z's currency for the purchase of United States goods.

Whether the balance of trade, i.e., value of exports minus the value of imports, will be improved depends on whether Z's demand for imports is elastic or inelastic and on whether United States' demand for Z's exports is elastic or inelastic. Devaluation makes imports more costly to Z, but if the demand for imports is inelastic, then a greater number of pesos will be spent on imports, worsening the balance of trade. Likewise Z's devaluation reduces the price of its exports to the United States. If the United States' demand for Z's exports is inelastic, then less will be spent on Z's exports after devaluation, working adversely to restore equilibrium in the balance of payments.

Some rule is needed to relate the required level of elasticities for devaluation to improve the balance of trade. The rule which serves this purpose is called the *Marshall-Lerner Conditions*. The Marshall-Lerner Conditions indicate that devaluation will improve the balance of trade if the sum of elasticities of demand exceeds 1, given permissively high elasticities of supply.[1]

The discussion of the Marshall-Lerner Conditions may be undertaken in terms of the currency of the devaluing country or in terms of the currency of the other country, but not in terms of both currencies. Since the discussion must be limited to one

---

[1] If the elasticities of supply are sufficiently small, devaluation will also improve the balance of payments when the sum of elasticities of demand is less than 1.

currency, the following illustration of the Marshall-Lerner Conditions will be limited to the consequences of different values for the elasticities in terms of pesos. In Table 10-1, the United States' elasticity of demand for Z's exports is assumed to be 2, and Z's elasticity of demand for imports is assumed to be $1\frac{1}{2}$, so that the sum of elasticities of demand is $3\frac{1}{2}$. A 10 percent devaluation is assumed. The price of Z's exports in terms of pesos remains unchanged. However, the dollar price of Z's exports is reduced 10 percent by devaluation. A 10 percent fall in price induces a 20 percent increase in quantity demanded when the elasticity of demand is 2. In row 1, peso price of exports is shown unchanged and quantity is shown to rise by 20 percent, so that receipts in pesos rise by approximately 20 percent. The price of Z's imports in terms of pesos rises by 10 percent as a result of devaluation. Given the elasticity of demand for imports of $1\frac{1}{2}$, quantity demanded falls by 15 percent. A 10 percent rise in price combined with a 15 percent fall in quantity leads to an approximately 5 percent fall in expenditure. The 20 percent increase in receipts combined with a 5 percent fall in expenditure leads to a reduced deficit and an improvement in the balance of trade.

In Table 10-2, each elasticity of demand is assumed to be $\frac{3}{4}$, so that the sum is $1\frac{1}{2}$, and a 10 percent devaluation is assumed. The price of Z's exports in terms of pesos remains unchanged. But the price of Z's exports in terms of dollars falls by 10 percent as a result of the 10 percent devaluation. A 10 percent fall in price must be accompanied by an increase of 7.5 percent in quantity,

Table 10-1

Elasticity of demand for exports = 2,
elasticity of demand for imports = $1\frac{1}{2}$
10% devaluation

$$\text{Elasticity} = \frac{\%dQ}{\%dP}, \text{ elasticity for exports} = \frac{20\%}{10\%},$$

elasticity for imports = $\dfrac{15\%}{10\%}$

	Change in Peso Price	Change in Quantity	Yields
Row 1	......	+20%	+20% receipts
Row 2	+10%	−15%	−5% expenditure
		Net improvement	25%

Table 10-2

Each elasticity of demand = $\frac{3}{4}$, sum = $1\frac{1}{2}$
10% devaluation

$$\text{Elasticity} = \frac{\%dQ}{\%dP} = \frac{7.5\%}{10\%} = \frac{3}{4}$$

	Change in Peso Price	Change in Quantity	Yields
Row 1	......	+7.5%	+7.5% receipts
Row 2	+10%	−7.5%	+2.5% expenditure
		Net increase in receipts	5.0%

to yield an elasticity of demand of $\frac{3}{4}$. In row 1, the price of exports in terms of pesos is shown unchanged, and the quantity of exports is shown to increase by 7.5 percent, so that receipts in terms of pesos rise by approximately 7.5 percent. The price of Z's imports in terms of pesos rises by 10 percent as a result of devaluation, as shown in row 2. The quantity of imports falls by 7.5 percent, to yield a coefficient of elasticity of $\frac{3}{4}$. The 10 percent increase in price and 7.5 percent fall in quantity yield a 2.5 percent increase in expenditure. The increase of 7.5 percent in receipts and 2.5 percent increase in expenditure result in a net increase in receipts of 5 percent to improve the balance of trade. Thus the sum of elasticities of demand exceeding 1 has brought an improvement in the balance of trade, and, thereby, contributes to improving the balance of payments.

In Table 10-3, it is assumed that each elasticity of demand is $\frac{1}{2}$, so that the sum of elasticities of demand equals 1. Again a

Table 10-3

Each elasticity of demand = $\frac{1}{2}$, sum = 1
10% devaluation in Z

$$\text{Elasticity} = \frac{\%dQ}{\%dP} = \frac{5\%}{10\%} = \frac{1}{2}$$

	Change in Peso Price	Change in Quantity	Yields
Row 1	......	+5%	+5% receipts
Row 2	+10%	−5%	+5% expenditure
		Net change	0

10 percent devaluation is assumed. The change in peso receipts from exports is shown in row 1; devaluation does not affect the peso price of exports. But, as a result of devaluation, the price of Z's exports is 10 percent cheaper in dollars. With an elasticity of demand for exports of $\frac{1}{2}$, quantity will increase by 5 percent upon a 10 percent fall in price. Thus peso receipts for exports will increase by approximately 5 percent. Whether the balance of trade is improved by devaluation also depends on what happens to peso expenditures on imports. The devaluation makes the peso price of all imports rise by 10 percent. Given the elasticity of demand for imports of $\frac{1}{2}$, this increase of 10 percent in price brings a fall of 5 percent in quantity demanded. Expenditure on imports rises by approximately 5 percent. Devaluation brought about an equal increase in export receipts and import expenditure. Thus if the sum of elasticities of demand is equal to 1, the trade balance will be unaffected by devaluation.

When the sum of elasticities of demand is greater than 1, devaluation improves the balance of trade; when it is equal to 1, devaluation leaves the size of the deficit unchanged. The consequences of devaluation when the sum of the elasticities of demand is less than 1 must now be considered. Again the peso price of exports is unaffected by devaluation, as shown in row 1 of Table 10-4, but the dollar price of Z's exports is 10 percent cheaper. The fall in price of 10 percent will induce an increase in quantity of 2.5 percent, with an elasticity of demand of $\frac{1}{4}$. With the peso price unchanged and quantity increased by 2.5 percent, receipts in pesos increase by approximately 2.5 percent. Devaluation increases the peso price of imports by 10 percent. Given the elasticity of demand of $\frac{1}{4}$, the 10 percent increase in price induces

Table 10-4

Each elasticity of demand = $\frac{1}{4}$, sum = $\frac{1}{2}$
10% devaluation in Z

$$\text{Elasticity} = \frac{\%dQ}{\%dP} = \frac{2.5\%}{10\%} = \frac{1}{4}$$

	Change in Peso Price	Change in Quantity	Yields
Row 1	......	+2.5%	+2.5% receipts
Row 2	+10%	−2.5%	+7.5% expenditure
		Net increase in expenditure	5.0%

a fall in quantity imports of 2.5 percent. A 10 percent increase in price combined with 2.5 percent fall in quantity yields a 7.5 percent increase in expenditure on imports. Receipts from exports increased by 2.5 percent; expenditure on imports by 7.5 percent. Devaluation, with the sum of elasticities of demand less than 1, results in expenditures increasing by more than receipts, thereby making the trade balance worse. Thus, when the sum of elasticities of demand for imports and exports exceeds 1, as stated in the Marshall-Lerner Conditions, devaluation improves the balance of trade and thereby contributes toward improving the balance of payments.

The Marshall-Lerner Conditions apply only to the demand for commodity exports and imports. The response of capital to devaluation must also be taken into consideration before it can be determined whether devaluation improves the balance of payments. Thus, if sufficient amounts of autonomous capital flowed into the devaluing country, it would be possible to have the sum of elasticities of demand less than 1, and devaluation would improve the balance of payments. If the country has investment opportunities and the devaluation is sufficient to allay fears of further devaluation, then capital will be induced to flow into the country in search of profits. Furthermore, if it is believed that devaluation will solve the "fundamental disequilibrium" in the economy, then the future growth of the economy and investment opportunities will appear more favorable to investors. It is also possible that the capital flow will be reduced as a result of devaluation; then devaluation with the sum of elasticities greater than 1 will increase the deficit. This would occur if capital were discouraged by the devaluation and investors feared further devaluation. Furthermore, devaluation makes foreign investment more costly to Z's residents. A United States asset selling for $1,000 will be more expensive in terms of pesos after devaluation. If devaluation discourages Z's residents from investing in the United States, then the balance of payments is better off. If Z's residents provide the larger number of pesos required, then the supply of pesos has increased, an adverse consequence for the balance of payments.

The Marshall-Lerner Conditions belong to microanalysis. In discussing responses along the supply and demand schedules, it is necessary to assume that income, all other prices, and costs remain unchanged. Movements along the demand schedule of an individual or supply curve of a firm in perfect competition will represent such small movements in relation to the total market. Total income, price of all other goods, and costs can reasonably be expected to remain constant; however, when talking about the supply of exports which may constitute 10 to 20 percent of national income, one cannot expect income, prices, and costs to remain unchanged. Changes in exports influence the level of income, wages, interest, and profits. When income changes, the demand schedule must shift. Changes in cost force the supply schedules to shift. Thus the changes in income and price force the schedules to shift and bring about a new equilibrium price and quantity; the elasticities measure only movements along the schedule, not the consequences of movements in the schedules themselves. The more important that trade is in national income, the greater the income and cost changes are likely to be; consequently, the prediction based on the Marshall-Lerner Conditions will tend to be more inaccurate. Thus an alternative system is needed which takes cognizance of the changes in income. Such an alternative is the *absorption approach* of S. S. Alexander.

The Absorption Approach

If a nation is utilizing less than its total output for consumption, investment, and government expenditure, then the remaining output will equal the amount by which exports exceed imports. Furthermore, only if imports exceed exports can the absorption of goods for consumption, investment, and government projects exceed production. Equation (10-1) states the

$$Y = C + I + X - M \tag{10-1}$$

$$Y - (C + I) = X - M \tag{10-2}$$

$$Y - A = X - M \tag{10-3}$$

definition of income, i.e., real income. In Equation (10-2), $C + I$ is transposed, and in Equation (10-3), A, absorption of goods, is substituted for $C + I$. This equation shows that real income, or output, minus absorption, or utilization of output, must equal exports minus imports. If real income exceeds absorption, then exports must exceed imports. Similarly, if real income is less than absorption, then exports must be less than imports.

Whether devaluation improves the balance of trade depends on whether a smaller amount of output is absorbed as a result of devaluation. If the change in output is greater than the change

$$dY - dA = dX - dM \tag{10-4}$$

in absorption, then the change in exports will exceed the change in imports, thereby improving the balance of trade. This is shown in Equation (10-4). Thus it is necessary to determine the various consequences of devaluation on output and absorption.

Absorption depends on real income and on other factors such as price. In Equation (10-5) the change in absorption is equal to

$$dA = e(dY) - D \tag{10-5}$$

the marginal propensity to absorb e multiplied by the change in income, where the marginal propensity to absorb is the sum of the marginal propensities to consume and to invest. D includes all the changes in absorption as a result of nonincome factors; i.e., D shows the changes in absorption at a given level of real income.

Equation (10-5) is substituted for dA in Equation (10-4) to yield

$$dY - e(dY) + D = dX - dM \tag{10-6}$$

Factor out dY to get

$$(1 - e) \, dY + D = dX - dM \tag{10-7}$$

As noted earlier, devaluation brings about an increase in the quantity of exports or an increase in real exports. If there are sufficient idle resources, real income will rise by the amount of increased exports times the international-trade multiplier. The increased output, or real income, induces changes in expenditure; the amount of increase in expenditure depends on the marginal propensity to absorb e. If the marginal propensity to absorb is greater than 1 (which it may be, since e equals the sum of the marginal propensity to consume and the marginal propensity to invest), then the increase in real income will induce a larger increase in expenditure, resulting in a worsening in the balance of payments. Only if e is less than 1 will increased production exceed increased absorption of goods so that the balance of payments will be improved.

Devaluation will tend to make the price of exports and imports rise in terms of the currency of the devaluing country. If the price of imports rises by more than the price of exports, then it is said that the terms of trade have moved against the devaluing country; the price of the goods it is buying has increased by more than the price of the goods it is selling. An adverse movement in the terms of trade serves to reduce a nation's real income. Thus real income falls and absorption falls by e. If e is greater than 1, the absorption of goods falls by more than real income, contributing to an improvement in the balance of payments.

Clearly, if there is full employment, no idle resources, and e is less than 1, then the income effects will not contribute to improving the balance of trade. If devaluation is to improve the balance of trade, it must do so through the nonincome effects D. One such nonincome effect is the real-cash-balance effect. If the money supply is kept constant and devaluation increases prices, the rising prices reduce the real value of cash balances. If individuals desire to maintain the real value of cash balance during a period of rising price, they will have to save more. Absorption must fall to allow this greater saving; the direct effect, then, is reduced absorption, contributing to an improvement in the balance of trade. The reduced expenditure on goods brings a fall in income; if e is greater than 1, the absorption will fall by more than income, contributing further to an improvement in the balance of trade.

If devaluation influences the distribution of income, then it will affect absorption. If income should be moved away from persons or areas with a high marginal propensity to absorb to those with low marginal propensities to absorb, then the absorption for the given level of real income will be reduced, thereby adding to an improvement in the balance of trade.

A third nonincome effect is that of a money illusion. If, when money income rises, people buy more believing that they are better off, even though prices have risen to such an extent that real income falls, then absorption is increased as a result of the money illusion. The pressure is adverse to improving the balance of trade.

A large number of other effects could be discussed. But the important point of the absorption approach is that the movements in the balance of trade must be looked at in relation to the entire economy. The elasticity approach of the Marshall-Lerner Conditions considers the balance of trade separately from the rest of the economy. The absorption approach considers both the country's total utilization of goods and its production of goods. A nation must be producing more than it is using to have a favorable balance of trade.

Conclusion

The current exchange system is a fixed-exchange-rate system; however, the exchange rate is allowed to fluctuate up to 1 percent each side of par. Most currencies are fixed in terms of dollars, and dollars are fixed in terms of gold. The United States buys and sells gold at specified rates. Other countries supply and demand their own currency for dollars to maintain the fixed rate of their currency to the dollar. Nations whose currency is under pressure may obtain loans from the IMF and may devalue up to 10 percent without consent of the IMF; greater devaluation requires the Fund's permission. The IMF is the watchdog of the system.

Whether devaluation will improve the balance of trade can be determined by using the Marshall-Lerner Conditions. These conditions state that devaluation will improve the balance of trade if the sum of elasticities of demand exceeds 1, assuming permissively large elasticities of supply. If a price elasticity is employed, the important income effects are omitted; consequently, only a partial answer is gained. Alternatively, a total elasticity may be employed; it relates the change in quantity from all direct and indirect forces resulting from a price change. Income effects are included. If the sum of total elasticities of demand exceeds 1, then when all changes are allowed for, receipts grow relative to expenditure, thereby indicating an improvement. When total elasticities are used, the whole mechanism becomes a truism; a sum greater than 1 means receipts increase relative to expenditure, an improvement in the balance of trade.

Alternatively, the absorption approach is deceptively simple. In equation form, it encompasses a large number of the factors determining the adjustment in the balance of trade. Conceptually, it is a neat mechanism; empirically, the absorption approach is less satisfying. Prediction is difficult, for some of the included forces cannot be quantified.

The consequences of capital flows must be introduced completely to predict the changes in the balance of payments resulting from devaluation.

Selected Readings

Books

Clement, M. O., R. L. Pfister, and K. J. Rothwell, *Theoretical Issues in International Economics*, Boston: Houghton Mifflin Co., 1967.

Einzig, Paul, *A Textbook on Foreign Exchange*, New York: St. Martin's Press, 1966.

Horie, Shiego, *The International Monetary Fund*, London: Macmillan and Co., 1964.

Johnson, H. G., "Towards a General Theory of the Balance of Payments," in his *International Trade and Economic Growth*, Cambridge: Harvard University Press, 1958.

Scammell, W. M., *International Monetary Policy*, London: Macmillan and Co., 1964.

Periodicals

A. E. A., *Index of Economic Journals*, classification no. 11.3313.

Alexander, S. S., "Effects of a Devaluation on a Trade Balance," International Monetary Fund, *Staff Papers*, April, 1952.

Alexander, S. S., "Effects of a Devaluation: A Simplified Synthesis of Elasticities and Absorption Approaches," *American Economic Review*, March, 1959.

Balogh, T., and P. P. Streeten, "The Inappropriateness of Simple 'Elasticity' Concepts in the Analysis of International Trade," *Bulletin of The Oxford University Institute of Economics and Statistics*, March, 1951.

Machlup, Fritz, "Elasticity Pessimism in International Trade," *Economia Internazionale*, February, 1950.

Machlup, Fritz, "Relative Prices and Aggregate Spending in the Analysis of Devaluation," *American Economic Review*, June, 1955.

Machlup, Fritz, "The Terms-of-Trade Effects of Devaluation upon Real Income and the Balance of Trade," *Kyklos*, 1956.

Orcutt, Guy, "Measurement of Price Elasticities in International Trade," *Review of Economics and Statistics*, May, 1950.

Sraffa, Piero, "The Laws of Returns under Competitive Conditions," *Economic Journal*, 1926.

Tsiang, S. C., "The Role of Money in Trade-balance Stability," *American Economic Review*, December, 1961.

11.

Monetary
and Fiscal
Policy

With the gold standard, it is income or price adjustments induced by the gold flow which make the internal economy adjust to a level consistent with equilibrium in the balance of payments. Alternatively, flexible exchange rates adjust the price of foreign exchange until autonomous supply and demand are equal. Fluctuations in the exchange rates may not induce equal changes in imports and exports; consequently, income adjustments are required. With the dollar-exchange standard there is no automatic adjustment process. Correction requires policy decision and action by the government concerned. One such policy action is devaluation. However, devaluation is usually a last resort. The nation will probably first try to correct disequilibrium by monetary and fiscal policy.

With the dollar-exchange standard, correction of a sizable

disequilibrium in the balance of payments may inevitably require some price and income adjustments. However, unlike the situation under the gold standard or fluctuating exchange rates, the officials have some leeway in timing and duration. If conditions require, the income adjustment may be postponed temporarily; furthermore, the government may choose a small adjustment over a long period or a large income adjustment over a short period. Alternatively, a nation may choose to allow its economy to grow more slowly than the rest of the world, thereby lowering its income relatively.

Fiscal Policy

Fiscal policy is the use of government account to influence the level of economic activity. The object is not to balance the government's budget but rather to allow surpluses and deficits as required for a stable economy. If the economy is at less than full employment, then the government allows its expenditure to exceed tax receipts in order to expand the economy to full employment. On the other hand, if the economy has gone beyond full employment to inflation, then aggregate demand for goods and services must be reduced by increasing taxes or lowering government expenditure.

One goal of fiscal policy is a stable economy with full employment without inflation. Another objective of fiscal policy is to maintain equilibrium in the balance of payments. Since the government's account can be used to influence income, and since imports, as has been shown, are a function of income, then the government's account can be used to influence the balance of payments. The model employed to discuss fiscal policy will be established first algebraically and then graphically. The discussion will be carried on in terms of the graphs.

National income Y is equal to consumption expenditure C plus investment expenditure I plus government expenditure G plus exports X minus imports M. The national incomes for W and Z are given by Equations (11-1) and (11-2).

$$Y^W = C^W + I^W + G^W + X^W - M^W \qquad (11\text{-}1)$$

$$Y^Z = C^Z + I^Z + G^Z + X^Z - M^Z \qquad (11\text{-}2)$$

Consumption is a function of income, but a linear consumption function is assumed for each country. Equation (11-3) gives the consumption function for country W, where 0.6 is the value of

$$C^W = 4 + 0.6Y^W \tag{11-3}$$

$$C^Z = 6 + 0.8Y^Z \tag{11-4}$$

the marginal propensity to consume. Z's consumption function is expressed by Equation (11-4), where the marginal propensity to consume is 0.8.

I and G are assumed to be autonomous and have the following given values:

$$I^W = 4, \quad G^W = 2 \tag{11-5}$$

$$I^Z = 4, \quad G^Z = 6 \tag{11-6}$$

Finally, W's marginal propensity to import is assumed to be equal to 0.1 and Z's marginal propensity to import is assumed to be equal to 0.2. Equations (11-7) and (11-8) give the imports of W and Z, respectively.

$$M^W = 0.1Y^W \tag{11-7}$$

$$M^Z = 0.2Y^Z \tag{11-8}$$

Equations (11-3) through (11-8) are substituted respectively into Equations (11-1) and (11-2) to yield Equations (11-9) and (11-10).

$$Y^W = (4 + 0.6Y^W) + 4 + 2 + X^W - 0.1Y^W \tag{11-9}$$

$$Y^Z = (6 + 0.8Y^Z) + 4 + 6 + X^Z - 0.2Y^Z \tag{11-10}$$

Transposing all Y's to the left and adding all constants yields

$$Y^W - 0.6Y^W + 0.1Y^W = 10 + X^W \tag{11-11}$$

$$Y^Z - 0.8Y^Z + 0.2Y^Z = 16 + X^Z \tag{11-12}$$

or

$$Y^W = 20 + \frac{1}{0.5} X^W \tag{11-13}$$

$$Y^Z = 40 + \frac{1}{0.4} X^Z \tag{11-14}$$

Since we are assuming a two-country model, W's exports are

Z's imports. Thus for X^W, $0.2Y^Z$ can be substituted. Likewise, $0.1Y^W$, W's imports, can be substituted for X^Z.

$$Y^W = 20 + \frac{2}{5} Y^Z \tag{11-15}$$

$$Y^Z = 40 + \frac{1}{4} Y^W \tag{11-16}$$

In Equation (11-15), W's income is equal to 20 of domestic expenditure $C + I + G - M$, plus the value of goods sold abroad $\frac{2}{5}Y^Z$. Similarly, Z's national income is equal to domestic utilization of domestic production, i.e., $(C + I + G - M)$, plus goods sold abroad.

Substitute the right side of Equation (11-16) for Y^Z in Equation (11-15).

$$Y^W = 20 + \frac{2}{5} (40 + \frac{1}{4} Y^W) \tag{11-17}$$

$$Y^W = 36 + \frac{1}{10} Y^W$$

$$Y^W = 40$$

Substitute the value of 40 for Y^W in Equation (11-16) to solve for Y^Z.

$$Y^Z = 40 + \frac{1}{4} (40) \tag{11-18}$$

$$Y^Z = 50$$

Knowing the income of W and Z, the values of C, X, and M can be determined. These are presented in Table 11-1.

Table 11-1

	W		Z	
Y Equation (11-17)	40		Equation (11-18)	50
C $4 + 0.6Y^W$	28		$6 + 0.8Y^Z$	46
I given as	4		given as	4
G given as	2		given as	6
X equals $0.2Y^Z$	10 ⎫ surplus		equals $0.1Y^W$	4 ⎫ deficit
M equals $0.1Y^W$	4 ⎭ of 6		equals $0.2Y^Z$	10 ⎭ of 6

The same relationship is shown graphically in Figure 11-1. W's consumption function, the slope of which is the marginal propensity to consume, is drawn in Figure 11-1a. Investment which is autonomous, i.e., not determined by income, is added to the consumption schedule to yield the $(C + I)$ schedule. Government spending, which is also autonomous, is measured vertically from the $(C + I)$ schedule to yield the $(C + I + G)$ schedule. All three schedules are parallel, and their slopes are determined by the marginal propensity to consume, since only consumption is a function of income. Imports are some function of income m, where m is the marginal propensity to import. These imports are included in the demand for goods for consumption, investment, and government spending. Subtracting imports from the $(C + I + G)$ schedule leaves domestic demand for domestic output, or $(C + I + G - M)$. Since imports are a function of income, the $(C + I + G - M)$ schedule has a slope different from the $(C + I + G)$ schedule. The marginal propensity to consume minus the marginal propensity to import gives the slope of the $(C + I + G - M)$ schedule.

The $(C + I + G - M)$ schedule shows the domestic demand for domestic output at different levels of income. Where this schedule crosses the 45-degree line gives the level of income determined by domestic demand for domestic output. The level of income beyond this depends on exports. The level of income determined by domestic demand for domestic output is transferred to Figure 11-1b by the dotted line. W's income beyond this level depends on foreign demand, i.e., Z's imports, for its output. Since the level of W's income depends on Z's imports and since Z's imports depend on its own income, W's income depends on Z's income. The mY^Z schedule shows W's income for alternative incomes in Z. It is thus not possible to determine W's income without knowing Z's income.

In Figure 11-1c, Z's consumption schedule is drawn where the slope is the marginal propensity to consume. Investment is assumed to be autonomous and is added to the consumption schedule, resulting in the $(C + I)$ schedule. Government expenditure is also assumed to be autonomous and is added to the $(C + I)$ schedule, giving the $(C + I + G)$ schedule. $(C + I + G)$ is the total expenditure on goods, some of which are imported. To derive the domestic demand for domestic output, it is necessary to subtract imports. Since imports are a function of income, subtracting imports from the $(C + I + G)$ schedule gives the

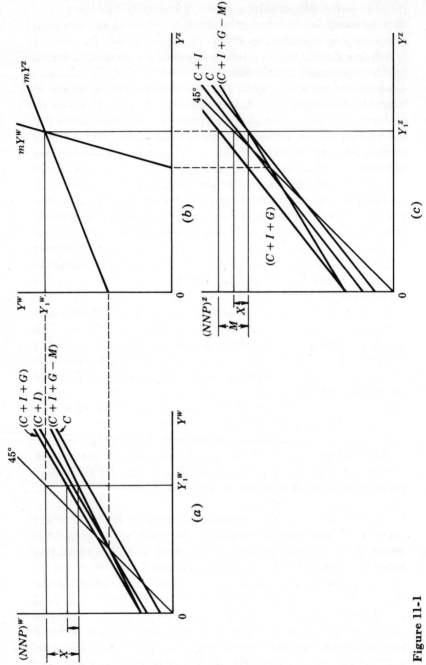

Figure 11-1

$(C + I + G - M)$ schedule, which has a different slope. The slope is equal to the marginal propensity to consume minus the marginal propensity to import.

Where the $(C + I + G - M)$ schedule crosses the 45-degree line gives the level of national income determined by the domestic demand for domestic output. This determined level of income is transferred to Figure 11-1b. Income beyond this level depends on exports, which depend on the level of income in W. The mY^W schedule shows levels of Z's income associated with different levels of income in W. The larger W's income, the larger its imports, and consequently the larger Z's exports and income.

The mY^Z schedule shows Z's income determined by the level of income in W. Likewise, the mY^W schedule shows W's income determined by the level of income in Z. The intersection of these two schedules gives the equilibrium income for the two countries. The level of income determined from W in Figure 11-1c is Y_1^W; this is transferred to Figure 11-1a. At Y_1^W, the total output is given by the 45-degree line; the domestic demand for domestic output is given by the $(C + I + G - M)$ schedule. The difference between output and domestic demand is exports, i.e., difference between the 45-degree line and the $(C + I + G - M)$ schedule. The difference between total demand for all goods $(C + I + G)$ and total demand for domestically produced goods $(C + I + G - M)$ represents imports. In the case of W, exports exceed imports.

The level of national income for Z determined in Figure 11-1b is transferred to Figure 11-1c. At Y_1^Z, the total demand is given by the $(C + I + G)$ schedule, and output is represented by the 45-degree line. Total demand for goods exceeds output; consequently the nation is consuming more than it is producing. The difference between demand for all goods at Y_1^Z and demand for domestically produced goods at Y_1^Z, $(C + I + G) - (C + I + G - M)$, is imports. The difference between production and demand for domestic output (the difference between the 45-degree line and the $(C + I + G - M)$ schedule) constitutes exports. As can be seen, imports exceed exports, and Z has a deficit.

The consequences of fiscal policies designed to bring equilibrium to the balance of payments can now be considered. First it will be assumed that Z acts to wipe out the deficit. W allows its income to change as a result of changes in Z but does not initiate any changes itself. Secondly, it will be assumed that W acts to wipe out the surplus, while Z reacts passively to any change. Thirdly, it will be assumed that both W and Z act to bring equilibrium to the balance of payments. Fourthly, it is assumed that prices, interest rates, level of capital flow, and exchange rates remain unchanged throughout.

Z, the deficit country, must reduce expenditure and income to bring equilibrium to the balance of payments. The contracted income induces imports to fall, thereby correcting the deficit in the balance of payments. However, the reduced imports are W's exports. The fall in exports reduces W's income, and consequently, its imports. Since W's imports are Z's exports, Z's exports fall, serving to mitigate the initial correction. Thus Z's imports must fall by the original amount of the deficit plus an amount equal to the fall in exports.

The graphs have been reproduced in Figure 11-2, except that the (C) and $(C + 1)$ schedules are omitted since they are not needed. Expenditure in Z, graph c, is reduced so that the $(C + I + G)$ schedule falls to $(C + I + G)'$. The $(C + I + G - M)$ schedule must also fall to $(C + I + G - M)'$, since its position depends on the position of the $(C + I + G)$ schedule.

Where the $(C + I + G - M)$ schedule crosses the 45-degree line gives the domestic demand for domestic output and the level of income resulting from this demand. This level of income is transposed to Figure 11-2b; income beyond this level depends on income in W. The mY^W line shifts to $(mY^W)'$. The intersection of mY^Z and $(mY^W)'$ determines income at $Y_2{}^Z$ and $Y_2{}^W$. As can be seen, income falls in both countries, further in Z. At $Y_2{}^W$, $(C + I + G)$ schedule crosses the 45-degree line, indicating that output is equal to demand. If demand is equal to output, then exports must be equal to imports. Clearly, if exports exceed imports, then output must exceed domestic absorption of goods. Similarly, if imports exceed exports, then absorption must exceed output. When absorption equals output, exports must equal imports. The total output is given by the 45-degree line at $Y_2{}^W$; the amount demanded for domestic utilization is given by the $(C + I + G - M)$ schedule, and the difference is exports. The difference between the $(C + I + G)$ schedule and the $(C + I + G - M)$ schedule at $Y_2{}^W$ is imports. As can be seen, the two distances are equal; exports equal imports.

At $Y_2{}^Z$, the $(C + I + G)$ schedule crosses the 45-degree line; absorption is equal to output. When absorption is equal to output, exports must equal imports. Naturally, in a two-country model, when one is in equilibrium, the other must be too.

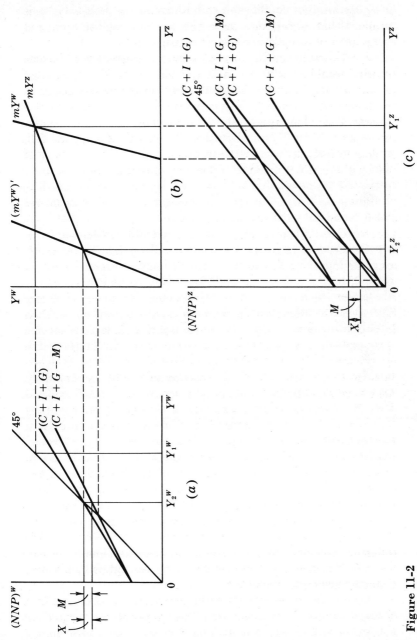

Figure 11-2

Although it has been shown that the reduced expenditure in Z has brought equilibrium to both countries' balance of payments, the question arises as to how much expenditure must be reduced to restore equilibrium. One answer is to take the present income Y_1^Z, subtract the level of income consistent with balance in the foreign account Y_2^Z and then divide by the appropriate multiplier to obtain the amount by which expenditure must be reduced. This, however, assumes that one knows the level of income in Z which is consistent with equilibrium in the balance of payments. In Figure 11-2c there is no indication of the level consistent with balance in the foreign account. The $(C + I + G)$ and the $(C + I + G - M)$ schedules must fall, but the point to which they must fall is not indicated. It is because the schedules must fall that it is impossible to determine the level of income consistent with balance.

However, when Z introduces an expenditure change, it has repercussions for country W. Income in W is related to income in Z, as Figure 11-2b shows. Thus the reduced expenditure in Z reduces both its income and W's income. As W's income falls, absorption falls, i.e., a movement along the $C + I + G$ and $C + I + G - M$ schedules. These schedules do not move; there is only a movement along the schedules themselves. Hence W's income must change to induce a movement along the $(C + I + G)$ schedule to the point where this schedule crosses the 45-degree line, for at this point demand equals output and, concomitantly, exports equal imports. At the point where W's surplus disappears, Z's deficit must also disappear, since there are only two countries.

$(C + I + G)$ equals output at Y_2^W. Y_2^W is transferred to Figure 11-2b. The $m Y^Z$ schedule shows the relationship of income in Z to income in W. For W's income to be Y_2^W, Z's income has to be Y_2^Z. Since Y_2^W is the level of income which restores balance to W's foreign account, then Z's income of Y_2^Z is also the level required for balance in its foreign account. Thus for Z to have an equilibrium in its balance of payments, its income must fall from Y_1^Z to Y_2^Z. This means that the $(C + I + G)$ schedule must fall until it crosses the 45-degree line at income Y_2^Z. At this point, its absorption equals output, which means exports must equal imports.

The level of income required to restore balance in the foreign account can be determined from the graph of the nation not acting to correct the deficit. This country's schedules do not move; the concern is only with movements along the schedules.

One can readily ascertain the level of income where balance has been restored to the foreign account, namely, the point where the $(C + I + G)$ schedule crosses the 45-degree line.

As can be seen in Figure 11-2, the deficit country has the largest fall in income. The country acting to correct the deficit through changes in expenditure must have the largest fall in income. This is due to the relative size of the investment multipliers. In Chapter 6, it was shown that if Z has a change in investment (or any expenditure), its income will change by

$$dY^Z = \frac{1 + (m^W/s^W)}{s^Z + m^Z + m^W(s^Z/s^W)} \, (-dI^Z)$$

and the repercussion for W depends on the following multiplier:

$$dY^W = \frac{(m^Z/s^Z)}{s^W + m^W + m^Z(s^W/s^Z)} \, (-dI^Z)$$

The 1 in the numerator of Z's multiplier effectively ensures that it will be larger. Thus Z's income will fall by a greater amount than will W's.

The amount by which Z's income must fall to correct a deficit by a given amount depends on: (1) Z's marginal propensity to import, (2) W's multiplier, (3) W's marginal propensity to import, and (4) Z's multiplier. The more responsive Z's imports are to change in income, i.e., a larger marginal propensity to import, the smaller will be the required changes in income to correct a deficit of given magnitude. The fall in Z's imports is reduced exports for W. W's income must fall, but a fall in W's income will result in a fall in its imports (which are Z's exports), serving to mitigate the correction to Z's balance of payments or requiring a larger fall in Z's income. The larger W's multiplier, the larger the fall in its income and imports, requiring a larger income change in Z. Also a large marginal propensity to import for a given size multiplier will serve greatly to reduce Z's exports for a given income change in W. Thus the larger W's marginal propensity to import, the larger the income fall required in Z to correct a deficit of a given amount. The reduced exports will induce a contraction in Z's income; the amount of the reduced income will depend on the size of Z's multiplier.

Thus for the deficit country to correct the disequilibrium requires deflation in the domestic economy. The question then is whether such deflation can be undertaken. If Y_1^Z in Figure

11-2 is a position of less than full employment, then Z would want to inflate to reduce the level of unemployment; such action would exacerbate the disequilibrium in the balance of payments. Thus the goals of fiscal policy in this situation have contradictory requirements. Fulfilling the requirement of full employment requires an expansionary fiscal policy; fulfilling the requirement of equilibrium in the balance of payments requires contractionary fiscal policy. The solution here is indeterminate. Each country in this situation will have to make a decision on the basis of its choices or welfare function.

On the other hand, if Y_1^Z is an inflationary level of income, then the requirements for the fulfillment of the two goals are consistent in direction. Contraction is needed to correct the deficit, and contraction will also reduce the level of inflation. For correction of the balance of payments, income must fall to Y_2^Z. It is not necessarily the case that a fall of $Y_1^Z Y_2^Z$ is required to correct the inflation. If a larger fall is required, then a move to Y_2^Z corrects the foreign account and reduces the level of inflation. If the government decides to reduce income below Y_2^Z to reduce the inflationary level further, then Z will not only eradicate the deficit but will also introduce a surplus at any income below Y_2^Z. This action makes W the deficit country and requires its action. If W corrects its new deficit by deflation, then Z's income will fall below full employment without inflation, creating unemployment in Z.

It is also possible that income need not fall by $Y_1^Z Y_2^Z$ to correct the inflation, but by something smaller. Thus the direction is the same for the two goals, but the amount of change is not. If the government acts to correct only the inflation, then it will still have a deficit, admittedly a smaller one. If the government reduces expenditure to lower income to Y_2^Z, unemployment will result. Again a choice between full employment and equilibrium in the balance of payments will have to be made.

Where a nation has a deficit and inflation, both requiring the same amount of reduced expenditure for their correction, the policy action is quite clear. The policy action from a political standpoint is also fairly clear in the case where a deficit occurs with inflation, but the inflation requires a greater fall in income than does the correction of the deficit. The difficulty arises, however, when income adjustment is required for the fulfillment of both goals, but correction of the deficit requires a larger change in income than does correction of inflation. Full correction of the deficit introduces unemployment. Finally, the country really finds itself torn by opposite goals when a deficit in the balance of payments is accompanied by unemployment. Correction of either worsens the other.

Next let us consider what happens when the nation with a surplus acts to correct the disequilibrium in the balance of payments. Income will have to be expanded to induce an increase in imports, thereby reducing the surplus. Expenditure might be increased by greater government spending or by reducing taxes to induce increased consumption or investment. The amount of the expenditure change will depend on the amount of the required change in income and the size of the multiplier.

Nation W in Figure 11-3 is going to introduce an increase in expenditure to reduce its surplus. The first question is one of how much it must increase expenditure and income to remove the surplus. W's $(C + I + G)$ and $(C + I + G - M)$ schedules will shift upward; the magnitude of the shift cannot be determined from Figure 11-3a. However, since Z is not introducing any expenditure changes, we can tell the level of income at which the foreign account is brought into equilibrium. This is where the $(C + I + G)$ schedule crosses the 45-degree line. At this point absorption equals output; thus exports must be traded for imports. Z's balance of payments is in equilibrium at Y_2Z. This level of income is transferred to Figure 11-3b, where the mY^W schedule shows the resulting level of income in Z for different levels of income in W. Since it is known that Z's income must be Y_2Z, then the level of income required in W is shown by the mY^W schedule to be Y_2^W. This level of income is transferred to Figure 11-3a. Thus we know that W's income must expand to Y_2^W; this level of income requires that the $(C + I + G)$ schedule shift to $(C + I + G)'$ and the $(C + I + G - M)$ to $(C + I + G - M)'$. The $(C + I + G - M)'$ schedule is the domestic demand for domestic output. Where this crosses the 45-degree line gives income resulting from domestic demand. Income beyond this level depends on exports. Therefore this level is transferred to Figure 11-3b. W's income as a function of Z's income is shown by $(mY^Z)'$. Where the $(mY^Z)'$ schedule and the mY^W schedule intersect determines the income in the two countries.

The increased expenditure in the surplus country causes both economies to expand. The size of the income change in W depends on: (1) W's marginal propensity to import, (2) Z's multiplier,

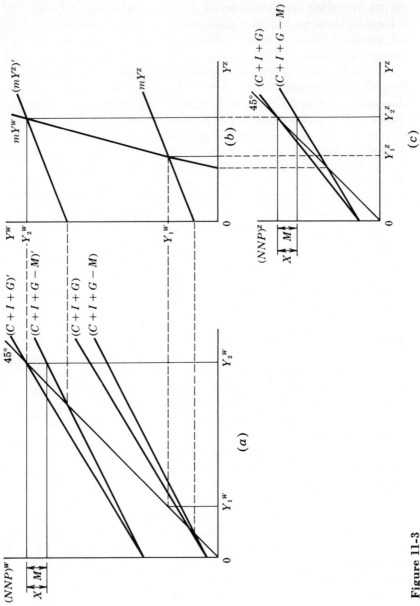

Figure 11-3

(3) Z's marginal propensity to import, and (4) W's multiplier. A large marginal propensity to import in W indicates that imports will change by a large amount as a result of a small increase in income. A surplus of given amount can be eradicated by a smaller income adjustment, the larger the marginal propensity to import. W's increased imports are Z's increased exports. Z's income will rise as a result of the increased exports; the increased income will be larger, the larger the multiplier. Since imports are a function of income, Z's imports will rise by more, the larger the multiplier. These increased exports for Z will serve to enlarge the surplus, requiring a larger income adjustment to wipe out the surplus. Also, a large marginal propensity to import in Z for a given size multiplier will result in the largest increase in imports for a given increase in income. W's exports will expand, and W's income will have to be increased further to remove the surplus. The increased exports will induce a large increase in W's income, the larger its multiplier.

Whether W can inflate its economy by $Y_1^W Y_2^W$ needs to be considered. Obviously, if W has unemployment, the correction of which requires income to expand by $Y_1^W Y_2^W$, then there is no problem. The expansion will correct both the surplus and the unemployment. However, if Y_1^W is a full-employment level of income, then the economy will have to choose between inflation and a surplus. Politically, it is usually more desirable to have a surplus than inflation. The authorities would be severely criticized for incurring inflation, where in many quarters a surplus is considered desirable. It is also possible for Y_1^W to be a level of income at less than full employment, but an increase in income of less than $Y_1^W Y_2^W$ is required to establish full employment. Again a choice between inflation and disequilibrium in the balance of payments must be made. Finally, it is possible that an increase in income of greater than $Y_1^W Y_2^W$ is required for full employment. If the economy goes beyond Y_2^W to realize full employment, then the economy will incur a deficit. This deficit will equal Z's surplus. If Z acts to correct this surplus, it will expand, with the result that its increased imports will induce W to expand beyond full employment to inflation.

By and large, the correction of deficits and surpluses through fiscal policy is going to require a choice between external and internal equilibrium. Only in cases where the deficit country has inflation equal to the amount by which income must be reduced to eradicate the deficit and where the surplus country has deflation equal to the amount by which income must be increased to correct the surplus is there no need to choose. All other combinations require a choice between internal and external equilibrium in the use of fiscal policy. A country's choice of internal equilibrium leaves the correction to the other country. However, if the second country acts to correct the external disequilibrium, then it forces the first country to move toward a position of internal disequilibrium.

Suppose that both nations decide to act to correct the disequilibrium in the balance of payments. Nation W inflates by an amount necessary to wipe out half of the surplus, and country Z deflates by an amount required to eradicate half of the deficit. In a two-country model, since the surplus of one country is equal to the deficit of the other one, the combined action of W and Z will wipe out the surplus or deficit. In Figure 11-4, expenditure rises in W so that the $(C + I + G)$ schedule moves upward by the amount of the increased expenditure to $(C + I + G)'$, and the $(C + I + G - M)$ moves to $(C + I + G - M)'$. Income moves from Y_1^W to Y_2^W. Expenditure in Z is reduced by the amount represented by the distance between the $(C + I + G)$ schedule and the $(C + I + G)'$, and the $(C + I + G - M)$ schedule becomes the $(C + I + G - M)'$ schedule. National income falls from Y_1^Z to Y_2^Z. As can be seen, income in Z changes by less than in W. The requirement is not that each country induce equal expenditure or income changes, but rather that each country adjust income and expenditure by the amount necessary to eradicate half the amount of the disequilibrium. Suppose that W's exports exceed imports by \$6 billion; then W must remove \$3 billion of the disequilibrium, and Z must act to remove the remaining \$3 billion. W must expand its income to induce an increase in imports until the difference in exports and imports is reduced to \$3 billion, the amount Z must act to correct. The amount by which income in W will have to expand depends on W's marginal propensity to import, Z's multiplier, Z's marginal propensity to import, and W's multiplier. If W has a large marginal propensity to import, then income will have to change by less to reduce the surplus by a given amount. As a result of W's increased imports, Z's exports and income increase. The amount by which income rises will depend on the size of Z's multiplier. This increase in Z will induce an expansion in Z's imports (which are W's exports), thereby enlarging W's surplus. Thus the larger Z's multiplier and its marginal propensity to import,

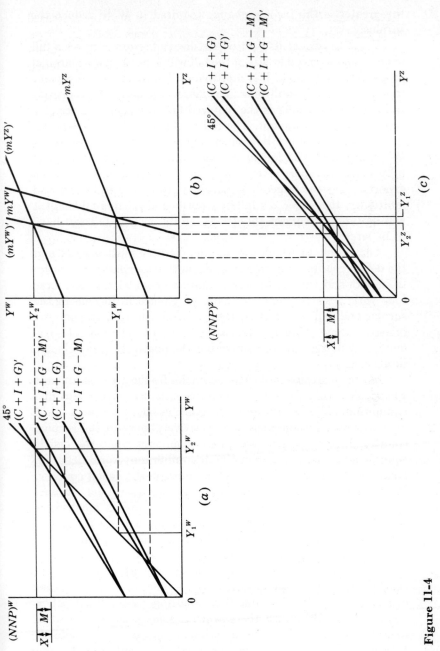

Figure 11-4

the greater is the income change required in W to reduce the surplus.

For Z to correct its part of the disequilibrium requires a fall in national income. The size of the fall will depend on Z's marginal propensity to import, W's multiplier, W's marginal propensity to import, and Z's multiplier. The larger Z's marginal propensity to import, the smaller is the required fall in income to correct a deficit of a given amount. The fall in Z's imports (W's exports) forces a contraction of W's income, the size of which depends on W's multiplier. The fall in income multiplied by the marginal propensity to import gives W's reduced imports, or Z's reduced exports. Thus the larger W's marginal propensity to import and multiplier, the larger Z's fall in exports, and the more difficult it will be for Z to correct the deficit, as the income fall will have to be larger.

The extent to which the surplus country must expand and the deficit country contract depends on the marginal propensities to import and the multipliers in the two countries. Since these four variables determine the required change in income in the surplus and deficit countries, they simultaneously determine the relative income change. The case represented in Figure 11-4 is one in which the surplus country has the relatively larger change in income.

Income increases in the two countries by the greatest amount when the surplus country alone attempts to correct the disequilibrium. This correction by the surplus country brings world inflation, with income increasing relatively more in the surplus country. Income falls by the greatest amount when the deficit country alone acts to correct the disequilibrium; world deflation results with income falling relatively more in the deficit country. Between these two extremes is the case where both act. Income in the surplus country will expand, but not by as much as it would if the surplus country alone acted to correct the disequilibrium, and income falls in the deficit country, but not by as much as when the deficit country alone acts.

Only in the rare situation where restoration of internal equilibrium—full employment without inflation—and external equilibrium require the same income change is the fiscal policy dictate clear. Otherwise there will be some trade-off between inflation and disequilibrium in surplus countries and a trade-off between unemployment and external disequilibrium in the deficit country. Since a surplus is not usually a problem to a country, a surplus country will probably act against inflation and allow the surplus. The deficit country with unemployment may not be willing to add to the unemployment as long as the correction of the deficit is not compelling. Fiscal policy will probably be used to restore full employment while other devices may be used in an attempt to correct the deficit.

Monetary Policy

By *monetary policy* we mean manipulation of the quantity of money in order to influence the interest rate. A rise in the interest rate is brought about to discourage investment and to induce a contraction in the economy. In order to effect an expansion in the economy, the interest rate is lowered to encourage investment. To the extent that monetary policy is used to influence the level of economic activity, the same problems exist as with fiscal policy. External and internal equilibrium may require contradictory monetary policies. As a matter of fact, the likelihood that internal and external equilibrium will require contradictory monetary policies is rather high. At this stage, the only difference in monetary and fiscal policy is that fiscal policy acts through *expenditure* and monetary policy acts through the *interest rate* to effect investment expenditure. The relative effectiveness of these two tools in inducing changes in income will not be discussed here.

With fiscal policy, income is changed to move exports and imports toward equilibrium. A surplus country expands imports to increase the autonomous supply of currency to equal autonomous demand. A deficit country lowers income to reduce imports, thus lowering autonomous supply toward autonomous demand and thereby moving the balance of payments toward equilibrium. Under monetary policy, the interest rate is lowered to encourage expansion which will in turn encourage imports. However, there is a second part. The lower interest rate will encourage an outflow of currency for investment abroad; consequently, there will be an increased supply of currency for investment. Thus commodity exports and imports do not have to change by so much to bring autonomous supply and demand toward equilibrium. The increased supply for investment reduces the amount by which imports need to expand to increase supply. Similarly, a deficit country increases the interest rate to lower expenditure and imports to move autonomous supply and demand toward equilibrium. The lower level of imports reduces supply. Furthermore, the increased rate of interest increases the demand for the currency for investment. Thus the increased interest rate acts to restore equilibrium by reducing the supply of currency for imports and increasing the demand for currency for investment.

The effectiveness of monetary policy depends on the elasticity of capital to changes in the interest rate and the sensitivity of investment to the interest rate. This discussion is beyond the scope of this work.

Conclusion

With exchange rates fixed and prices inflexible (at least downward), corrections fall to income changes if direct controls are not to be used. This means that the deficit country corrects excess absorption over output by decreasing output, because absorption will fall by more than output. To expand output to allow the high level of absorption is not possible. The expanded output would have to be traded for imports to restore equilibrium. But there is no reason why foreigners will want to buy these expanded exports; only if prices fall will there be an increased demand for exports and if prices are inflexible, there will be no increased demand. Thus the correction must be reduced income to reduce imports.

The surplus country might be in a better position to restore equilibrium. However, surplus countries with full employment are usually unwilling to inflate. For example, until the spring of 1968, France had been acquiring reserves, and the French franc had become one of the strongest currencies in Europe. De Gaulle was particularly critical of the deficit in the United States balance of payments and maintained that the United States must reduce its deficit. United States capital had been flowing to Europe buying up industry. It was this capital flow and a favorable current account which made for France's surplus.

In the spring of 1968, French unions struck for a higher standard of living. There was considerable criticism of the government's holding of the country's savings in idle reserves rather than investing them to promote growth and a higher standard of living. During the strike, a proportion of French reserves were used up. Furthermore, the higher standard of living obtained by the workers brought a deficit to the balance of payments. In the fall of 1968, there was heavy speculation against the franc—devaluation was anticipated. Western nations extended credit to France to forestall devaluation, and France introduced commodity controls. In the fall of 1968, the French government decided not to devalue and expressed the opinion that Germany, a surplus country, should appreciate its currency.

This episode raises a question as to what are adequate reserves. When a currency in a matter of months can go from one of the strongest to one of the weakest, there is a serious question as to the stabilty of the system and the magnitude of required reserves to allow more orderly adjustment to change.

If devaluation and income changes are to be avoided, then price must be made to adjust to allow external balance. A feasible method of effecting such price change in nonplanned economies has not been found. Thus we are left with the contradictions of internal and external equilibrium. The external imbalance can more easily be ignored in the short run or until the day of absolute necessity.

Selected Readings

Books

American Enterprise Institute, *International Payments Problems*, Washington, D.C.: American Enterprise Institute.

Baldwin, Robert E., *Trade, Growth, and the Balance of Payments*, Chicago: Rand McNally, 1965.

Caves, Richard and Harry Johnson, *Readings in International Economics*, Homewood: Richard D. Irwin, 1968.

Fellner, William, *Maintaining and Restoring Balance in International Payments*, Princeton: Princeton University Press, 1966.

Machlup, Fritz, *International Trade and National Income Multiplier*, New York: Kelley, 1961.

Meade, J. E., *Balance of Payments*, London: Oxford University Press, 1955.

Periodicals

A. E. A., *Index of Economic Journals*, classification nos. 11.322 and 11.323.

Collery, A., "A Full Employment, Keynesian Theory of International Trade," *Quarterly Journal of Economics*, August, 1963.

Dosser, D., "National-Income and Domestic-Income Multipliers and Their Application to Foreign-aid Transfers," *Economica*, n.s. February, 1963.

Flanders, M. J., "The Balance-of-Payments Adjustments Mechanism: Some Problems of Model-building," *Kyklos*, 1963.

Gilbert, M., "Reconciliation of Domestic and International Objectives of Financial Policy: The European Countries," *Journal of Finance*, May, 1963.

Gorden, W. M., "The Geometric Representation of Policies to Attain Internal and External Balance," *Review of Economic Studies*, October, 1960.

Hein, J., "Monetary Policy and External Convertability: The German Experience, 1959–1961," *Economia Internationale*, August, 1964.

Johnson, Harry, "Fiscal Policy and the Balance of Payments in a Growing Economy," *Malayan Economic Review*, April, 1964.

Macesich, G., "The Quantity Theory and the Income Expenditure Theory in an Open Economy: Canada, 1926-1958," *Canadian Journal of Economics*, August, 1964.

Mundell, R. A., "The Appropriate Use of Monetary and Fiscal Policy for Internal and External Stability," International Monetary Fund, *Staff Papers*, March, 1962.

Takayama, A., "Stability in the Balance of Payments: A Multi-country Approach," *Journal of Economic Behavior*, October, 1961.

12.

Commercial Controls

Correcting the disequilibrium in the balance of payments by devaluing the currency and by employing fiscal and monetary policy has been considered. Whether devaluation will improve the balance of payments cannot easily be predetermined; it is possible that devaluation will enlarge the deficit. Monetary and fiscal policy may be so engaged in stabilizing the domestic economy as to preclude its use for external stability; or at best fiscal and monetary policy may be available to effect only a partial correction. An alternative is the imposition of direct controls on the autonomous demand for foreign currency for the purposes of investing abroad and importing goods.

Exchange Controls

The *exchange control* may be undertaken by requiring that all earned foreign exchange be sold to the government or central bank for resale to importers. Alternatively, the government may leave the exchange market free but require persons buying the currency on the exchange market to have a license or permit to purchase a specified amount of foreign exchange. The licenses would serve to limit the demand for foreign exchange; presumably, licenses to purchase foreign exchange would be issued in total value equal to the amount of foreign exchange earned.

In the first case, where the government monopolizes the sale of foreign exchange, all foreign currency earned from exports and from foreigners investing in the country must be sold to a government agency or the central bank, which in turn allocates the currency among demanders for permitted transactions. In this way the government restricts the currency to approved transactions. Since only the currency received is sold, autonomous demand is limited to autonomous supply, thereby maintaining equilibrium in the balance of payments.

To ensure that the system works, the government must be certain that it is receiving all the currency earned abroad. Nonreporting and failure to sell the currency to the authorities must be kept to a minimum. Steps must also be taken to ensure that reports of sales abroad do not misrepresent the currency earned. Tight surveillance is necessary if the sale of the currency on the black market is to be avoided.

Furthermore, the government must inspect the mail to prohibit the outflow of currency. A resident of W could send his currency to a resident of Z; the Z resident could exchange at his bank the W currency for his own currency. Through the nation's central bank, the bank would present the currency to the central bank of W for redemption. Thus a resident could obtain unlimited foreign exchange by having a foreigner convert the currency for him.

Instead of inspecting the mail, the government could announce that it would not buy its currency from any foreign central bank. Consequently, foreign central banks would not accept that currency, and foreigners would be unable to convert it. Such a currency is said to be inconvertible. Supplies held outside the country would sell cheaply; tourists would be able to buy below the official exchange rate and take the currency with them upon a visit to the issuing country. If this action is to be stopped, then the customs would have to search for the currency.

Furthermore, the resident of W might be able to trade with a resident of Z a domestically produced good for an import good. This barter transaction would avoid the currency exchange altogether. Alternatively, if the W resident desires to travel in Z, he might find someone to extend him Z's currency in exchange for a deposit in W. Again a commercial transaction would have been made without resorting to the currency market. The government authorities would be deprived of the currency earned from exports and from visits of foreign tourists. A large investigating staff would be required to forestall these barter arrangements.

Instead of monopolizing the foreign currency earned, the W government may, alternatively, require licenses to exchange W currency for any other currency; in this manner, the supply of W currency would be limited to demand so that the central bank would not have to buy any excess supply of W currency for gold to maintain the exchange rate. However, any nonresident could supply W currency to the market without a license. The W government would have to prevent its residents from supplying W currency to foreigners who could supply this currency to the market.

Direct controls for their efficient operation require extensive government intervention into the economy. As some men spend their ingenuity in devising controls, others devise means, both legal and illegal, to circumvent them. Controls must constantly be expanded. The effectiveness of the controls themselves is beyond the scope of this text. In the discussion it will be assumed that the controls are effective, but it must be pointed out that this is an heroic assumption. First capital controls and then commodity controls will be discussed.

Capital Controls

Control of capital for the purpose of maintaining equilibrium in the balance of payments is authorized in the Bretton Woods Agreement. It must be recognized, however, that in regulating capital it is not always easy to define what in fact constitutes capital. Loopholes will be sought out and the effectiveness of the legislation reduced.

Suppose country W has a deficit and introduces restrictions on the outflow of capital but does not introduce any restrictions on the current-account items. Suppose further that the controls effectively reduce the capital outflow by $10 billion. Whether the balance of payments is improved by $10 billion depends on what happens to investment expenditure in the two countries. First assume that W's capital is diverted to domestic investment, which expands by 10, and Z's investment expenditure falls by 10 as a result of the loss of the inflow of capital.

To determine the change in income in the two countries and the resulting change in imports, the investment multipliers of Chapter 6 must be used. The increased investment expenditure in W brings the following change in income:

$$dy^W = \frac{1 + (m^Z/s^Z)}{s^W + m^W + m^Z(s^W/s^Z)} (10) \tag{12-1}$$

The resulting increased imports bring an expansion in Z of

$$dy^Z = \frac{(m^W/s^W)}{s^Z + m^Z + m^W(s^Z/s^W)} (10) \tag{12-2}$$

The decreased investment expenditure in Z brings the following fall in Z's income:

$$dy^Z = \frac{1 + (m^W/s^W)}{s^Z + m^Z + m^W(s^Z/s^W)} (-10) \tag{12-3}$$

W's income falls as a result of the fall in Z's income:

$$dy^W = \frac{(m^Z/s^Z)}{s^W + m^W + m^Z(s^W/s^Z)} (-10) \tag{12-4}$$

The total change in W's income is given by the sum of Equations (12-2) and (12-4):

$$dy^W = \frac{1 + (m^Z/s^Z)}{s^W + m^W + m^Z(s^W/s^Z)} (10)$$
$$+ \frac{(m^Z/s^Z)}{s^W + m^W + m^Z(s^W/s^Z)} (-10) \tag{12-5}$$

or $$dy^W = \frac{1}{s^W + m^W + m^Z(s^W/s^Z)} (10)$$

The total change in Z's income is the sum of Equations

(12-2) and (12-3):

$$dy^Z = \frac{(m^W/s^W)}{s^W + m^Z + m^W(s^Z/s^W)} \; (10)$$

$$+ \frac{1 + (m^W/s^W)}{s^Z + m^Z + m^W(s^Z/s^W)} \; (-10) \quad (12\text{-}6)$$

or $\quad dy^Z = \dfrac{-1}{s^Z + m^Z + m^Z(s^Z/s^W)} \; (10)$

The change in W's income times its marginal propensity to import gives the change in imports:

$$dM^W = \frac{m^W}{z^W + m^W + m^Z(s^W/s^Z)} \; (10) \qquad (12\text{-}7)$$

The change in Z's income times its marginal propensity to import gives Z's changed imports:

$$dM^Z = \frac{-m^Z}{s^Z + m^Z + m^W(s^Z/s^W)} \; (10) \qquad (12\text{-}8)$$

The change in W's balance of payments will be improved by the decreased capital outflow of 10, made worse by the decreased exports of.

$$\frac{-m^Z}{s^Z + m^Z + m^W(s^W/s^W)} \; (10)$$

and worse by the increased imports of

$$\frac{m^W}{s^W + m^W + m^Z(s^W/s^Z)} \; (10)$$

The balance of payments equation is:

$$dB^W = 10 + \left[\frac{-m^Z}{s^Z + m^Z + m^W(s^Z/s^W)} \right] 10$$

$$- \left[\frac{m^W}{s^W + m^W + m^Z(s^W/s^Z)} \right] 10$$

$$(12\text{-}9)$$

or $\quad dB^W = \left[1 - \dfrac{m^Z}{s^Z + m^Z + m^W(s^Z/s^W)} \right.$

$$\left. - \frac{m^W}{s^W + m^W + m^Z(s^W/s^Z)} \right] 10$$

Table 12-1

	m^Z	s^Z	m^W	s^W	dB^W	dY^W	dY^Z	dM^W	dM^Z
A	0.2	0.2	0.2	0.2	3.3	+16.6	−16.6	+3.3	−3.3
B	0.1	0.2	0.2	0.2	4.0	+20.0	−20.0	+4.0	−2.0
C	0.2	0.1	0.2	0.2	2.5	+12.5	−25.0	+2.5	−5.0
D	0.2	0.2	0.1	0.2	4.0	+20.0	−20.0	+2.0	−4.0
E	0.2	0.2	0.2	0.1	2.5	+25.0	−12.5	+5.0	−2.5

In row A of Table 12-1, the marginal propensities to save and to invest in both countries are assumed to be equal to 0.2. These values are plugged into Equation (12-9) to derive the overall improvement in the balance of payments as a result of reducing the outflow of capital by $10 billion. As shown in the column designated dB^W, W's balance of payments improves by $3.3 billion, not by the $10 billion of reduced capital. The reason the balance of payments improved by only a proportion of the reduced capital outflow can be seen from the next four columns. W's income increased as a result of the capital being diverted to the domestic market, and Z's income fell as a result of the reduced foreign investment expenditure. W's imports rose by $3.3 billion, an adverse effect on the balance of payments. Z's imports fell by $3.3, thereby reducing W's exports by that amount. Thus the current account of W's balance of payments incurs a deficit of 6.6. The improvement of 10 in the capital account and deterioration of 6.6 in the current account make for an overall improvement of $3.3 billion.

The results given in row A are determined by the assumed values of the propensities. In rows B through E the value of one of the propensities is changed to set off the consequences of different size propensities. In row B the value of Z's marginal propensity to import is lowered, while all other propensities have the same value as in row A. With the smaller marginal propensity to import in Z, the improvement in W's balance of payments is greater than that in row A. W's income rises by more and Z's income falls by more. Also W's imports expand by a greater amount and Z's imports contract by a smaller amount. Thus, while W's imports increase by a larger amount than in row A, its exports (Z's imports) contract by a smaller amount, with the result that the overall improvement in W's balance of payments is greater. The increase in imports of 4 plus the fall in exports of 2 yields a current-account deficit of 6. The improvement of 10 in the capital account and deterioration of the current account of 6 yields an improvement in the balance of payments of 4. Clearly, a smaller marginal propensity to import in the country receiving capital will contribute to a larger correction in the balance of payments in the country controlling the capital outflow.

In row C, Z's marginal propensity to import is reduced while all other propensities have the same value as in row A. The correction to W's balance of payments is less than that in row A. A small marginal propensity to save in the receiving country serves to diminish the size of the correction provided to the balance of payments in the country controlling the capital outflow. The small marginal propensity to save in Z results in a small income increase in W and a large income fall in Z. Consequently, W's imports rise by little, but Z's imports fall by a great deal. W's increased imports of 2.5 plus reduced exports of 5 add a deficit entry of 7.5 to the current account. The improvement of 10 in the capital account and deficit of 7.5 in the current account yield an improvement in the balance of payments of 2.5.

In row D the value of W's marginal propensity to import is lowered, all other propensities have the same values as given in row A. The lower marginal propensity in W brings about a larger correction in the balance of payments. Country W has a greater income increase and Z has a larger fall. However, W's imports increase by less and its exports decrease by more; the consequence of the increased imports and decreased exports is a deficit entry of 6 in the current account. The improvement of 10 in the capital account and deficit of 6 in the current account yield an overall improvement of $4 billion.

In row E all propensities are the same as in row A, except for W's marginal propensity to save, which is smaller. As a result of assuming a smaller marginal propensity to save, the improvement in the balance of payments is less. W's income rises by more and Z's income falls by less; consequently, W's imports rise by more while its exports fall by less. Imports rise by 5 and exports fall by 2.5, contributing a deficit of 7.5 to the current account. The addition of a deficit of 7.5 combined with the improvement of 10 in the capital account yields an overall improvement of $2.5 billion.

In summary, small marginal propensities to import in both

countries result in the greatest amount of improvement in the balance of payments from a specific amount of capital control. Also, large marginal propensities to save in both countries allow the country introducing capital control to achieve the greatest correction in the balance of payments.

The improvement in W's balance of payments is accompanied by an increase in its income and by a fall in Z's national income. If W is initially at a position of less than full employment, then it may be willing to allow the expansion. If the income expansion achieved here is not sufficient to restore full employment, then further expansion of income must be considered. Such additional expansion will induce an expansion of imports and a deterioration in the balance of payments; further capital controls will be required. Whether a further amount of capital can be restricted depends on the amount of the original capital outflow.

The resulting fall in Z's income will be acceptable only if Z has an inflationary economy requiring a fall equal to or more than that brought about by W's control of capital.

However, it might be the case that W is not willing to allow its economy to expand, and Z might not be willing to allow its economy to contract. First we will consider the case where W acts to prevent its economy from expanding, and then the case where Z acts to prevent its economy from contracting.

Again it is assumed that W effectively reduces the capital outflow by 10. This capital is diverted to domestic investment, but this increased investment expenditure is neutralized by reduced government expenditure of 10. Thus national income will not change as a result of the introduction of capital controls.

Z's loss of foreign capital of 10 is assumed to bring about a reduction of 10 in domestic investment. Clearly then, an expenditure change is going to occur in Z but not in W as a direct result of W's controlling the outflow of capital.

Equations (12-3) and (12-4) reveal the income changes in both countries resulting from the reduced investment expenditure in Z. These income changes multiplied by the respective marginal propensity to import yield the change in imports.

$$dM^Z = M^Z \left[\frac{1 + (m^W/s^W)}{s^Z + m^Z + m^W(s^Z/s^W)} \right] - 10 \qquad (12\text{-}10)$$

$$dM^W = M^W \left[\frac{(m^Z/s^Z)}{s^W + m^W + m^Z(s^W/s^Z)} \right] - 10 \qquad (12\text{-}11)$$

The change in W's balance of payments will be equal to the reduced capital of 10 plus the change in exports minus the change in W's imports. In Equation (12-12) Z's imports are W's exports:

$$dB^W = 10 + \left[-M^Z \frac{1 + (m^W/s^W)}{s^Z + m^Z + m^W(s^Z/s^W)} \right] 10$$

$$- \left[-M^W \frac{(m^Z/s^Z)}{s^W + m^W + m^Z(s^W/s^Z)} \right] 10$$

$$\text{or} \quad dB^W = \left[1 - M^Z \frac{1 + (m^W/s^W)}{s^Z + m^Z + m^W(s^Z/s^W)} \right. \tag{12-12}$$

$$\left. + M^W \frac{(m^Z/s^Z)}{s^W + m^W + m^Z(s^W/s^Z)} \right] 10$$

The balance-of-payments correction in each of the five rows of Table 12-2 is greater than in the equivalent row in Table 12-1. W's action to prevent the diverted capital from expanding the domestic economy served to bring about a larger correction to W's balance of payments. Since Z's income and imports fall, W's exports and income fall. The fall in W's exports is greater in every row of Table 12-2 than Table 12-1. Thus the larger loss of exports is going to require a larger fall in imports to bring about a given amount of correction to the balance of payments. W's income must fall to induce a reduction in imports; a fall in W's income is crucial to the correction. If income were not allowed to fall as a result of reduced exports, then the correction would be considerably smaller, but not as small as in Table 12-1 where W's income increased.

A small marginal propensity to import and a large marginal propensity to save in the country originally receiving capital make

Table 12-2

	m^Z	s^Z	m^W	s^W	dB^W	dY^W	dY^Z	dM^W	dM^Z
A	0.2	0.2	0.2	0.2	$6\frac{2}{3}$	$-16\frac{2}{3}$	$-33\frac{1}{3}$	$-3\frac{1}{3}$	$-6\frac{2}{3}$
B	0.1	0.2	0.2	0.2	8	-10	-40	-2.0	-4.0
C	0.2	0.1	0.2	0.2	5	-25	-50	-5.0	-10.0
D	0.2	0.2	0.1	0.2	6	-20	-30	-2.0	-6.0
E	0.2	0.2	0.2	0.1	7.5	-25	-37.5	-5.0	-7.5

for a larger correction to the balance of payments of the country restricting the outflow of capital. Furthermore, a small marginal propensity to save and a large marginal propensity to import in the country controlling the outflow of capital make for a larger correction in that country's balance of payments.

The third and final case to consider is where the country controlling the outflow allows the diverted capital to expand its national income, but the other nation replaces the reduced foreign investment expenditure with an equal amount of government expenditure. W's controls then will result in a direct change in expenditure in W but not in Z. Equations (12-1) and (12-2) will show the results for national income in W and Z. m^W multiplied by W's change in income reveals W's change in imports:

$$dM^W = M^W \frac{1 + (m^Z/s^Z)}{s^W + m^W + m^Z(s^W/s^Z)} \text{ (10)} \qquad (12\text{-}13)$$

The change in Z's imports is equal to m^Z multiplied by Z's change in income.

$$dM^Z = M^Z \frac{(m^W/s^W)}{s^Z + m^Z + m^W(s^Z/s^W)} \text{ (10)} \qquad (12\text{-}14)$$

The change in W's balance of payments will be equal to the reduced capital of 10 minus the change in W's imports plus the change in W's exports (Z's imports).

$$dB^W = 10 - \left[M^W \frac{1 + (m^Z/s^Z)}{s^W + m^W + m^Z(s^W/s^Z)} \right] 10$$
$$+ \left[M^Z \frac{(m^W/s^W)}{s^Z + m^Z + m^W(s^Z/s^W)} \right] 10$$

$$(12\text{-}15)$$

$$\text{or} \quad dB^W = \left[10 - M^W \frac{1 + (m^Z/s^Z)}{s^W + m^W + m^Z(s^W/s^Z)} + \right.$$
$$\left. M^Z \frac{(m^W/s^W)}{s^Z + w^Z + m^W(s^Z/s^W)} \right] 10$$

The balance-of-payments correction in each row of Table 12-3 is greater than that in Table 12-1. Z acting to prevent its income from falling as a result of the decreased foreign capital serves to enlarge the correction to W's balance of payments. However, Z's income will then rise as a result of the increase in W's income and imports. If Z also acts to neutralize the secondary

Table 12-3

	m^Z	s^Z	m^W	s^W	dB^W	dY^W	dY^Z	dM^W	dM^Z
A	0.2	0.2	0.2	0.2	$6\frac{2}{3}$	$+33\frac{1}{3}$	$+16\frac{2}{3}$	$+6\frac{2}{3}$	$+3\frac{1}{3}$
B	0.1	0.2	0.2	0.2	6	+30	+20.0	+6.0	+2.0
C	0.2	0.1	0.2	0.2	5	+37.5	+25.0	+7.5	+5.0
D	0.2	0.2	0.1	0.2	8	+40.0	+10.0	+4.0	+2.0
E	0.2	0.2	0.2	0.1	5	+50.0	+25.0	+10.0	+5.0

increase in income resulting from increased export expenditure, then Z's imports will not be induced to expand. The correction afforded W's balance of payments will be less.

Large values for Z's marginal propensities to import and to save contribute to a large correction of W's balance of payments. Also a large propensity to save and a small marginal propensity to import in W act to enlarge the correction to W's balance of payments.

What would happen if income in neither country were allowed to change? Then imports in neither country would change. The change in the balance of payments would be the reduced capital outflow of $10 billion.

The correction to W's balance of payments, then, is greatest when both nations act to prevent income changes. The next largest correction comes when only one of the countries acts to reduce the direct income consequences of the reduced capital flow: the size of the correction depends in part on the propensities to save and import in the two countries. The correction will be least when neither country acts to prevent income changes.

Commodity Controls

Besides controlling capital, the nation confronted with a deficit may try to reduce expenditure on items in the current account. It may attempt to discourage private donations to receivers outside the country. Furthermore, it may decide to discourage foreign travel. Travel restrictions will most likely divert travel and vacation expenditure to the domestic economy. This will force national income to rise and reduce foreign income. The analysis of the consequence is the same as that presented above for capital restrictions.

To reduce its deficit, country W may discourage imports so as to reduce the demand for foreign currency, or it may subsidize exports to increase the supply of foreign currency. W's success in reducing imports and expanding exports will have income repercussions for both countries. If W's expenditure is diverted from imports to domestically produced goods, then W's income will rise as a result of the increased expenditure. Z's income will fall as a result of the decreased exports (W's imports). Furthermore, W's income will rise as a result of the increased exports brought about by the subsidy. If Z's residents divert expenditure from domestic output to the purchase of subsidized goods from W, then Z's income will fall. The increase in W's income, resulting from expanding exports and diverting expenditure from imports to domestic output, will serve to induce an expansion in imports. The fall in Z's income, resulting from reduced exports and expenditure diverted from domestic output to imports, will serve to reduce imports. The correction afforded W's balance of payments from the imposition of a tariff and exports subsidy will depend on: (1) the size of the correction of the balance of trade provided directly by the controls, (2) the amount of the income change in the two countries, and (3) income effects on imports and exports in the two countries.

The surplus country may also act to correct the disequilibrium in the balance of payments. Nation Z may subsidize imports to encourage a demand for foreign goods and currency, or it may tax exports to discourage the earning of foreign currency. Subsidizing imports may divert expenditure from domestic production to the imports; if this occurs, then income will fall by the amount of reduced imports times the foreign-trade multiplier. A tax on exports will discourage them; and if these goods are not purchased on the domestic market, a fall in income will also result. The deflationary consequences will tend to make these corrections unacceptable to the surplus country. A surplus is not usually a sufficient inconvenience to induce a nation to suffer deflation. Possibly if the nation had a sufficiently inflationary economy, it would be willing to undertake these steps.

A nation with a deficit in its balance of payments is one that is trying to absorb more than it is producing. The deficit can be corrected by reducing the absorption so as to diminish the indebtedness to other nations. Alternatively, the nation can increase output to bring its production up to a level consistent with its absorption. A production subsidy would work in this direction. If the nation has unutilized resources and a marginal propensity to absorb of less than 1, then more goods will be produced than absorbed. These extra goods must either be exported to pay for the imports or be substituted for imports. If the price of these goods does not fall, there is little reason to expect exports to rise. Whether these goods can be substituted for imports depends on whether the increased output serves similar ends to the imports. If the nation does not have unutilized capacity, then it may not be possible to increase output. A production subsidy will only create inflation, making imports an even better bargain and reducing the competitive position of its exports.

The nation with a surplus is producing more than it is absorbing. To reduce the surplus requires either curtailing production or increasing absorption. A production tax could be employed to reduce output. Such a device might create unemployment and slow down the growth rate of the nation; neither consequence is likely to be acceptable.

The advantage of imposing commodity controls in the form of tariffs, quotas, and subsidies over straight devaluation is the obvious discrimination which may be achieved. The controls may be applied discriminately to the various goods traded and to commodities from various countries. If devaluation brings forth a greater expenditure on the higher-priced imports, then it enlarges the deficit. However, it is possible to impose tariffs on imports whose elasticities are high, thereby reducing the expenditure on these goods and contributing to an improvement in the balance of payments. Likewise, the subsidizing of exports could be selective. Only those exported goods with high elasticities of demand would be subsidized; the fall in price resulting from the subsidy would induce an increase of foreign expenditure on these goods, thereby improving the balance of payments. Furthermore, a subsidized good should have a high elasticity of supply, the higher return inclusive of subsidy should encourage expanded output for sale abroad.

Also the tariffs may be applied to goods from countries with which the nation has a deficit and not to goods coming from nations with which trade is balanced or in surplus. If a subsidy on exports is employed, then it can be made to apply to nations with which trade is in deficit.

Although the commodity controls allow for discrimination in their implementation, instituting such a policy is extraordinarily difficult. If discrimination is to be based on commodities with high elasticities, it must be possible to define and classify the goods so that the good will always come under the proper schedule. Studies on tariffs have shown that a particular commodity may appropriately be taxed under several schedules with the tariff ranging tenfold. For example, is an *aftaba* (an Iranian coffee urn) a cooking utensil or an item of household decoration? These two categories have different tariffs.

Using the controls to discriminate against the trade of different nations is also hazardous. If a particular commodity has a high tariff from one exporting country and a low tariff from another exporting country, the good may be shipped from the first exporting country to one that has to pay a high tariff, then to the second exporting country which has to pay the low tariff, and then from the second exporting country to the importing country at the low tariff for goods coming from the second.

Obviously nations do not like to be discriminated against. International relations are made difficult by these controls. Often the slow removal of such barriers after they have served their useful purpose is a further thorn in the use of controls.

Although direct controls have many advantages in the abstract, the introduction of these controls requires a great amount of government intervention and supervision. The cost may be more than the gain.

Conclusion

Direct controls have been widely used to restore equilibrium in the balance of payments. In the 1960s, the United States introduced both a tariff on capital flows and a voluntary control. During the early 1960s, foreign securities were being sold in large amounts in the New York money market. The result, of course, was an outflow of dollars at a time of deficit in the balance of payments. An increase in the interest rate would have served to discourage the foreign securities; however, the higher interest rate would have induced a fall in domestic investment expenditure, resulting in a fall in income and employment. Since the economy was already at less than full employment, there was a general reluctance to employ devices which would expand the level of unemployment. In 1963 the interest equalization tax was introduced. This measure increased the cost to foreigners of obtaining funds on the American money market by 1 percent. The result was that securities tended to seek out European money markets.

In 1965, the Voluntary Credit Restraint Program was initiated. The United States government asked the business community to reduce investment abroad, remit dividends more rapidly, and finance abroad their foreign operations. It was hoped that these measures would bring about a 5 percent improvement in the balance of payments.

Restrictions on capital flows for balance-of-payments reasons are widespread. For example, Spain allows domestic industry to invest in foreign firms only if the foreign firm is in the same line of business. Furthermore, the foreign investment is allowed only if it will serve to increase Spanish exports.

As tariffs imposed to protect domestic industry are being removed, restrictions in commodities are being imposed for balance-of-payments reasons. France with its Common Market countries reduced tariffs to allow for more competition in the market, but decided to impose tariffs in 1968 during the rapid deterioration in the balance of payments. New Zealand has a complicated "category" system for grouping goods and issuing import licenses. The categories are devised to restrain imports and to ensure that essential commodities are given priority with respect to the limited foreign exchange.

Selected Readings

Books

A. E. A., *Readings in International Economics*, Homewood: Richard D. Irwin, 1968.

Baldwin et al., *Trade, Growth and the Balance of Payments*, Chicago: Rand McNally and Co., 1965.

Fellner, William, et al., *Maintaining and Restoring Balance in International Payments*, Princeton: Princeton University Press, 1966.

Johnson, Harry G., *The World Economy at the Crossroads*, New York: Oxford University Press, 1965.

Kindleberger, Charles P., *Foreign Trade and the National Economy*, New Haven: Yale University Press, 1962.

Meade, J. E., *The Balance of Payments*, London: Oxford University Press, 1951.

Salant, Walter S., and Beatrice N. Vaccara, *Import Liberalization and Employment*, Washington, D.C.: The Brookings Institution, 1961.

Periodicals

A. E. A., Index of Economic Journals, classification no. 11.34.

Aufricht, H. "Exchange Taxes," *Zeitschrift für Nationalokonomie*, May, 1962.

Bhagwati, J., "Indian Balance of Payments Policy and Exchange Auctions," *Oxford Economic Papers*, February, 1962.

—— "On the Underinvoicing of Imports," *Institute of Economics and Statistics Bulletin*, November, 1964.

Birnbaum, E. A., and M. A. Qureshir, "Advance Deposit Requirement for Imports," International Monetary Fund, *Staff Papers*, November, 1960.

Bruton, H. J., and S. R. Bose, "The Export Bonus Scheme: A Preliminary Report," *Pakistan Development Review*, 1962.

Nair, K. N. B., "Exchange Control and Economic Planning in Underdeveloped Countries," *Indian Journal of Economics*, October, 1959.

Salant, W. S., "The Balance-of-Payments Deficit and the Tax Structure," *Review of Economics and Statistics*, May, 1964.

Tew, B., "The Use of Restrictions to Suppress External Deficits," *Manchester School of Economic and Social Studies*, September, 1960.

13.

Multiple Exchange Rates

Policy instruments so far discussed for correcting a disequilibrium in the balance of payments have been monetary and fiscal policy, capital controls, and commodity controls. Commodities may be controlled by tariffs or by quantitative restrictions. The quantitative restriction limits the total value of a commodity to be imported annually. The restriction reduces the supply and forces up the domestic price; importers are able to buy cheaply abroad and sell at a high price on the domestic market. If demand is inelastic, revenue received by importers rises. The excess revenue may be absorbed by the government through taxes or by the auctioning of import licenses. A tariff, on the other hand, restricts the import of a good and allocates the resulting price difference to the government in the form of the duty. Multiple exchange rates will likewise influence the level of trade and thereby improve the balance of payments and provide revenue.

Balance of Payments

Devaluation allows the price mechanism to ration more effectively the limited supply of foreign currency, providing the sum of elasticities of demand exceeds 1. If the elasticities of demand are less than 1, devaluation will worsen the balance of payments. When the elasticities are less than 1, appreciation will improve the balance of payments. These elasticities are an average for all goods imported and exported; some of these goods have high and some low elasticities. Instead of devaluing the currency for all goods imported and exported, devaluing the currency for goods with an elasticity greater than 1 and appreciating the currency for goods with an elasticity less than 1 will be more effective.

For purposes of illustration, suppose country Z's imports are valued at ₱400, of which ₱200 is spent on good A and ₱200 on good B, and its exports equal ₱200, of which ₱100 is received from good C and ₱100 from good D. The elasticity of demand for good A is assumed to be $\frac{1}{4}$ and for good B $2\frac{1}{4}$, so that the elasticity of demand for imports is $1\frac{1}{4}$. The elasticity of demand for good C is $\frac{1}{4}$ and for good D is $2\frac{1}{4}$, so that the elasticity of demand for exports is also $1\frac{1}{4}$. This information is set out in Table 13-1.

Consider now a straight devaluation of 10 percent to correct the deficit. As shown in Table 13-2, devaluation forces the price of imports up by 10 percent, and with an elasticity of $1\frac{1}{4}$, the quantity imported falls by 12.5 percent, yielding a net expenditure fall of approximately 2.5 percent. The 2.5 percent fall in expenditure multiplied by the value of imports yields the money value of the fall in imports, ₱10. Devaluation does not change the peso price of exports, so no price change for exports is shown

Table 13-1

	Imports		Exports	
Good	A	B	C	D
Value	₱200	₱200	₱100	₱100
Elasticity	$\frac{1}{4}$	$2\frac{1}{4}$	$\frac{1}{4}$	$2\frac{1}{4}$
Total value		₱400		₱200
Elasticity (average)		$1\frac{1}{4}$		$1\frac{1}{4}$

Table 13-2

Elasticity of imports $1\frac{1}{4}$, of exports $1\frac{1}{4}$, total $2\frac{1}{2}$
10% devaluation

	P	Q	Yields		
Imports	+10%	−12.5%	−2.5%	change expenditure or	₱10.00
Exports	.....	+12.5%	+12.5%	receipts or	₱25.00
				Improvement	₱35.00

in Table 13-2. However, the price of Z's exports in foreign currency falls by 10 percent. The 10 percent fall in price induces foreigners to increase the quantity of goods purchased from Z by 12.5 percent, given an elasticity of $1\frac{1}{4}$. No change in the peso price of exports combined with a 12.5 percent increase in quantity sales brings an increase in receipts of 12.5 percent, which amounts to ₱25. The fall in expenditure of ₱10 and increase in receipts of ₱25 equal an improvement in the balance of payments of ₱35.

Suppose instead of straight devaluation, country Z introduces multiple exchange rates, appreciating the rate for goods with low elasticities and depreciating the rate for goods with high elasticities. In Table 13-3, the consequences of appreciating the currency by 10 percent for goods A and C and depreciating the

Table 13-3

Appreciate currency by 10% for goods A and C
Elasticity of demand for import A $\frac{1}{4}$, for export good C $\frac{1}{4}$.

	P	Q	Yields		
Imports	−10%	+2.5%	−7.5%	expenditure or	₱15.00
Exports	.....	−2.5%	−2.5%	receipts or	₱2.50
				Improvement	₱12.50

Devalue currency by 10% for goods B and D
Elasticity of demand for import B $2\frac{1}{4}$, for export D $2\frac{1}{4}$.

	P	Q	Yields		
Imports	+10%	−22.5%	−12.5%	expenditure or	₱25.00
Exports	.....	+22.5%	+22.5%	receipts	₱22.50
				Improvement	₱47.50
				Total decrease in expenditure	₱40.00
				Total increase in receipts	₱20.00
				Total improvement	₱60.00

currency by 10 percent for goods B and D are shown. Appreciating by 10 percent the currency rate for import A serves to make imports 10 percent cheaper in terms of pesos. The 10 percent fall in the peso price induces a 2.5 percent increase in quantity demanded, given the elasticity of $\frac{1}{4}$. Expenditure in terms of pesos falls by approximately 7.5 percent, or ₱15. The peso price of exports is not affected. The price in foreign currency is 10 percent higher, with the result that quantity falls by 2.5 percent. The unchanged peso price combined with a 2.5 percent fall in quantity yields a 2.5 percent fall in receipts, or ₱2.50. The appreciation of the currency by 10 percent for import A and export C brings an improvement of ₱12.50 in the balance of payments.

Also shown in Table 13-3 is the consequence of devaluing the currency by 10 percent for import B and export D. The devaluation increases the import price by 10 percent with the result that the quantity imported falls by 22.5 percent, given the elasticity of $2\frac{1}{4}$. The 10 percent increase in price and 22.5 percent fall in quantity imported effect a fall in expenditure of approximately 12.5 percent, or ₱25. The devaluation does not affect the peso price of exports. However, the foreign price falls by 10 percent, so quantity exported rises by 22.5 percent. The unchanged peso price and the 22.5 percent increase in quantity exported amount to an increase in exports of approximately 22.5 percent, or ₱22.50. The combined devaluation of the exchange rates for import B and export D makes for an improvement in the balance of payments of ₱47.50.

The bottom of Table 13-3 shows that the result of appreciating the currency for import A and export C and devaluating the currency for import B and export D is an improvement in the balance of payments by an amount equal to ₱60. Compare this with the improvement of ₱35 achieved by straight devaluation of 10 percent. Obviously, multiple exchange rates can be more effective in correcting a deficit than can a straight devaluation.

It was indicated in Chapter 10 that elasticities did not indicate the change in the balance of payments because the income changes were not included, unless one uses total elasticities instead of price elasticities. Price elasticities have been used here; the changes in income must be taken into consideration. The improvement of ₱60 in Z's balance of trade consists of ₱40 reduced expenditure on imports and ₱20 in increased sales. The foreign country finds exports down by ₱40 and the domestic expenditure diverted to the purchase of ₱20 imports. Thus, in this foreign country, expenditure on domestic output is down by ₱60. If the government does not act to replace this expenditure, then income will fall by ₱60 times the multiplier. This fall in income will reduce imports from Z, thereby reducing the improvement in the balance of payments below ₱60.

Similarly, if Z's reduced expenditure on imports of ₱40 is diverted to domestic goods, then domestic expenditure will rise by the ₱40 plus the ₱20 of increased exports. National income will rise by ₱60 times the multiplier, if the government does not act to reduce expenditure by that amount. The increase in income will induce an increase in imports, restricting the improvement in the balance of payments to less than the initial improvement of ₱60.

Clearly, if neither country acts to prevent the expenditure changes resulting from Z's introduction of multiple exchange rates, then the improvement in Z's balance of payments will be the lesser of the two and substantially below the initial improvement of ₱60. The size of the multiplier in both countries and the size of the marginal propensities are crucial in determining the amount by which the correction to Z's balance of payments will fall below the initial correction of ₱60. A large multiplier in the other country will result in a large fall in income and imports (Z's exports). Also a large marginal propensity to import in the other country will result in a larger fall in imports for a given change in income. This large reduction in exports for Z will reduce substantially the correction afforded the balance of payments. Furthermore, a large multiplier in Z will serve greatly to expand income and induced imports, with the result that the correction to the balance of payments will be less than the initial ₱60. And a large marginal propensity to import will induce a large increase in imports from a given amount of increase in income; the larger the marginal propensity to import, the smaller the actual correction in comparison with the initial correction.

If either country acts to prevent the income change, then the correction to Z's balance of payments will more nearly approximate the initial correction of ₱60. If the other country expands domestic expenditure to compensate for the reduced sales to Z and expenditure diverted to Z's exports, then the other country's imports will not fall to reduce Z's exports. Z's maintaining its income at an unchanged level will leave the correction to the balance of payments.

Revenue

Most taxes are market-oriented, with the possible exception of a head tax. Goods may be taxed upon the sale to the consumer—a sales tax; salary, income (wages), and profits may be taxed—income tax. A production tax is usually levied on goods brought to the market by the producer. The market creates a boundary over which goods or income crossing must pay the appropriate tax. Furthermore, the market gives value to those goods and services, so ad valorem taxes may be levied.

The less market-oriented an economy, the more difficult it is to determine sales, output, and income. Few records are available upon which to assess sales, production, or income taxes when the producer is also the consumer. Nonmarket-oriented production is indicative of most underdeveloped countries. One of the limited number of goods crossing the market is foreign exchange; therefore it is exposed to taxation.

The difference in the prices at which the government buys foreign exchange and sells it equals the amount of the tax. It may have a single purchase price and a single sale price. Alternatively, the government may discriminate by establishing a series of purchasing prices so as to maximize revenue. It may further discriminate by having a series of selling prices depending on the category of the commodity.

The revenue will be the difference between the purchase price and the sale price of currency times the number of units of foreign exchange sold. If the revenue is to be large, the high exchange rate must not discourage imports. To obtain the maximum revenue, goods with low elasticities should be charged the higher price, since these goods are not sensitive to price. The multiple rates can be determined by elasticity; the more inelastic the demand for an import, the higher the rates charged.

The price given for foreign exchange to exporters will depend on the elasticity of supply. A good with an inelastic supply will be sold abroad in only slightly reduced quantity as a result of the smaller amount of domestic currency given for the foreign exchange. In effect, the domestic currency is devalued in the purchase of foreign exchange from exporters, and the currency will be devalued most for highly inelastic goods.

Regulating Trade

If we define the nondiscriminatory equilibrium exchange rate as the one which equates autonomous supply and demand for foreign currency, then the amount by which any rate for imports exceeds this equilibrium rate constitutes a subsidy on imports. For example, assume the equilibrium rate is 50 cents per peso. If the rate is set at 60 cents per peso, then an import costing $3 sells for 5 pesos. At the equilibrium exchange rate, it would sell for 6 pesos. Overvaluing the exchange rate serves to subsidize this import by 1 peso. Likewise, the amount by which any exchange rate on imports falls below this equilibrium rate is equivalent to a tax on imports. Establishing various rates at which the government sells foreign currency to importers allows for subsidizing and taxing imports to different degrees.

The amount by which exchange rates for exports exceed the equilibrium exchange rate constitutes a tariff, and the amount by which the exchange rate falls below the equilibrium rate constitutes a subsidy on exports. A multiple-rate system may be devised so that various commodities are given different subsidies or taxed.

The manner in which subsidies and tariffs regulate trade has been discussed in Chapter 4. That discussion applies here where the tariff or subsidy is built into the exchange-rate system, the consequences of this measure with alternative elasticities and repercussions for maximizing world production and trade need not be repeated.

It must be realized that the above discussion centers around the departure of an exchange rate for a particular good from an equilibrium rate. Now what are the consequences of initiating a multiple rate to correct a disequilibrium in the balance of payments? The prevailing rate being above an equilibrium rate made for the deficit. This high rate was serving to subsidize imports and tax exports and thereby disrupt trade. From this nonequilibrium rate, multiple rates are introduced to correct the deficit; the rate is appreciated for some goods and depreciated for others. The important question is whether this reduces the restraints to the maximization of world production and trade.

Those multiple rates which are depreciated from the prevailing rate toward the equilibrium rate serve to reduce the subsidy on imports and the tariff on exports, thereby contributing to the maximization of world production and trade. If the rate is depreciated below the equilibrium rate, then imports are no longer being subsidized and exports taxed; instead, the imports are taxed and the exports are subsidized. A large reallocation of resources is required. The maximization of world trade and production deteriorates only if the rate is depreciated to the extent that imports are more restricted and exports more subsidized than the initial rate served to subsidize import and tax exports.

Appreciating the rate for some goods further above the prevailing rate serves to increase the import subsidy and the export tax, thereby enlarging the distortion of world production and trade. For a deficit country, the appreciation of the exchange rate further distorts world production and trade; depreciation may improve, depending on how far the depreciation goes.

Administration

Three primary advantages for administration are (1) revenue can be collected without the need of a competent civil service, (2) response to the balance of payments is more flexible, and (3) responses may not require legislative action.

An equitable sales or income tax requires a trained civil service to devise the reporting forms, to train the public in the filing of the tax return, to audit the tax return, and to investigate to ensure honest reporting. The nation may have difficulty in recruiting a civil service in the numbers required; furthermore, if trained persons are in short supply, there is a question as to whether this makes the best use of their talents. Also, those filing taxes will need at least a rudimentary education. Alternatively, revenue can be obtained more readily through multiple rates. The government need only give the bank schedules for the purchase and the sale of foreign exchange; the difference would be deposited to the government's account.

However, a policing problem remains. If revenue is to be earned, the price paid to exporters for earned foreign exchange will be below the market price. Exporters will be tempted to sell the exchange on the black market at a higher rate. Furthermore, the multiple rates sometimes allow the import and export of a good at sizable profits. For example, if exports are subsidized by the government purchasing foreign exchange at a premium, then it may be profitable to import a good by buying a currency at a low rate and reexporting it, selling the foreign exchange at a premium. Thus the policing job is not limited to ensuring that foreign currency is sold to the bank, but it must also ensure that goods are not reexported.

Multiple exchange rates may allow a more flexible response to balance-of-payments pressures. If the demand at the bank exceeds supply, then the rates need further adjustment to equate autonomous supply and demand. Thus the market mechanism provides the government with a guide in its attempt to retain balance in the foreign account. Tariffs and quantitative restrictions are not nearly so adjustable in bringing equilibrium to the balance of payments. Changes in tariffs and quotas usually require legislative action, whereas setting the multiple exchange rates is often left to the government.

As has been shown, multiple exchange rates contain tariffs and subsidies. Therefore they may encourage or discourage trade in certain commodities. Rates which are devised to control commodity trade may be rationalized as needed for revenue or taxed to allow balance-of-payments corrections without disrupting economic development. In this manner a nation is able to impose tariffs and subsidies and also circumvent agreements on tariffs and subsidies.

Given the fact that a multiple-exchange-rate system may be useful for maintaining equilibrium in the balance of payments, obtaining revenue, and regulating trade, some choices must be made. Just as it was shown in Table 4-1 that a tariff cannot achieve a large revenue and a large degree of protection, similarly a multiple-exchange-rate system cannot be used for both protection and revenue. Obtaining revenue requires that the quantity of goods traded not be greatly reduced. If persons decide not to purchase the foreign good because of the high price of foreign currency, then the government would sell little foreign currency and gain little revenue. Thus if the elasticities of supply and demand in all countries are small, then increasing the price of foreign currency will provide a large revenue. Imports which are greatly discouraged by the higher price of foreign exchange would require a very small increase in the price of foreign exchange, i.e., a very small tariff, to maximize revenue to the government, and a large increase to reduce imports to provide protection to domestic producers.

Protection and improving the balance of payments require the same action on the importing of goods. That which provides protection reduces the demand in terms of foreign currency. It is this fact which makes it possible for a country to use multiple exchange rates to serve as a tariff while claiming that their only purpose is to correct a deficit in the balance of payments.

Buying foreign exchange at a rate above the equilibrium serves to subsidize exports. If supply is elastic, exports will tend to increase by a large amount. If foreign demand is elastic, a small decrease in price will result in the larger quantity demanded. The total expenditure in the foreign currency will be greater, thereby contributing to a correction in the balance of payments. However, if the foreign demand is inelastic, a large decrease in price will be required to bring about an increase in quantity demanded. The total revenue in foreign currency will be reduced, with adverse effects on the balance of payments. Furthermore, if the elasticity of supply is small, the subsidy will induce a very small increase in exports. A foreign elasticity of demand of less than 1 will result in an adverse movement in the balance of payments; a higher elasticity will yield a small improvement in the balance of payments.

Conclusion

Multiple exchange rates have been used primarily by under-developed countries; they allow more effective control of the balance of payments. The system allows for disguised subsidies and taxes on foreign trade. Finally, the system can be administratively desirable for obtaining revenue. The shortcomings are that corrections to the balance of payments bring a distortion to the maximization of world production and trade. Extensive policing is required to ensure the full functioning of the system.

Selected Readings

Books
A. E. A., *Readings in International Economics*, Homewood: Richard D. Irwin, 1968.
Ellsworth, P. T., *The International Economy*, New York: The Macmillan Co., 1964.
Harrod, Roy, and D. C. Hague, *International Trade Theory in a Developing Country*, London: Macmillan and Co., 1963.
Kindleberger, Charles P., *International Economics*, Homewood: Richard D. Irwin, 1963.
Meade, J. E., *Trade and Welfare*, London: Oxford University Press, 1955.

Ward, Richard, *International Finance*, Englewood Cliffs: Prentice-Hall, 1965.

Periodicals

A. E. A., *Index of Economic Journals*, classification no. 11.34.

Bernstein, Edward M., "Some Economic Aspects of Multiple Exchange Rates," International Monetary Fund, *Staff Papers*, 1950–1951.

deVries, Margaret G., "Multiple Exchange Rates: Expectations and Experiences," International Monetary Fund, *Staff Papers*, June, 1965.

Schlesinger, Eugene, *Multiple Exchange Rates and Economic Development*, Princeton: Princeton Studies in International Finance, 1952.

Sherwood, Joyce, "Revenue Features of Multiple Exchange Rate Systems: Some Case Studies," International Monetary Fund, *Staff Papers*, 1956–1957.

14.

International Reserves

As discussed earlier, imports are a function of price and income. Given income and price levels in the two countries, there is an exchange rate which will maintain equilibrium in the balance of payments in both countries. Should income or prices rise in one of the countries, then that country will incur a deficit if the exchange rate is not allowed to change. Likewise, the introduction of tariffs, subsidies, and taxes will bring about a disequilibrium in the balance of payments.

In Figure 14-1, the assumed levels of income and prices in countries *W* and *Z*, together with the value of the exchange rate, maintain balance in the foreign accounts of the two countries. An increase in *W*'s income or prices will weigh down its side to a deficit and cause a surplus in *Z*. The correction may take the form of reducing *W*'s income and increasing *Z*'s; maintaining

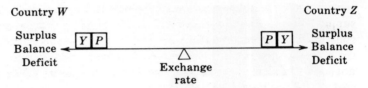

Country _W_   Country _Z_

Surplus   Surplus
Balance   Balance
Deficit   Exchange   Deficit
                       rate

Figure 14-1

equilibrium in this manner typifies the gold standard. Alternatively, the exchange-rate fulcrum may be allowed to move freely to maintain balance, i.e., a flexible-exchange-rate system.

With the dollar-exchange standard there is no automatic adjustment. The nation must finance its deficit while devising and implementing a policy. A nation may decide to devalue, i.e., move the exchange-rate fulcrum of Figure 14-1 to the left. Alternatively, the nation may employ monetary or fiscal policy to reduce income and prices, or it may employ commodity controls to reduce the quantity of imports for a given level of income. Subsidizing domestic output may also be undertaken, providing there is excess capacity.

If nations may incur deficits, then a reserve from which to finance the deficit will be required. If a nation's experience shows that deficits tend to be small and quickly corrected, then a large reserve may not be necessary. On the other hand, if deficits prove to be rather intransigent to correction, a large reserve might be required. For example, Great Britain in November of 1967 devalued from $2.80 per pound sterling to $2.40. In addition, a number of sales taxes were imposed and limits to increases to income were extended to reduce absorption. By the end of 1968, Great Britain was still incurring large deficits in its current account. The British public appears to be anticipating further sales taxes and is buying now to avoid them. The result is continued pressures on the balance of payments.

Reserves

A deficit occurs when the autonomous supply of a nation's currency exceeds the autonomous demand. The central bank of the deficit country is obligated to buy up the excess supply, thereby preventing it from driving down the exchange rate. At the fixed exchange rate, autonomous supply must equal autonomous demand plus accommodating demand. Obviously the central bank cannot use its own currency to buy up the excess supply; some other international medium of exchange must constitute the accommodating demand for the nation's currency. Gold has long served this purpose; however, gold output has not kept up with its demand for monetary purposes. While the cost of mining gold has been rising, the price of gold has been fixed at $35 an ounce. Fixing exchange rates has created a demand for gold as reserves; fixing the price of gold has limited its supply. A supplement to gold is needed to fill the demand for reserves.

As long as the United States is able and willing to fulfill its obligation of buying and selling gold at the fixed rate, a dollar is as good as $\frac{1}{35}$ ounce of gold. If all nations have faith in the United States' willingness to convert dollars for gold, dollars will serve as an international medium of exchange, accepted in settlement of all foreign accounts. Holding dollars on deposit in an American bank earns interest, whereas gold does not earn interest and involves a storage cost. Thus a nation may find dollars preferable to gold and build its reserves primarily of dollars. As long as the dollar is secure, it constitutes an excellent reserve and medium of international exchange.

How do dollars become available, or how are they supplied for reserve purposes? Nations wishing to acquire dollar reserves must run a surplus, i.e., earn more dollars than they spend. The difference may be maintained on deposit in New York as a reserve. If these nations are running a surplus, then the United States must be running a deficit. It is, then, the United States deficit which serves to create dollar reserves.

The United States Deficit

Table 14-1 gives the balance of payments of the United States for 1947 through 1966. The United States has run a deficit on liquidity basis every year since 1950, except 1957, for which a surplus of $578 million is recorded. In the late 1950s and early 1960s the annual deficit ranged between $2 and $3 billion. In 1965 and 1966 the deficit was restricted to $1.3 billion.

For most years the deficit enlarged the "liquid liabilities to foreign official holders and other foreign holders." Drawing on United States gold and reserves played a smaller part in accommodating the United States deficit. Since 1947, only on six occasions has as much as 50 percent of the deficit been financed by giving up United States gold and reserves: 1950, 50 percent;

Table 14-1 Balance of payments of the United States (millions of dollars)

Year	Balance on Goods and Services	Remittances and Pensions	U.S. Government Grants and Capital, Net	U.S. Private Capital, Net	Foreign Capital, Net	Errors and Unrecorded Transactions	Balance Liquidity Basis	Change in Gold, Convertible Currencies and IMF Gold Tranche Increase	Change in Liquid Liabilities to Foreign Official Holders and Other Foreign Holders Decrease
1947	11,529	-728	-6,121	-987	-432	949	4,210	-3,315	-895
1948	6,440	-631	-4,918	-906	-361	1,193	817	-1,736	919
1949	6,149	-641	-5,649	-553	44	786	136	-266	130
1950	1,779	-533	-3,640	-1,265	181	-11	-3,489	1,758	1,731
1951	3,671	-480	-3,191	-1,048	540	500	-8	-33	41
1952	2,226	-571	-2,380	-1,160	52	627	-1,206	-415	791
1953	386	-644	-2,055	-383	146	366	-2,184	1,256	928
1954	1,828	-633	-1,554	-1,622	249	191	-1,541	480	1,061
1955	2,009	-597	-2,211	-1,255	297	515	-1,242	182	1,060
1956	3,967	-690	-2,362	-3,071	615	568	-973	-869	1,842
1957	5,729	-729	-2,574	-3,577	545	1,184	578	-1,165	587
1958	2,206	-745	-2,587	-2,936	186	511	-3,365	2,292	1,073
1959	147	-815	-1,986	-2,375	736	423	-3,870	1,035	2,835
1960	4,001	-697	-2,769	-3,879	365	-922	-3,901	2,145	1,756
1961	5,509	-722	-2,780	-4,180	707	-904	-2,370	606	1,764
1962	5,045	-778	-3,013	-3,425	1,021	-1,053	-2,203	1,533	670
1963	5,853	-891	-3,581	-4,456	689	-285	-2,671	378	2,293
1964	8,462	-896	-3,560	-6,542	685	-949	-2,800	171	2,629
1965	6,944	-1,024	-3,375	-4,743	278	-415	-1,335	1,222	113
1966	5,102	-1,010	-3,446	-4,213	2,512	-302	-1,357	568	789

1958, 67 percent; 1960, 55 percent; 1962, 70 percent; and 1965, 90 percent. Obviously other nations have been willing to hold United States liabilities; these liabilities are convertible and constitute international liquidity and reserves.

Nations running a surplus are accumulating dollars. These dollars can be used to buy goods anywhere in the world, since the dollar is accepted as international currency. If nations decide not to spend their net foreign earnings, then they may decide to hold the dollars on deposit in a New York bank and thereby earn interest. These deposits constitute part of the nation's reserves.

International liquidity is created by the United States deficit and by the surplus nation being willing to hold dollars. Confidence in the dollar's ability to remain convertible and retain its value is essential.

As long as nations are trying to build reserves, the deficit on liquidity basis is no problem. The excess supply of dollars on commercial transactions—commodities and capital—is being absorbed by increased "liquid liabilities to foreign official holders and other foreign holders." However, once foreign nations have acquired adequate dollar reserves, the excess supply of dollars on commercial transactions will have to be reduced, since they will not be held for reserves but converted to gold. Thus once foreigners reduce their acquisition of dollars for reserves and liquidity, the United States must correct its balance of payments. The need for correction, in this case, comes not from changes in the commerical transactions but from changes in desires of foreigners. If the United States does not correct the flow of dollars, foreign central banks will be presenting them for conversion into gold. This continual deficit and reduced gold stock may serve to weaken confidence in the dollar. Fears of devaluation of the dollar will serve to bring dollars out of reserves for conversion to gold.

The problem for the United States can be considerably greater than the current deficit. If the nations wish to reduce their stocks of dollar reserves, the number of dollars presented for conversion to gold will be considerably greater than the amount of the dollar deficit for any year. This really shows the instability of the system; once nations wish to stop holding dollars, the number presented for conversion may be extremely large, and the current deficit may represent only a small proportion. Consequently, eradicating the deficit is going to shut down a rather small part of the total supply of dollars being presented for conversion.

When a nation is building a reserve, it runs a surplus. The surplus may be the result of absorption being less than output. A nation is saving, and the saving takes the form of international reserves of dollars and gold. Alternatively, the surplus can be the result of a capital inflow; the nation is losing its commercial assets and gaining foreign currency. The nation's savings are no longer held in the form of domestic assets, but in the form of reserves. As long as the nation is willing to keep its savings in the form of reserves of dollars, there is no problem. If a nation wishes to hold its reserves in gold, there is only a limited amount of gold the United States can supply. Eventually the United States must act against the sale of gold. The only way the United States can do this is to limit the supply of dollars to be converted.

To correct the deficit, the United States could devalue and thereby reduce the price of exports to foreigners and increase the price of imports to Americans. Supposedly sales of exports would increase and the purchase of imports would fall. The fall in imports would reduce expenditure and income in foreign countries. The fall in income would induce a fall in savings; the fall in savings would tend to reduce the countries' ability to add to their reserves.

Alternatively, the United States might try to correct the deficit by reducing foreign aid for both military and development purposes. Since our current account is in surplus, it is often argued that the deficit is the consequence of the United States giving too much aid; aid should be reduced to correct the deficit. If foreign aid were reduced by an amount equal to the deficit, the deficit might be entirely wiped out, or it might only be reduced. If the aid were being held as reserves, then cutting it out would reduce the net supply of dollars by that amount. However, if some of the aid were used directly or indirectly to buy goods from the United States, then the dollar supply would be reduced by the amount of the reduced aid, and the demand for dollars would be reduced by the proportion of the aid used to purchase United States exports. With both supply and demand falling, the deficit would not be eradicated.

It has also been suggested that the United States appreciate the price of gold to, say, $70 an ounce, while maintaining the price relationships of the currencies. In other words, all currencies would be devalued in terms of gold but not in terms of one another. This would greatly increase the value of the United States' reserves and probably strengthen confidence in the dollar. Opposition to this action is based both on political and economic arguments. The political argument concerns nations which would gain especially by the revaluation of gold—Russia and the Union of South Africa. Because of the cold war, we do not wish to improve the economic position of Russia by offering a higher price to its gold-mining industry. Likewise, there is general reluctance to assist the racist government of the Union of South Africa to improve its economic well-being. More important though, there is no reason to believe that the new price will serve to bring gold forth automatically in the right quantities needed for reserves. Digging gold in one part of the world to bury in another part is a misallocation of resources when the same goals can be achieved by other means. The revaluation of gold will help those nations which have been embarrassing the United States by converting dollars for gold; the gold will be worth more dollars. Our friends who have been holding dollars will be relatively worse off from assisting us.

Speculation

Speculators attempt to earn a profit by outguessing the changes in the value of a currency. The speculation may take the form of buying the currency at a low rate and selling it at a higher rate. Alternatively, the speculators may obtain a loan in a currency expected to fall in value and sell the foreign exchange; they expect to be able to buy the exchange at a lower rate in the future. If the currency is not expected to be devalued, the speculation will take place within the support points, if the support points are sufficiently large to allow a profit from a correct guess. If revaluation is expected, then there will be pressure for the rate to go outside the support points; it will be retained within these points only by official intervention. If the official intervention is able to convince speculators that the currency will not be revalued, then speculation will return to within the support points. If the official intervention is not able to convince speculators with the limits of resources available, then revaluation will occur.

Until the first part of 1968, the United States has interpreted its obligation to buy or sell gold at $35 an ounce, plus or minus handling charges, as a duty to maintain the world price of gold at $35 an ounce. Thus the United States bought or sold gold to maintain this rate. Recently the United States has provided large amounts of gold to the world market. To support the United States in maintaining the price of gold, the gold pool was formed, consisting of the United States, Belgium, Germany, Italy, the Netherlands, Switzerland, and the United Kingdom; France recently withdrew. Fearing a serious depletion in its gold reserve, the United States, after consulting with the other nations, has decided not to defend the market price of gold; the free market gold price will be allowed to fluctuate. The United States will, however, continue to buy and sell gold at $35 an ounce from all central banks. This is an attempt to separate the financial demand for gold from the speculative demand. The problem with a two-track market in this commodity is that some central banks will be tempted to buy gold from the United States at $35 an ounce and sell at any free market price above this. To prevent the United States resources of gold from going on the market in this manner, the United States has threatened not to sell gold to any nation selling it on the free market.

The purpose of resorting to the two-track market is to prevent the speculation on the upward valuation of gold from disrupting international finance. During 1968 gold prices have risen as persons feared the devaluation of the pound, the dollar, and the franc. Under the old system the United States would have had to defend the price of gold on each occasion.

The speculation threatened to induce a run on United States gold. As speculators moved out of any currency in favor of gold, the metal's price was under pressure to rise. But as the United States sold gold, concern began to spread as to whether the United States had sufficient supply to maintain its price. As the concern grew, the demand for gold rose further. A situation similar to a run on the bank could be set off purely by speculative behavior. Under the two-track system, the United States reserves are not depleted by speculation, and doubt as to the stability of the United States to redeem dollars at the rate of $35 an ounce of gold is not fostered.

Eurodollar

The *Eurodollar* is a United States dollar deposit which has been redeposited in a European bank. A deposit denominated in dollars, not local currency, is made in a European bank; the

European bank may lend the dollars or convert them and loan in some other money.

Because of legal restrictions, deposits held in the United States banks have earned relatively low interest rates. Most European banks are not allowed to borrow abroad without the permission of the central authorities, but the banks may accept deposits in any currency. Thus by offering higher rates on United States deposits, the European banks have been able to acquire a large number of them.

The importance of the Eurodollar to the discussion here is to show the extent to which the dollar is truly an international currency. Even though the United States deficit is being questioned in many quarters, the dollar in various forms, such as the Eurodollar, continues to become even more important in international finance. Thus we have on the one hand the expanding importance of the dollar in international finance, and on the other hand the inability of the United States to maintain the price of gold. Has the world lost confidence in the dollar, or is it about to lose confidence?

Adequacy of Reserves

Reserves are created by the United States deficit and by foreign monetary authorities' willingness to hold dollars. Once a nation decides it has sufficient dollar deposits, it merely converts any additional dollars received for gold. The drawing on United States gold requires a correction in the balance of payments to reduce the supply of dollars. However, a nation's reluctance to acquire further dollar deposits does not necessarily mean that the nation is satisfied with the level of its reserves—gold, IMF position, and foreign currencies. The unwillingness to acquire further dollar deposits may be based on fear of devaluation or restrictions on conversion to gold.

Whether international reserves are adequate depends on the goals to be fulfilled by the mechanism. Large reserves reduce the need to rely on adjustments in the exchange rate to correct disequilibrium in the balance of payments. Thus the amount of reserves required will depend on the nation's attitude toward relying on the exchange mechanism. Some nations, such as the reserve-currency countries, can depend on the exchange mechanism only as a final resort. A currency is acceptable as a reserve only if its value in terms of gold is secure; continual revaluations would make gold preferable. The reserve-currency countries, such as the United States and England, will need large reserves of gold to hold them over any deficit.

The level of desired reserves depends also on the duration of the business cycle and the degree of synchronization of growth rates. As a nation's income rises and falls, its imports will expand and contract, thereby inducing deficits and surpluses. Furthermore, as nations grow at different rates, a particular nation's imports and exports will increase by different amounts. Unless there is a peculiar type of synchronization, a nation's balance of payments will fluctuate between varying degrees of deficit and surplus over time. It is extremely unlikely that any nation will sustain for a prolonged period a perfect equilibrium of autonomous supply and demand of foreign exchange. The more typical situation will be disequilibrium—deficits and surpluses. The need for reserves will depend on the nation's particular cycle of surplus and deficit in the balance of payments.

As pointed out, reserves are acquired by demanding less foreign exchange than supplied. It also means that a nation is consuming less than its total output; some of its savings are being held in the form of idle reserves. The building of reserves comes at the cost of a higher standard of living, less consumer goods, or less investment and a slower growth rate. There are limits to which nations are willing to forestall increases in the standard of living or investment. Recent events in France show that the unions are unwilling to allow the nation to build up reserves at the cost of a higher standard of living. Furthermore, some nations simply cannot afford the luxury of maintaining reserves. Underdeveloped nations short on consumer and investment goods are unable to maintain reserves for future use. These nations will tend to employ any reserves received, then maintain the balance of payments through controls.

Although an adequate level of world reserves cannot be set with any precision, two extreme positions must be avoided. World reserves must not be so scarce as to disrupt trade patterns. It would seem that this extreme position could easily be described and set forth; this is not the case. For to say that "reserves must not be so low as to disrupt trade patterns" suggests that some sort of optimal trade pattern exists. But as we have seen, the optimal trade pattern has already been greatly disrupted by subsidies, taxes, tariffs, quotas, overvalued exchange rates, and undervalued exchange rates. It cannot easily be determined whether the level of reserves is serving to mitigate the disruption provided by these other controls or whether they are serving to enhance the disruption. What is a normal or appropriate level of trade in such a world?

On the other side, the amount of the reserves created must not be so large as to create inflation which cannot be controlled by the individual countries. Unfortunately this involves the distribution of reserves. If the quantity of reserves is in the hands of a few countries, then the reserves may be considered to be inadequate. However, further creation of reserves may result in their transfer to those nations already having large reserves in exchange for consumer or investment goods. The recipient countries will incur further inflation, and some nations will continue to be without reserves.

Thus to say the level of international reserves is adequate or inadequate requires a number of subjective judgments: (1) a judgment as to whether the revaluation of the exchange rate should be used more readily, (2) a judgment as to the part of the surplus or deficit which is cyclical and self-correcting, and (3) a judgment as to whether additional reserves would improve the trade pattern or lead to world inflation. These are points about which experts can disagree.

Conclusion

The key currency is subjected to greater uncertainty than any other currency. It may run long deficits as nations accumulate the currency to build reserves to strengthen their own world position. As long as nations demand the currency for purposes of building up reserves, this demand is autonomous, and the key currency does not really have a deficit. But this large stock of money held abroad which is able to come onto the market for conversion to gold at any time makes the key currency highly vulnerable.

Confidence is crucial to the whole system. As long as there is confidence in the key currency, it will be acceptable internationally and will therefore serve as an international medium of exchange and store of value. The amount of gold backing the currency will matter little. Once confidence is lost, only if the amount of key currency held abroad is not more than the amount of gold held by the key country can the currency be bought up without difficulty. Loss of confidence is unlikely in this case.

Beyond this ratio of key currency held abroad to gold, loss of confidence will result in a large number of currency units sold on the market for gold. As gold flows out, loss of confidence will spread; more currency will be put onto the market to be purchased by the central bank of the key country. If the run on the key currency is not stopped, the international financial system will break down.

The key currency is caught between two forces. Providing international liquidity is one goal; maintaining a balance of payments which will not result in a large debt is a second goal. The international financial position of the key country is a matter of concern to the entire international community.

Selected Readings

Books

American Enterprise Institute, *International Payments Problems*, Washington, D.C.: American Enterprise Institute, 1966.

Clement, Pfister, and Rothwell, *Theoretical Issues in International Economics*, Boston, Houghton Mifflin Co., 1967.

Einzig, Paul, *A Textbook on Foreign Exchange*, London: Macmillan and Co., 1966.

Hansen, Alvin H., *The Dollar and International Monetary System*, New York: McGraw-Hill, 1965.

Harris, Seymour, *International and Interregional Economics*, New York: McGraw-Hill, 1957.

Harrod, Roy, *The Dollar*, New York: W. W. Norton and Co., 1963.

Salant, Walter S., *The United States Balance of Payments in 1968*, Washington, D.C.: The Brookings Institution, 1963.

Ward, Richard, *International Finance*, Englewood Cliffs: Prentice-Hall, 1965.

Yeager, Leland B., *International Monetary Relations*, New York: Harper and Row, 1966.

Periodicals

A. E. A., *Index of Economic Journals*, classification no. 11.331.

Aliber, R. Z., "The Costs and Benefits of the U.S. Role as a Reserve Currency Country," *Quarterly Journal of Economics*, August, 1964.

Altman, O. L., "Euro-dollars: Some Further Comments," International Monetary Fund, *Staff Papers*, March, 1965.

———— "Foreign Markets for Dollars, Sterling and Other Currencies," International Monetary Fund, *Staff Papers*, December, 1961.

———— "International Liquidity and the Balance of Payments," International Monetary Fund, *Staff Papers*, November, 1965.

Beza, S. T., and G. Patterson, "Foreign Exchange Guarantees and the Dollar," *American Economic Review*, June, 1961.

Einzig, Paul, "Some Recent Changes in the Euro-dollar System," *Journal of Finance*, September, 1964.

Floyd, J. E., "The Overvaluation of the Dollar: a Note on the International Price Mechanism," *American Economic Review*, March, 1965.

Klopstock, F. H., "The International Money Market Structure, Scope and Instruments," *Journal of Finance*, May, 1965.

McKinnin, R. I., "Optimum Currency Areas," *American Economic Review*, September, 1963.

Salant, W. S. "The Reserve Currency Role of the Dollar: Blessing or Burden to the United States," *Review of Economics and Statistics*, May, 1964.

15.

International Monetary Plans

A key currency has to serve both as a domestic and as an international medium of exchange. The key country is unable to adjust the value of the currency without taking into consideration the consequences for the reserves of other countries; furthermore, the currency is subject to greater uncertainty as nations' demand for it fluctuates with reserve requirements. Speculation, with large hoards of currency being held externally, can create serious problems in maintaining the value of the currency and confidence in it.

If a separate international medium of exchange could be instituted, then no currency would need to serve both national and international monetary requirements. The international currency would have to be acceptable as an international medium of exchange and a trustworthy store of value. With proper international cooperation, this currency could replace gold. The volume of such currency could be made more dependent on the needs of international finance and less on other extraneous factors, such as mining costs.

Keynes Plan

Of the several plans offered during World War II for the establishment of an international monetary system, one was put forth by the British Government. The British economist J. M. Keynes was the main architect, and his name is now associated with it. This plan is very clearly written; important parts of it are reproduced here.

International Clearing Union[1]

I.—The Objects of the Plan

ABOUT the primary objects of an improved system of International Currency there is, to-day, a wide measure of agreement:—

a. We need an instrument of international currency having general acceptability between nations, so that blocked balances and bilateral clearings are unnecessary; that is to say, an instrument of currency used by each nation in its transactions with other nations, operating through whatever national organ, such as a Treasury or a Central Bank, is most appropriate, private individuals, businesses and banks other than Central Banks, each continuing to use their own national currency as heretofore.

b. We need an orderly and agreed method of determining the relative exchange values of national currency units, so that unilateral action and competitive exchange depreciations are prevented.

c. We need a *quantum* of international currency, which is neither determined in an unpredictable and irrelevant manner as, for example, by the technical progress of the gold industry, nor subject to large variations depending on the gold reserve policies of individual countries; but is governed by the actual current requirements of world commerce, and is also capable of deliberate expansion and contraction to offset deflationary and inflationary tendencies in effective world demand.

d. We need a system possessed of an internal stabilising mechanism, by which pressure is exercised on any country whose balance of payments with the rest of the world is departing

[1] British Information Services, *International Clearing Union*, April 8, 1943.

from equilibrium in either direction, so as to prevent movements which must create for its neighbours an equal but opposite want of balance.

e. We need an agreed plan for starting off every country after the war with a stock of reserves appropriate to its importance in world commerce, so that without due anxiety it can set its house in order during the transitional period to full peacetime conditions.

f. We need a central institution, of a purely technical and non-political character, to aid and support other international institutions concerned with the planning and regulation of the world's economic life.

g. More generally, we need a means of reassurance to a troubled world, by which any country whose own affairs are conducted with due prudence is relieved of anxiety, for causes which are not of its own making, concerning its ability to meet its international liabilities; and which will, therefore, make unnecessary those methods of restriction and discrimination which countries have adopted hitherto, not on their merits, but as measures of self-protection from disruptive outside forces.

4. The proposal is to establish a Currency Union, here designated an *International Clearing Union*, based on international bank-money, called (let us say) *bancor*, fixed (but not unalterably) in terms of gold and accepted as the equivalent of gold by the British Commonwealth and the United States and all the other members of the Union for the purpose of settling international balances. The Central Banks of all member States (and also of non-members) would keep accounts with the International Clearing Union through which they would be entitled to settle their exchange balances with one another at their par value as defined in terms of bancor. Countries having a favourable balance of payments with the rest of the world as a whole would find themselves in possession of a credit account with the Clearing Union, and those having an unfavourable balance would have a debit account. Measures would be necessary (see below) to prevent the piling up of credit and debit balances without limit, and the system would have failed in the long run if it did not possess sufficient capacity for self-equilibrium to secure this.

5. The idea underlying such a Union is simple, namely, to generalise the essential principle of banking as it is exhibited within any closed system. This principle is the necessary equality of credits and debits. If no credits can be removed outside the clearing system, but only transferred within it, the Union can never be in any difficulty as regards the honouring of cheques drawn upon it. It can

make what advances it wishes to any of its members with the assurance that the proceeds can only be transferred to the clearing account of another member. Its sole task is to see to it that its members keep the rules and that the advances made to each of them are prudent and advisable for the Union as a whole.

II.—The Provisions of the Plan

3. The member States will agree between themselves the initial values of their own currencies in terms of bancor. A member State may not subsequently alter the value of its currency in terms of bancor without the permission of the Governing Board except under the conditions stated below; but during the first five years after the inception of the system the Governing Board shall give special consideration to appeals for an adjustment in the exchange value of a national currency unit on the ground of unforeseen circumstances.

4. The value of bancor in terms of gold shall be fixed by the Governing Board. Member States shall not purchase or acquire gold, directly or indirectly, at a price in terms of their national currencies in excess of the parity which corresponds to the value of their currency in terms of bancor and to the value of bancor in terms of gold. Their sales and purchases of gold shall not be otherwise restricted.

5. Each member State shall have assigned to it a *quota*, which shall determine the measure of its responsibility in the management of the Union and of its right to enjoy the credit facilities provided by the Union. The initial quotas might be fixed by reference to the sum of each country's exports and imports on the average of (say) the three pre-war years, and might be (say) 75 percent of this amount, a special assessment being substituted in cases (of which there might be several) where this formula would be, for any reason, inappropriate. Subsequently, after the elapse of the transitional period, the quotas should be revised annually in accordance with the running average of each country's actual volume of trade in the three preceding years, rising to a five-year average when figures for five post-war years are available. The determination of a country's quota primarily by reference to the value of its foreign trade seems to offer the criterion most relevant to a plan which is chiefly concerned with the regulation of the foreign exchanges and of a country's international trade balance. It is, however, a matter for discussion whether the formula for fixing quotas should also take account of other factors.

6. Member States shall agree to accept payment of currency balances, due to them from other members, by a transfer of bancor to their credit in the books of the Clearing Union. They shall be

entitled, subject to the conditions set forth below, to make transfers of bancor to other members which have the effect of overdrawing their own accounts with the Union, provided that the maximum debit balances thus created do not exceed their quota. The Clearing Union may, at its discretion, charge a small commission or transfer fee in respect of transactions in its books for the purpose of meeting its current expenses or any other outgoings approved by the Governing Board.

7. A member State shall pay to the Reserve Fund of the Clearing Union a charge of 1 percent per annum on the amount of its average balance in bancor, whether it is a credit or a debit balance, in excess of a quarter of its quota; and a further charge of 1 percent on its average balance, whether credit or debit, in excess of a half of its quota. Thus, only a country which keeps as nearly as possible in a state of international balance on the average of the year will escape this contribution. These charges are not absolutely essential to the scheme. But if they are found acceptable, they would be valuable and important inducements towards keeping a level balance, and a significant indication that the system looks on excessive credit balances with as critical an eye as an excessive debit balances, each being, indeed, the inevitable concomitant of the other. Any member State in debit may, after consultation with the Governing Board, borrow bancor from the balances of any member State in credit on such terms as may be mutually agreed, by which means each would avoid these contributions. The Governing Board may, at its discretion, remit the charges on credit balances, and increase correspondingly those on debit balances, if in its opinion unduly expansionist conditions are impending in the world economy.

8. *a.* A member State may not increase its debit balance by more than a *quarter* of its quota within a year without the permission of the Governing Board. If its debit balance has exceeded a quarter of its quota on the average of at least two years, it shall be entitled to reduce the value of its currency in terms of bancor provided that the reduction shall not exceed 5 percent without the consent of the Governing Board; but it shall not be entitled to repeat this procedure unless the Board is satisfied that this procedure is appropriate.

b. The Governing Board may require from a member State having a debit balance reaching a *half* of its quota the deposit of suitable collateral against its debit balance. Such collateral shall, at the discretion of the Governing Board, take the form of gold, foreign or domestic currency or Government bonds, within the capacity of the member State. As a condition of allowing a member State to increase its debit balance to a figure in excess of a half of its quota, the Governing Board may require all or any of the following measures:—

    i. a stated reduction in the value of the member's currency, if it deems that to be the suitable remedy;

    ii. the control of outward capital transactions if not already in force; and

    iii. the outright surrender of a suitable proportion of any separate gold or other liquid reserve in reduction of its debit balance.

c. If a member State's debit balance has exceeded *three-quarters* of its quota on the average of at least a year and is excessive in the opinion of the Governing Board in relation to the total debit balances outstanding on the books of the Clearing Union, or is increasing at an excessive rate, it may, in addition, be asked by the Governing Board to take measures to improve its position, and, in the event of its failing to reduce its debit balance accordingly within two years, the Governing Board may declare that it is in default and no longer entitled to draw against its account except with the permission of the Governing Board.

d. Each member State, on joining the system, shall agree to pay to the Clearing Union any payments due from it to a country in default towards the discharge of the latter's debit balance and to accept this arrangement in the event of falling into default itself. A member State which resigns from the Clearing Union without making approved arrangements for the discharge of any debit balance shall also be treated as in default.

9. A member State whose credit balance has exceeded *half* of its quota on the average of at least a year shall discuss with the Governing Board (but shall retain the ultimate decision in its own hands) what measures would be appropriate to restore the equilibrium of its international balances, including—

a. Measures for the expansion of domestic credit and domestic demand.

b. The appreciation of its local currency in terms of bancor, or, alternatively, the encouragement of an increase in money rates of earnings.

c. The reduction of tariffs and other discouragements against imports.

d. International development loans.

10. A member State shall be entitled to obtain a credit balance in terms of bancor by paying in gold to the Clearing Union for the credit of its clearing account. But no one is entitled to demand gold from the Union against a balance of bancor, since such balance is available only for transfer to another clearing account. The Governing Board of the Union shall, however, have the discretion to distribute any gold in the possession of the Union between the members possessing credit balances in excess of a specified proportion of their quotas, proportionately to such balances, in reduction of their amount in excess of that proportion.

11. The monetary reserves of a member State, viz., the Central Bank or other bank or Treasury deposits in excess of a working balance, shall not be held in another country except with the approval of the monetary authorities of that country.

III.—What Liabilities Ought the Plan to Place on Creditor Countries?
7. It is not contemplated that either the debit or the credit balance of an individual country ought to exceed a certain maximum—let us say, its *quota*. In the case of debit balances this maximum has been made a rigid one, and, indeed, counter-measures are called for long before the maximum is reached. In the case of credit balances no rigid maximum has been proposed. For the appropriate provision might be to require the eventual cancellation or compulsory investment of persistent bancor credit balances accumulating in excess of a member's quota; and, however desirable this may be in principle, it might be felt to impose on creditor countries a heavier burden than they can be asked to accept before having had experience of the benefit to them of the working of the plan as a whole. If, on the other hand, the limitation were to take the form of the creditor country not being required to accept bancor in excess of a prescribed figure, this might impair the general acceptability of bancor, whilst at the same time conferring no real benefit on the creditor country itself. For, if it chose to avail itself of the limitation, it must either restrict its exports or be driven back on some form of bilateral payments agreements outside the Clearing Union, thus substituting a less acceptable asset for bancor balances which are based on the collective credit of all the member States and are available for payments to any of them, or attempt the probably temporary expedient of refusing to trade except on a gold basis.

8. The absence of a rigid maximum to credit balances does not impose on any member State, as might be supposed at first sight, an unlimited liability outside its own control. The liability of an individual member is determined, not by the quotas of the other

members, but by its own policy in controlling its favourable balance of payments. The existence of the Clearing Union does not deprive a member State of any of the facilities which it now possesses for receiving payment for its exports. In the absence of the Clearing Union a creditor country can employ the proceeds of its exports to buy goods or to buy investments, or to make temporary advances and to hold temporary overseas balances, or to buy gold in the market. All these facilities will remain at its disposal. The difference is that in the absence of the Clearing Union, more or less automatic factors come into play to restrict the volume of its exports after the above means of receiving payment for them have been exhausted. Certain countries become unable to buy and, in addition to this, there is an automatic tendency towards a general slump in international trade and, as a result, a reduction in the exports of the creditor country. Thus, the effect of the Clearing Union is to give the creditor country a choice between voluntarily curtailing its exports to the same extent that they would have been involuntarily curtailed in the absence of the Clearing Union, or, alternatively, of allowing its exports to continue and accumulating the excess receipts in the form of bancor balances for the time being. Unless the removal of a factor causing the involuntary reduction of exports is reckoned a disadvantage, a creditor country incurs no burden but is, on the contrary, relieved, by being offered the additional option of receiving payment for its exports through the accumulation of a bancor balance.

IV.—Some Advantages of the Plan
10. The plan aims at the substitution of an expansionist, in place of a contractionist, pressure on world trade.

11. It effects this by allowing to each member State overdraft facilities of a defined amount. Thus each country is allowed a certain margin of resources and a certain interval of time within which to effect a balance in its economic relations with the rest of the world. These facilities are made possible by the constitution of the system itself and do not involve particular indebtedness between one member State and another. A country is in credit or debit with the Clearing Union as a whole. This means that the overdraft facilities, whilst a relief to some, are not a real burden to others. For the accumulation of a credit balance with the Clearing Union would resemble the importation of gold in signifying that the country holding it is abstaining voluntarily from the immediate use of purchasing power. But it would not involve, as would the importation of gold, the withdrawal of this purchasing power from circulation or the exercise of a deflationary and contractionist pressure on the whole world, including in the end the creditor country itself.

Under the proposed plan, therefore, no country suffers injury (but on the contrary) by the fact that the command over resources, which it does not itself choose to employ for the time being, is not withdrawn from use. The accumulation of bancor credit does not curtail in the least its capacity or inducement either to produce or to consume.

12. In short, the analogy with a national banking system is complete. No depositor in a local bank suffers because the balances, which he leaves idle, are employed to finance the business of someone else. Just as the development of national banking systems served to offset a deflationary pressure which would have prevented otherwise the development of modern industry, so by extending the same principle into the international field we may hope to offset the contractionist pressure which might otherwise overwhelm in social disorder and disappointment the good hopes of our modern world. The substitution of a credit mechanism in place of hoarding would have repeated in the international field the same miracle, already performed in the domestic field, of turning a stone into bread.

14. It should be much easier, and surely more satisfactory for all of us, to enter into a general and collective responsibility, applying to all countries alike, that a country finding itself in a creditor position *against the rest of the world as a whole* should enter into an arrangement not to allow this credit balance to exercise a contractionist pressure against world economy and, by repercussion, against the economy of the creditor country itself. This would give everyone the great assistance of multilateral clearing, whereby (for example) Great Britain could offset favourable balances arising out of her exports to Europe against unfavourable balances due to the United States or South America or elsewhere. How, indeed, can any country hope to start up trade with Europe during the relief and reconstruction period on any other terms?

16. It must, however, be emphasized that the provision by which the members of the Clearing Union start with substantial overdraft facilities in hand will be mainly useful, just as the possession of any kind of reserve is useful, to allow time and method for necessary adjustments and a comfortable safeguard behind which the unforeseen and the unexpected can be faced with equanimity. Obviously, it does not by itself provide any long-term solution against a continuing disequilibrium, for in due course the more improvident and the more impecunious, left to themselves, would have run through their resources. But, if the purpose of the overdraft facilities is mainly to give time for adjustments, we have to make sure, so far as possible, that they *will* be made. We must have, therefore, some rules and some machinery to secure that

equilibrium is restored. A tentative attempt to provide for this has been made above. Perhaps it might be strengthened and improved.

17. The provisions suggested differ in one important respect from the pre-war system because they aim at putting some part of the responsibility for adjustment on the creditor country as well as on the debtor. This is an attempt to recover one of the advantages which were enjoyed in the nineteenth century, when a flow of gold due to a favourable balance in favour of London and Paris, which were then the main creditor centres, immediately produced an expansionist pressure and increased foreign lending in those markets, but which has been lost since New York succeeded to the position of main creditor, as a result of gold movements failing in their effect, of the breakdown of international borrowing and of the frequent flight of loose funds from one depository to another. The object is that the creditor should not be allowed to remain entirely passive. For if he is, an intolerably heavy task may be laid on the debtor country, which is already for that very reason in the weaker position.

18. If, indeed, a country lacks the productive capacity to maintain its standard of life, then a reduction in this standard is not avoidable. If its wage and price levels in terms of money are out of line with those elsewhere, a change in the rate of its foreign exchange is inevitable. But if, possessing the productive capacity, it lacks markets because of restrictive policies throughout the world, then the remedy lies in expanding its opportunities for export by removal of the restrictive pressure. We are too ready to-day to assume the inevitability of unbalanced trade positions, thus making the opposite error to those who assumed the tendency of exports and imports to equality. It used to be supposed, without sufficient reason, that effective demand is always properly adjusted throughout the world; we now tend to assume, equally without sufficient reason, that it never can be. On the contrary, there is great force in the contention that, if active employment and ample purchasing power can be sustained in the main centres of the world trade, the problem of surpluses and unwanted exports will largely disappear, even though, under the most prosperous conditions, there may remain some disturbances of trade and unforeseen situations requiring special remedies.

VII.—The Control of Capital Movements

32. There is no country which can, in future, safely allow the flight of funds for political reasons or to evade domestic taxation or in anticipation of the owner turning refugee. Equally, there is no country that can safely receive fugitive funds, which constitute an

unwanted import of capital, yet cannot safely be used for fixed investment.

33. For these reasons it is widely held that control of capital movements, both inward and outward, should be a permanent feature of the post-war system. It is an objection to this that control, if it is to be effective, probably requires the machinery of exchange control for *all* transactions, even though a general permission is given to all remittances in respect of current trade. Thus those countries which have for the time being no reason to fear, and may indeed welcome, outward capital movements, may be reluctant to impose this machinery, even though a general permission for capital, over a period.

35. The advocacy of a control of capital movements must not be taken to mean that the era of international investment should be brought to an end. On the contrary, the system contemplated should greatly facilitate the restoration of international loans and credits for legitimate purposes in ways to be discussed below. The object, and it is a vital object, is to have a means—

a. of distinguishing long-term loans by creditor countries, which help to maintain equilibrium and develop the world's resources, from movements of funds out of debtor countries which lack the means to finance them; and

b. of controlling short-term speculative movements or flights of currency whether out of debtor countries or from one creditor country to another.

36. It should be emphasised that the purpose of the overdrafts of bancor permitted by the Clearing Union is, not to facilitate long-term, or even medium-term, credits to be made by debtor countries which cannot afford them, but to allow time and a breathing space for adjustments and for averaging one period with another to all member States alike, whether in the long run they are well-placed to develop a forward international loan policy or whether their prospects of profitable new development in excess of their own resources justifies them in long-term borrowing. The machinery and organisation of international medium-term and long-term lending is another aspect of post-war economic policy, not less important than the purposes which the Clearing Union seeks to serve, but requiring another, complementary institution.

Gold as international exchange leaves the volume of the world's reserves dependent upon the output of the gold-mining industry, rather than the world need for reserves. The Keynes

Plan has the clearing union create for each nation a quota or reserve, which is a deposit with the clearing union. The deposit may be transferred in making payments among member nations, but deposits may not be withdrawn. The deposit, expressed in a monetary unit called *bancor*, is similar to a country having a checking account with a world bank; each country makes payment by drawing on its account and deposits foreign earnings to it.

These reserves are not unlimited and do not delay indefinitely the necessary corrections. As a matter of fact, the plan requires adjustment on the part of both the debtor and creditor nations. The plan pressures adjustment by charging interest of 1 percent on either a credit or debit entry in excess of one-half of the quota. It is unlikely that a 1 percent interest rate will be very effective in inducing nations to maintain low debit or credit accounts; however, a higher rate could be set which would induce nations to act to maintain low accounts.

The clearing union can take much more effective action against a debtor nation. Before giving the debtor nation permission to extend its debit balance beyond half its quota, it may require the debtor (1) to devalue, (2) to control the outflow of capital, or (3) to surrender gold or liquid reserves to reduce debit balances. The debtor nation will be required to correct its deficit; the reserves only provide the nation with the time necessary to devise the appropriate action.

An additional pressure on the creditor nation to correct its surplus is the suggestion that a nation's surplus with the clearing union either be cancelled after a predetermined period or be invested. This item is not set forth very forcibly, and without it there is little that can be done to induce the surplus nation to act to correct its disequilibrium. It is important to note, however, that this plan stresses the point that the obligation to correct disequilibrium lies with both the debtor and the creditor.

The clearing union is like a world bank with which each country holds deposits; these deposits can be used in making payment among member nations. Furthermore, no nation may withdraw its deposits; they can be used only for settling international accounts. The clearing union acts as a central bank in that it may adjust upward or downward the amount of international reserves. If it fears world inflation, it may reduce proportionately each country's quota, or if it desires to expand the world economy, it may enlarge each country's quota.

The main criticism of the Keynes Plan is that it has a bias toward inflation. Reserves or quotas are simply created by the clearing union, and as nations draw upon their accounts, international money is created. Just as money is created in the domestic monetary system by borrowing, international reserves are created by drawing upon the country's account up to its quota. Furthermore, the size of these quotas may grow with the expansion of international trade; thus even more reserves can be created. The system is further inflationary to the extent that the correction is brought about by the surplus country.

The International Monetary Fund

The Keynes Plan was by and large rejected in favor of a plan by Harry Dexter White of the United States to set up the International Monetary Fund (IMF). The International Monetary Fund attempts to prohibit competitive devaluation by requiring permission to devalue by more than 10 percent of the original par value. This is much less rigid than the Keynes Plan, which would allow without the permission of the clearing union only one devaluation of not more than 5 percent to a country. Furthermore, the Keynes Plan recognizes the need for devaluation to correct a deficit and may even require such action before a country can have further recourse to expanding its debt with the clearing union. The International Monetary Fund is much more reluctant to have devaluation used as a means of correcting a deficit and simultaneously opposes trade controls. The adjustment must then be through income and prices, a means for correcting the disequilibrium which is distasteful to most nations concerned with maintaining full employment. Furthermore, unlike the Keynes Plan, the International Monetary Fund can only give permission for devaluation; it cannot request or require it.

In the Keynes Plan, deposits, which could be used in exchange among members, are created by countries drawing against their quota. The International Monetary Fund, in contrast, has a subscription-reserve system. Each country places on deposits with the Fund 25 percent of its quota in gold and the remaining 75 percent in its own currency. Thus the Fund has an amount of each member's currency which it might sell to those requiring these currencies. The Fund does not lend; it exchanges currencies.

Any nation may purchase any other nation's currency, as long as the Fund's-holding of the purchasing nation's currency does not increase by 25 percent during any period of one year. Furthermore, the Fund's holding of any country's currency must not exceed 200 percent of the quota. Since the original subscription consisted of 75 percent of the quota in a nation's currency, a country can make purchases up to 125 percent of its quota. A member does not have an automatic right to obtain currency from the IMF. For purchases beyond 25 percent of the quota, a nation must obtain the Fund's permission. This permission will be dependent upon the purchasing country having an acceptable program to reduce the deficit.

Every five years the Fund is to consider the adequacy of reserves. The Fund may only propose an adjustment in the quotas; for such changes to go into effect requires four-fifths majority of the voting power. Such expansion of quotas means that member countries deposit with the Fund more gold and more of their own currency.

The Fund is a "currency-exchange" system rather than a deposit-creating system. As such there is no multilateral clearing as in Keynes's clearing union, and each country is required to keep its balance convertible.

Because the International Monetary Fund is a currency-exchange organization, it runs the risk of running out of any particular country's currency. To overcome this danger, the Fund does not make permanent sales; instead, nations are expected to repurchase their own currency with gold or other foreign exchange. Furthermore, charges of $\frac{1}{2}$ percent on each purchase are imposed. An additional percentage is charged on the average daily balance of a nation's currency in excess of its quota; the rate is dependent on the amount of the daily average in excess of the quota and the duration it has been in excess. The higher the average daily balance and the longer the period, the greater the rate.

Furthermore, if the Fund's holding of any currency is greatly reduced by demand, then the Fund may declare the currency "scarce." The amount of the "scarce currency" which any nation is allowed to purchase is restricted. Nations may discriminate against goods from a country whose currency is scarce.

With the International Monetary Fund unable to create international money or deposits, and with the gold output being inadequate for the increased needs for reserves, some commercial instrument must be used to fill the gap. This gap is filled by the key currencies.

The difficulty with using the key currencies for international reserves is that confidence is maintained by having the key currency convertible into gold. The key countries' stocks of gold set the limits to the amount of international reserves that can be created. In Keynes's clearing union, the deposits served only as international reserves and could not be redeemed for gold. These deposits could be used in exchange because every nation agreed to accept them. Thus the clearing union was concerned only with the volume of reserves needed for the unimpeded flow of trade, without regard to redemption.

Triffin Plan

The object of the Triffin Plan is to reorganize the International Monetary Fund so that it will more nearly resemble Keynes's clearing union. Professor Triffin feels that the present IMF does not serve the needs of international commerce, particularly insofar as providing liquidity is concerned.

Somewhat like Keynes's clearing union, Triffin would have the IMF loan to underdeveloped nations to create deposits, expressed in bancor units. To forestall the fears of inflation which were responsible for the rejection of the Keynes Plan, Triffin suggests that bancor creation should be limited by the needs of international liquidity. One means of restricting the increase in bancor is to set a limit of 3 to 5 percent per annum to the growth of international reserves, including gold. Triffin argues that international reserves must expand at some rate so as not to be a drag on the expansion of trade. This position suggests the quantity theory of money in which a relation between money and prices or output is postulated. More specifically, it is kin to Professor Milton Friedman's position in which he argues that domestic money needs to expand smoothly at some rate to maintain the economy at an equilibrium growth rate.

Reserves are to be expanded so that international trade will be allowed to continue to grow; it is assumed that the further growth of international trade is desirable. It must be remembered, however, that the reserves are needed to cover deficits. If the exchange rates were allowed to adjust automatically, there would be equilibrium in the balance of payments and no need for reserves. The reserves are not necessarily needed for growth, but for disequilibrium growth. It cannot be assumed that trade growth resulting in disequilibrium in the balance of payments is desirable.

Keynes's clearing union has its deposits created through loans, and the present IMF's reserves are the result of subscriptions of each member. Triffin would have each country subscribe 20 percent of monetary reserves to the IMF; additional deposits would be created through loans.

All members would agree to accept deposits in settlements of accounts. To induce creditor nations to hold deposits with the IMF, the earnings would be divided pro rata among creditors. However, any nation would have the right to convert to gold its deposits beyond the subscription quota.

The essence of the Triffin Plan then is that the IMF would have a subscription quota paid in gold, foreign exchange, and credit accounts previously accumulated with the Fund. These quotas would be used, as they are at the moment, to sell members other currencies. The Fund would be able to create further deposits by lending to underdeveloped countries; it is here that international currency or reserves would be accepted by all members in settling accounts. Countries being net creditors would earn interest on other deposits; however, any nation may convert deposits into gold in excess of the subscription quota.

The Triffin Plan allows the IMF to expand world liquidity by limited amounts annually. The deposits denominated in bancor would serve as reserves, and since these deposits could be converted into gold and would be accepted among all members, they serve as reserves to back national currencies. It would be expected that these reserves would displace the present key currencies, which alone would be an important achievement.

The Triffin Plan does little to provide the IMF with a mechanism for correcting disequilibrium in the balance of payments. Introducing a corrective mechanism into the IMF is probably more important than providing a mechanism for adjusting international liquidity, particularly since it has not been shown that there is a relationship between liquidity and the volume of trade. Furthermore the Triffin Plan, unlike the Keynes Plan, makes no attempt to place some of the responsibility for correcting the disequilibrium on the creditor nation. Instead the creditor nation is allowed to convert deposits into gold.

Rio de Janeiro Conference

In the fall of 1967 a conference of the 106 nations of the International Monetary Fund met to consider alterations to the IMF. The main proposals were concerned with the shortage of gold and the need for international liquidity.

Under the new arrangements, each country is given a special drawing right against which a country can borrow to settle international accounts. Thus the IMF would be creating deposits by loaning as in the Keynes and Triffin Plans. Only a drawing in excess of 70 percent of a country's allocations need be repaid. Thus deposits are created which will change hands.

No nation need accept another country's payment in drawing rights beyond twice its own allocation. These special drawing rights serve only as a limited mechanism of exchange. Further negotiations will be required to reduce these limitations.

What we have here is a first step toward a Keynes Plan. It is hoped that we will soon be able to go to a point where liquidity will be created solely by the IMF. Furthermore, the IMF needs stricter corrective requirements than those presently agreed upon. The corrective requirement should place the burden both on the debtor and the creditor.

Conclusion

Fully automatic mechanisms for maintaining equilibrium in the balance of payments, such as the pure gold standard or flexible exchange rates, may be undesirable because of the required income adjustments. Pressures to inflation and unemployment are also undesirable. Nonautomatic systems are desirable if they can provide authorities time to devise monetary and fiscal policies which will allow the adjustment to come in the least painful form. National income may be adjusted to external pressure, but the adjustment may be controlled as to the sectors affected and the allocation of the cost among the various sectors. The time and duration of the adjustment are also important factors to be considered and not left to automation. The nonautomatic systems are undesirable to the extent that they postpone the adjustment and make the inevitable adjustment greater in the future. The nonautomatic systems are best in dealing with temporary disorders which do not really require income to adjust; here the automatic systems would put the economy through unnecessary or temporary income adjustment.

Selected Readings

Books

Gowda, K. Venkatagiri, *International Currency Plans and the Expansion of World Trade*, New York: Asia Publishing House, 1964.

Hansen, Alvin, *The Dollar and International Monetary System*, New York: McGraw-Hill Book Co., 1965.

Harrod, Roy, *Reforming the World's Money*, London: MacMillan, 1965.

Horie, Shigeo, *The International Monetary Fund*, London: MacMillan and Co. Ltd., 1964.

Scammell, W. M., *International Monetary Policy*, London: MacMillan, 1964.

Triffin, Robert, *Gold and the Dollar Crises*, New Haven: Yale University Press, 1960.

Periodicals

A. E. A., *Index of Economic Journals*, classification nos. 11.330 and 11.3331.

Altman, O. L., "The Management of International Liquidity," International Monetary Fund, *Staff Papers*, July, 1964.

Bernhard, R. C., "Triffin's Prescription of International Liquidity," *Western Economic Journal*, 1965.

Fleming, J. M., "The Fund and International Liquidity," International Monetary Fund, *Staff Papers*, July, 1964.

Malkiel, B. G., "The Rejection of the Triffin Plan and the Alternative Accepted," *Journal of Finance*, 1963.

Veit, O., "Gold Exchange Standard and World Monetary Reform," *German Economic Review*, 1963.

Wald, H. P., "On the Evolving Strategy of International Monetary Cooperation," *Social Research*, January, 1962.

Williamson, J., "Liquidity and the Multiple Key-currency Proposal," *American Economic Review*, January, 1963.

16.

State Trading

The classical theory of international trade was formulated primarily for the purpose of giving direction on questions of international trade policy confronting Great Britain. It was, furthermore, inferred by some members of the classical school that the policy conclusions of the theory were applicable to all nations. This inference led to the more formalized conclusion that free trade promoted the well-being of each nation simultaneously with that of the international community.

While the classical theory was employed to demonstrate that welfare was maximized under free trade, tariffs were admitted to be necessary in a specific situation, namely defense. The allowance of a tariff in one country, however, might necessitate corrective measures in other countries in order to ensure the maximization of world well-being and to maintain equilibrium. Thus, it is argued, should any nation for any conceivable reason impose a tariff, it would not necessarily be to the advantage of international welfare for all nations to maintain a free trade position. For example, should the United States impose a tariff on watches, Switzerland might have to subsidize its exports of watches in order to maintain the level of trade; or if the United States were its major market, it might have to impose a tariff against the United States' exports for balance-of-payments reasons and possibly to maintain the terms of trade, given that the elasticities were of the right magnitude.

The basic assumption underlying the classical theory, that each nation's welfare coincided with the maximization of international welfare, inhibited any substantial investigation of a nation's welfare apart from the international welfare. Although the classical theory was correct as it pertained to the international community as a unit, the assumption that national and international welfare were necessarily interdependent has not been borne out. A particular nation may be able to increase its own national income at the expense of other nations by imposing tariffs or by playing the game otherwise than set out in classical theory. One nation could impose a tariff and thereby reduce the price of imports, subject to the condition that no nation were sufficiently injured to invite retaliation, or if it could be supposed that no nation would retaliate in fear that such action might continue to the point of no trade.

All governments have expanded in varying degrees their jurisdiction to encompass many economic activities, with the stated intention of stabilizing the internal economy and ensuring full employment. The resulting substitution of policy decisions for market decisions has limited the applicability of free trade. For, contrary to classical assumptions, the internal economy is often stabilized at the expense of the world economy, frequently resulting in a general misallocation of resources and disequilibrium in the balance of payments, together with expensive delays in the return of capital. Determined to maintain full employment and promote economic growth, most countries, in good mercantilist fashion, prefer a favorable balance of trade (i.e., to export more than they import). The exchange rate is not determined by forces freely operating in the international market and often has little relationship to one compatible with a competitive international equilibrium; it is authoritatively set by governments with the intention of equalizing a balance of payments already distorted by existing artificial barriers to trade.

The instruments governments may use to interfere in the free course of trade on behalf of their citizenry are numerous and have varying degrees of effectiveness. The protective tariff and the quota are among the most venerable devices. Cartels, clearing agreements, multiple exchange rates, and undervalued exchange rates are the more fashionable and specific tools now found in the bag of protectionism. *State trading*, defined as the purchase or sale of goods by the government or agent of the government, is the acme of protective instruments and can serve the objectives of all these other devices. A tariff can be used to regulate the price of the foreign commodity on the home market; but quantity demanded at any particular price is left unregulated. A quota fixes the quantity importable of a commodity but leaves its price to the market mechanism. Overvalued exchange rates promote imports and impede exports, and the opposite is true of undervalued exchange rates. A state trading organization as a big buyer or seller on the international market and monopolist on the internal market has a unique opportunity to influence simultaneously the purchase price, quantity purchased, and sale price.

The establishment of state trading organizations is not primarily associated with any particular set of economic conditions. Its institution is conditioned by political factors, and its incorporation depends on a government's broadening its conception of political sovereignty to include economic activities, and more specifically international economic activities, usually with the objective of improving the well-being of its nationals.

State Trading and the Planned Economy

Under partial control, the government's interference in the economy is not all-embracing. A simple tariff or quota may be sufficient to prevent external forces from hampering the internal plans for full employment and growth. Or, if an infant industry with sufficient potential for future economies of scale cannot presently pay the market price for foreign raw materials, a specific subsidy may be justifiable during the period of growth, provided such measures are not allowed to become permanent.

Both quotas and tariffs are only limits to trade; there is no assurance that the quantity will not still fluctuate within the ceiling set by these trade barriers and interfere with the internal plan for price stabilization. A subsidy may also prove too expensive or too unpredictable for budgeting the annual expenditure. Thus as planning becomes more comprehensive and as nationalization is undertaken, a government monopoly of all foreign trade might prove more practicable.

Devising a policy which would win the support of the agrarian proletariat without alienating the industrial workers has often been one of the foremost problems confronting Socialists. Clearly, a program designed to improve the economic position of the farmer by stabilizing agricultural prices at a high level will be costly to urban workers and will reduce their real income, if compensating measures are not made. A possible solution which does not improve the lot of one group to the detriment of the other to so great an extent would be to institute a state trading monopoly which could buy grain on the external market at a low price and grain on the internal market at a high price and sell at some average price, or even subsidize the sale of grain if the tax structure is progressive. With this in mind, Jean Jaures proposed to the French Chamber of Deputies in 1894 that an import monopoly of grain be substituted for the tariff system.

The British Labour Party at the 1931 Conference passed its first resolution supporting state trading. It was only a limited endorsement of state trading, under which some categories of imports and no exports were to come under a government monopoly. "Import boards" were to be established for foodstuffs, raw materials, and a few manufactured commodities. The primary object of these "import boards" was to exploit the position of a strong monopolistic buyer, who would have been able to obtain goods more cheaply than private traders. Furthermore, the state trading agency was expected to enter long-term contracts which were to be designed to stabilize prices.

Presently, the Soviet Union has all its foreign trade under state trading. The theoreticians of communism considered foreign trade monopolies indispensable to the type of state they strove to evolve; the Communist state would have to be insulated from all imperialistic practices and exploitations of capitalist countries. Lenin emphatically laid down the argument for foreign trade monopolies. He said:

Strengthen and regulate those state monopolies, which have already
been put into effect and then prepare the monopolization of foreign
trade by the state; without this monopolization we shall not be able
to separate ourselves from foreign capital and from paying tribute.[1]

When Private Trade Diminishes

Probably a more important impetus to the intermittent growth
of state trading has been international crises rather than any
movement toward the controlled economy. For one type of
international crisis, a depression, the theoretical arguments for
unhampered international trade not only fail to refute the
arguments for protectionism and state trading but may also be
so used as a support for a policy for reducing foreign trade. In a
period of depression a country has unutilized resources, and
therefore it does not have to produce less of A in order to produce
more of B. The opportunity cost is said to be zero. International
trade, understandably, diminishes during a recession. Nations
may, furthermore, construct tariff barriers, simply because the
closed multiplier is larger and more conducive to fiscal policy.

During a depression, the balance of payments may become
unfavorable; this is especially likely for a fully industrialized
country which has to import most of its food. Devaluation during
a crisis is often suspected to be an attempt to export internal
difficulties. Nations with a favorable balance of payments will be
quick to claim injury and even retaliate in order to maintain
their favorable position and protect their economy. Therefore,
devaluation may possibly become competitive and intensify the
instability.

Countries which are primary producers have also brought
many exports under state trading during a depression in an
attempt to forestall falling prices on the international market
and in order to circumvent the problems involved in a mal-
functioning market system. The theoretical reasons for state
trading are three: First, a nation alone or in collusion with other
countries may attempt to control the quantity of a commodity

[1] J. N. Hazzard, "State Trading in History and Theory," *Law and Contemporary Problems*, vol. 24 p. 245. Spring, 1959. Quoted from Sochinenica,
Collected Works, 3d ed., 1928–1937, p. 449.

on the market in order to affect its price. Second, a country which desires to increase exports could allow its prices to be bargained down to a level which would be equivalent to devaluation without inviting retaliation. Third, a nation may be able to barter its exports which are unfavorably received on the international market for desired commodities which may be in a similar situation.

It must not, however, be overlooked that state trading may be the only means of increasing world trade during an international crisis in which the exchange rates are fixed and left unadjusted in fear of competitive devaluation. Cleverly handled state trading can be used to reduce prices of exports and yet make dumping difficult to define, discrimination vague, and retaliation cumbersome.

War, probably, has been responsible for a greater degree of state trading than any other international crisis. The international trade channels are more completely destroyed during war than during a depression. Furthermore, many commodities are strategically essential and shipping facilities are scarce; both require government action. The value of state trading was learned during World War I, and a rapid shift to this trading organization was made at the outset of World War II.

Neutrals have often found it advantageous to institute state trading during a major war. The primary purpose is certainty of destination. By state trading, a nation can be sure its exports are not going to any of the belligerents and ensure its neutrality. Without the services of foreign shipping, a neutral may also have to resort to state trading in order to ensure that the more essential commodities are given priority with respect to the limited shipping facilities.

Inconvertible currencies and the dollar shortage have both been a major impetus to bilateralism and state trading. State trading may be bilateral, which is usually equivalent to barter, or unilateral, depending on whether money or goods are exchanged. When the money market hampers trade because currencies are either scarce or inconvertible, barter will be used. These barter agreements, unlike those agreements during the depression which had exports as their motive, were negotiated by the importing countries primarily to obtain essential imports under the conditions of a deficit in the balance of payments.

Latin America in the postwar period serves as an excellent example of countries resorting to barter in the face of a dollar shortage. Most Latin American nations accumulated dollar reserves during the war. After the war, these reserves were quickly reduced, and a dollar shortage began to arise. These Latin American countries instituted state trading to prevent the use of their limited dollar resources for intra-Latin American trade.

The supposition that an abundance of goods and a normal flow of money would cancel the motives for state trading, except in the case of the fully planned economy, has not been substantiated; overproduction of a commodity has also resulted in the introduction of state trading of a good. Wheat was in abundance in 1949, and the International Wheat Agreement was organized to guarantee the sale and purchase of a quantity of wheat within a predetermined price range. Members of the International Wheat Agreement state traded 53 percent of their exports for the crop year 1949–1950 and 52 percent of their exports for the crop year 1950–1951. Likewise, 81 percent of the imports for the crop year 1949–1950 and 77 percent of the imports for the crop year 1950–1951 were under state trading. An agreement in which each nation promises to buy or sell a specific quantity of wheat within a preestablished price range may encourage state trading. A government may subsidize its exporters or importers to induce them to fulfill the country's obligations, but it may be easier for the government to perform the actual transaction itself, when the price is not an incentive to private traders.

State Trading and International Organizations

International organizations such as the Organization for European Economic Cooperation, General Agreement on Tariffs and Trade, and the International Monetary Fund have unwittingly abetted the employment of state trading by failing to enjoin effectively state monopolies within their stated objectives. One of the primary purposes of those supernational bodies is to encourage a greater amount of international trade; these organizations obligate member nations to reduce barriers to trade, prohibit discrimination, and disallow the depreciation of a nation's currency without the consent of the particular organization. Nevertheless, under such commitments, which relinquish a limited degree of economic sovereignty to an international body, state trading, which is not effectively regulated by these bodies, offers a means to circumvent less desirable aspects of the agreement while remaining within the formal code of the charter. For example, a policy of disallowing the unauthorized depreciation of a currency is not applicable to barter transactions where the exchange rate is of limited importance.

State trading is mentioned in the charters of these international bodies, but the regulations pertaining to it are vague, general, and ineffective. The International Trade Organization directs its members' state-trading agencies to act like private companies without indicating nonpermissible activities. Therefore, monopolistic and monopsonistic activities, which may include market discrimination, go unregulated.

Conclusion

The classical model is a normative expression of the mechanism of international trade for the maximization of international welfare. It is hardly applicable to a world lacking a homogeneous technology, characterized by inflexible exchange rates, and bent upon emphasizing the national economy at the expense of the international economy. State trading is not a new technique for solving the national economic problems. It serves the strong and the weak, poor and the rich, the prosperous and the depressed.

Selected Readings

See *Law and Contemporary Problems*, Vol. 24, nos. 1 and 2, 1959.

Index

Index

Balogh, T., 185
Bank of England, 148
Bank Act, 146
Bardham, P., 58
Barkin, S., 74
Barter terms of trade, 14, 41
Beckmann, M. J., 43
Belgium, 147, 244
Bernhard, R. C., 268
Bernstein, Edward, 235
Beza, S. T., 249
Bhagwati, J., 58, 224
Bieda, K., 74
Bilateral trade, 274
Birnbaum, E. A., 224
Bose, S. R., 224
Brazil, 164
Bretton Woods, 169
British Labour Party, 272
Brown, A. J., 43
Bruton, H. J., 112, 224
Buchanan, N. S., 43

Cairnes, J. E., 49
Canada, 49, 73, 148, 164–167
Capital, 99–112, 118, 125
  long-term, 99–102, 118, 121,
    125
  short-term, 99–101, 118, 125
  transfer payment, 100
Capital account, 118–119
Capital controls, 211–219
Capital transfer, 120–123
Cartel, 271
Cassell, G., 149
Caves, Richard, 42, 58, 167,
  207
Chancellor's letters, 146
Chile, 164
Clearing agreements, 271

Clement, M. O., 184, 248
Clemhout, S., 43
Coefficient of elasticity, 62
Collery, A., 94, 207
Colombia, 164
Commodity controls, 219–222
Common Market, 47, 223
Comparative advantage, 2–6,
  22, 46, 47, 51, 56, 57, 59
Competition, 51, 52
Concorde, 73
Constant costs, 6–10, 22, 31
Constant returns to scale, 10
Consumption effect of tariff,
  63, 66, 67
Consumption subsidy, 70, 71
Consumption tax, 71
Current account, 117–118

Defense, 71
de Gaulle, Charles, 206
Denmark, 147
Devaluation, 175–184, 207
deVries, Margaret, 235
Dollar-exchange standard,
  169–185, 187
Dosser, D., 94, 207

Eastham, H. C., 167
Eastham, K. K., 42
Economies of scale, 52, 57
Edgeworth box diagram, 38–41
Einzig, Paul, 185, 248, 249
Elasticity, 62
  coefficient of, 62
  unitary, 62
Ellsworth, P. T., 42, 58, 149,
  234
Employment act, 94

Inelastic schedule, 62
Infant-industry argument,
71–72
Ingram, J. C., 167
Interest equalization tax, 222
Interest rate, 100, 153–154,
205
International monetary fund,
(IMF), 169, 174, 175, 184,
263–267, 275
International price, 36–41
International Wheat Agree-
ment, 275
Investment, 79, 80, 102–103,
111, 152–154, 159–164
Investment multiplier, 90–93,
96–98
Isard, Walter, 58
Isocost curve, 16–20
Isoproduct curve, 18–20
Italy, 147, 244

Japan, 46
Jasay, A. E., 112
Jaures, Jean, 272
Johnson, Harry, 185, 207, 208,
223
Jones, M. C., 58
Jones, R. W., 43

Kemmerer, E. W., 149
Kemp, M. C., 58
Kenen, P., 132, 150
Kennedy Round, 73, 94
Key currency, 247, 251
Keynes Plan, 252–267
Kindleberger, C. P., 43, 94,
223, 234

Klein, T. M., 132
Klopstock, F. H., 249
Kreinin, M. E., 113

LaBarge, R. A., 132
Latin America, 50, 274, 275
Leighton, Richard, 132, 167
Leiter, R. D., 75
Leontief, W., 43
Liquidity, 237–248
Localization of industry, 56–57
Long-term capital, 99–102, 118,
121, 125

Macesich, G., 208
Machlup, Fritz, 94, 112, 132,
185, 207
McKenzie, L. W., 43
McKinnin, R. I., 249
Majumdar, T., 43
Malkiel, B. G., 268
Marginal propensity to import,
82, 106
Marginal propensity to save,
78–79, 106–108
Marginal rate of psychological
substitution, 24–36
Marginal rate of transforma-
tion, 8–16, 33
Marsh, Donald, 43, 58, 94,
149
Marshall-Lerner conditions,
176–181
Meade, J. E., 43, 74, 75, 132,
168, 207, 223, 234
Meek, P., 113
Monetary policy, 187–208
Montias, J. M., 58